ROGET'S THESAURUS

For home, school and office

A-Z for easy reference

Clear & easy-to-read format

Key words in bold type

**A dictionary of synonyms
and antonyms**

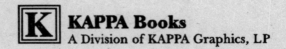

KAPPA Books
A Division of KAPPA Graphics, LP

CONTENTS

SYNONYMS...

Are those words which appear under the alphabetical listing. All have the same meaning.

ANTONYMS...

Are those words which appear under the alphabetical listing preceeded by the word "Antonyms:." All have the opposite, or different, meanings.

PHRASES...

Are listed alphabetically, with single words following them to define their meanings.

PARTS OF SPEECH...

a—adjective
adv—adverb
Bot.—botany
conj—conjunction
n—noun
pl—plural
prep—preposition
pron—pronoun
sing—singular
v—verb

A

abandon, v. desert, forsake, forego, discard, relinquish. *Antonyms:* maintain, continue.

abase, v. degrade, dishonor, reduce, humiliate.

abdomen, n. belly, paunch.

abduction, n. kidnapping, child-stealing, man-stealing.

abide, v. dwell, stay, continue, remain.

ability, n. competence, efficiency, aptitude, capacity. *Antonyms:* inability.

able, a. competent, qualified, capable, talented, clever.

abnormal, a. irregular, exceptional, unusual. *Antonyms:* normal.

abode, n. residence, habitation, dwelling, sojourn.

abolish, v. annul, nullify, invalidate, revoke, destroy. *Antonyms:* confirm, establish.

abound, v. be plentiful, teem, swarm.

abridge, v. shorten, diminish, curtail.

abrupt, a. hasty, rough, rude, curt, jagged, rugged.

abscess, n. ulcer, fester.

absence, n. nonattendance; want. destitution, privation.

absolute, a. unconditional, unrestricted, uncontrolled, supreme; consummate, faultless.

absorb, v. engulf, overwhelm, swallow up; suck up, engross, occupy, monopolize.

abstain, v. refrain, withhold, deny one's self. *Antonyms:* indulge.

absurd, a. ridiculous, preposterous, irrational, inconsistent.

abundance, n. sufficiency, plenty, profusion, exuberance, overflow.

abuse, v. misapply, misuse, desecrate, violate, profane.

acceptance, n. approval, favorable reception: acceptableness. *Antonyms:* rejection.

accessory, a. accompanying, accessary, subservient, subsidiary.

accommodation, n. adaptation, adjustment: complaisance; favor, kindness.

account, n. calculation, record, tab; registry, register; recital, relation, narrative, report, portrayal, description, opinion; value.

accumulation, n. hoard, aggregation, accruement.

achieve, v. accomplish, realize, effect, attain.

acrobat, n. bitterness, rancor, sharpness.

action, n. agency, operation, activity; pl. conduct, deeds; lawsuit, *Antonyms:* inaction, inactivity.

active, a. brisk, nimble, agile, sprightly, spirited; strenuous, diligent. *Antonyms:* inactive, passive.

actual, a. real, veritable. *Antonyms:* potential, nominal.

adapt, v. adjust, conform.

addict, v. habituate, accustom.

adequacy, n. sufficiency. *Antonyms:* inadequacy, insufficiency.

admissible, a. allowable, permissible. *Antonyms:* inadmissable.

adorn, v. decorate, beautify, grace, garnish, beset. *Antonyms:* disfigure, mar, deform.

advance, v. progress, increase; promote, elevate; enhance. *Antonyms:* retreat, decline.

advantage, n. superiority, mastery, ascendancy; benefit, avail. *Antonyms:* disadvantage.

adversary, n. enemy, foe,

opponent, antagonist.

advice, n. counsel, information, report.

advise, v. counsel, warn; inform, notify, acquaint, tell; advise with, consult.

advocate, n. defender, apologist, upholder, promoter.

affectionate, a. devoted, fond, loving, ardent.

afflict, v. persecute, distress, trouble, harass.

agency, n. operation, action, mediation, means.

agent, n. representative, substitute, procurator, proctor, solicitor. *Antonyms:* principal, chief.

aggravate, v. intensify, enhance, increase; irritate.

agree, v. concur, accord, chime, harmonize; accede, comply, assent, consent, grant. *Antonyms:* disagree, differ.

agriculture, n. farming, geoponics, agronomy.

ailment, n. disorder, complaint, illness.

alarm, v. terrify, scare, appall, unnerve, frighten.

alienate, v. transfer, demise, assign; estrange, wean.

alleviate, v. mollify, lessen. moderate, relieve.

allow, v. permit, consent to; suffer, endure.

allowance, n. permission, admittance, tolerance, sufferance, assent. *Antonyms:* disallowance, refusal.

allude, v. refer, advert, suggest

amaze, v. astonish, astound, surprise, stagger, dumfound.

ambiguous, a. indefinite, vague, doubtful.

amiable, a. gracious, benign, good-natured, obliging.

amuse, v. entertain, recreate, please.

analogy, n. similarity, agreement, correspondence.

anatomy, n. dissection; body, structure, skeleton.

ancestor, n. forefather, primogenitor, forbear.

ancient, a. old, archaic, antique, primitive, pristine.

angelic, a. cherubic, celestial, heavenly, divine.

anguish, n. agony, distress, torture, misery, remorse.

animate, v. vitalize, quicken, inspirit, rouse.

animosity, n. rancor, hatred, virulence.

announce, v. proclaim, publish, advertise, trumpet. *Antonyms:* suppress, reserve, withhold, hush-up.

annoy, v. trouble, bother, pester, aggravate, chafe.

antagonist, n. opponent, foe, adversary, rival.

anterior, a. prior, before, previous.

anticipate, v. expect, preclude, obviate.

anxiety, n. apprehension, solicitude *Antonyms:* indifference, assurance.

anxious, a. apprehensive, concerned, worried. *Antonyms:* unconcerned, assured.

apathy, n. dispassion, indifference, unconcern.

apparent, a. visible, manifest, obvious, evident; seeming, specious.

appendage, n. pedicle, appendix, attachment.

appetite, n. desire for food, hunger; desire. *Antonyms:* aversion, distaste.

applause, n. acclaim, cheers. *Antonyms:* hooting, derision.

appliance, n. device, facility.

applicant, n. candidate, petitioner, suitor.

apply, v. utilize, practice.

appreciate, v. value, esteem,

prize.

apprehend, v. arrest, seize; understand, consider, believe.

appropriate, a. fitting, proper, apposite, pertinent., *Antonyms:* inappropriate.

aptitude, n. proneness, propensity, leaning, inclination. *Antonyms:* inaptitude.

ardent, a. zealous, warm, passionate, fervent, enthusiastic.

aristocracy, n. peerage, nobility, patriciar order *Antonyms:* commonalty, peasantry.

armory, n. arsenal.

aromatic, a. fragrant, balmy, spicy, savory.

arouse, v. excite, rouse, stimulate, awaken, revive.

arrest, v. apprehension, capture, detention; custody, duress; stoppage, restraint.

arrogance, n. insolence, haughtiness, lordliness.

article, n. thing, commodity; portion, clause, stipulation.

artifice, n. finesse, craft, guile, diplomacy.

ashamed, a. confused, mortified, disconcerted. *Antonyms:* unashamed, brazen-faced.

aspect, n. appearance, look; view, scene, prospect.

assent, n. consent, agreement, concurrence; placet. *Antonyms:* dissent, declension.

assert, v. affirm, state, say, predicate, maintain.

assets, n. pl. resources, property, effects, possessions.

assign, v. allot, appoint; transfer, make-over, convey.

assistant, a. helping, auxiliary, aider, ally, aid, accomplice, subsidiary.

assurance, n. surety, promise; confidence, conviction, assuredness; audacity.

asylum, n. retreat, sanctuary.

atrocious, a. heinous, felonious, infamous, outrageous.

attain, v. achieve, compass, gain.

attend, v. guard, look after; accompany, escort; pay regard. attention, n. regard, consideration, alertness, watchfulness, notice civility, courtesy. *Antonyms:* inattention, slight, disregard.

attitude, n. posture, position, pose.

attract, v. allure, entice, draw, decoy, interest, engage, induce. *Antonyms:* repel, repulse.

attribute, v. impute, assign, refer, trace.

audacious, a. presumptuous, impudent, brazen, unabashed.

authentic, a. genuine, trustworthy, credible.

author, n. creator, originator, father, writer.

authorize, v. empower, commission; sanction, warrant, justify, confirm.

automatic, a. self-propelling, self-moving.

auxiliary, n. assistant, helper.

average, a. medium, ordinary, mediocre, middling.

aversion, n. dislike, antipathy loathing.

avoid, v. evade, shun, elude, shirk, parry.

awaken, v. wake, awake, rouse, arouse, excite.

aware, a. conscious, apprised, mindful.

awkward, a. clumsy, ungraceful, gawky, ungainly, inelegant, unskillful, uncourtly, embarrassing. *Antonyms:* graceful, courtly, elegant, clever.

awry, a. distorted, wry crooked, askant, perverse.

axle, n. arbor, spindle.

B

babble, n. gabble, chatter; murmur, purl.

baby, n. infant, babe, suckling. see child.

bachelor, n. celibate.

back, a. posterior, dorsal, neural; remote, distant, frontier; rear, reverse.

backbone, n. spine, spinal column, chine.

backdown, n. surrender, recession, withdrawal.

backhouse, n. outhouse, privy, water-closet, latrine.

backslide, v. break faith, relapse, desert, fall away.

backward, a. reverse, regressive; retrospective; reluctant, loath, unwilling; dull, inapt.

bad, a. evil, wicked, immoral, corrupt, sinful, demoralized, sinister, vicious.

badge, n. device, emblem, ensign, star, insignia.

badinage, n. raillery *Antonyms:* innocent), banter.

baffle, v. balk, disconcert, frustrate, thwart, circumvent.

bag, n. sack, pouch, knapsack, pocket, satchel, suitcase, gunny sack.

baggage, n. luggage, traps.

bail, n. security, surety, vadium.

bait, n. lure, enticement, temptation, decoy, allurement; kibbling.

balcony, n. gallery, terrace.

balk, v. frustrate, baffle, foil, disappoint.

ball, n. sphere, globe, pellet; pommel; baseball, football, basket-ball, tether-ball.

ballast, n. steadiness, self-control, stability, judgement.

balm, n. ointment; mitigant, nepenthe, balsam.

banal, a. commonplace, hack-neyed, trite.

banality, n. platitude, commonplace.

bandage, v. deligate, swathe.

bandit, n. outlaw, brigand, footpad, desperado.

banish, v. exile, expatriate, relegate; drive away, dismiss.

banister, n. baluster.

bank, n. mound, pile, ridge, dike, heap, drift, embankment; brink.

bankrupt, a. insolvent; depleted, impoverished.

banner, n. flag, standard, ensign, banderole, colors, pavilion.

banquet, n. junket, regalement, feast.

banter, n. joking, jesting, pleasantry, badinage, chaff.

baptism, n. baptizing; parabaptism, pedobaptism; hypothetical baptism.

barbarian, a. barbarous, savage, rude, uncivilized.

barbarous, a. uncivilized, barbarian, inhuman, brutal.

bare, a. naked, nude, undressed, unveiled, exposed, undraped, unadorned, empty.

barefaced, a. unmasked, undisguised, glaring, shameless, audacious.

bargain, v. stipulate, agree, covenant; barter.

bark, v. peel, flay, skin, decorticate; bay, yelp, yap.

barn, n. stable.

barrel, n. cask, cade, hogshead, keg, rundlet; [of wine] 31-1/2 gallons.

barren, a. sterile, agenestic, unprolific; unproductive, unfruitful, unfertile, desert.

barrier, n. obstruction, impediment, obstacle, hindrance, barricade.

barter, n. traffic, exchange, trade, business.

base, n. basis, bottom, foundation, groundwork.

baseboard, n. mopboard, scrubboard.

basement, n. cellar.

bashful, a. over-modest, diffident, coy, sheepish.

basis, n. foundation.

bask, v. luxuriate, revel.

basket, n. hamper, creel, hanaper, tumbril, canister, bassinet, punnet, wicker.

batch, n. quantity, lot, assortment, collection.

bate, n. puer, grainer.

bath, n. ablution, lavement; bathroom, lavatory.

bathe, v. lave, wash; foment; surround, envelop, enwrap.

baton, n. staff, wand.

batten, v. fatten.

batter, v. smite, pelt, assault; demolish, shatter.

battle, n. engagement, fight, encounter, skirmish, contest, combat, strife.

bauble, n. trinket, plaything.

bay, n. bight, frith, fiord, bayou; recess, alcove, sinus.

beach, n. shore, strand, shingle, marge.

beacon, n. balefire, signal fire; signal, pharos.

beads, n. pl. rosary; [beaded trimming]; chaplet.

beak, n. bill, nib, mandible; prow, bow, rostrum.

beam, n. girder, joist; ray, gleam.

bear, v. endure, tolerate, stand, undergo, brook, submit to, suffer, carry.

beard, n. whiskers; goatee, mustache; awn, arista.

bearing, n. mien, carriage, port, demeanor, air, deportment; endurance.

bearish, a. discourteous, boorish, rude; ursine.

beast, n. brute; quadruped; monster, brute.

beat, v, forge, malleate, beetle, weld, hammer; belabor, maul,

buffet, flagellate.

beau, n. lover, sweetheart, gallant, swain, flame.

beautiful, a. fair, lovely, handsome, personable, elegant, exquisite. *Antonyms:* homely, ugly, repulsive, hideous, inelegent.

becloud, v. dim, cloud, obscure.

becoming, a. appropriate, fit, seemly, befitting. *Antonyms:* unbecoming.

bed, n. berth, bunk, couch, cot; pallet, mattress; cradle, trundle-bed; deposit, seam.

bedbug, n. chinch.

bedim, v. obscure, becloud, overcast.

bedlam, n. madhouse, insane asylum; babel, pandemonium.

beehive, n. beehouse, apiary.

beetle, n. mallet [heavy]; scarabee, clock.

befall, v. happen, supervene.

befitting, a. suitable, proper, seemly, meet, applicable.

befuddle, v. confuse, mystify.

beg, v. beseech, implore.

beget, v. procreate, generate.

beggar, v. impoverish, ruin; exhaust, surpass, go beyond.

begin, v. commence; arise, spring, originate.

beguile, v. insnare, mislead, lure, deceive, cheat.

behave, v. deport one's self, act.

behead, v. decapitate, execute.

beholden, a. obliged, indebted, bound.

being, n. existence, entity. *Antonyms:* nonexistence, nonentity.

belch, v. expel, throw up.

belfry, n. bell-tower.

belief, n. persuasion, faith; conviction, assurance, confidence; creed, opinion. *Antonyms:* doubt, disbelief, skepticism.

belittle, v. decry, disparage.

A
B

bell, n. campana, curfew, gong.

belligerent, a. at war, militant; bellicose.

bell-ringer, n. sexton, campanologist.

bell-tower, n. belfry, campanile.

belly, n. abdomen, paunch; recesses.

belly-ache, n. colic, gripes.

belonging, n. appendage, appurtenance, accessary.

below, adv. under, beneath, underneath.

belt, n. girdle; girth, surcingle, cestus; zone.

bemoan, v. lament, deplore.

bench, n. form; workbench.

bend, v. curve, flex, crook; direct, turn, apply; stoop, incline; yield.

beneficent, a. benevolent, charitable, magnanimous.

benefit, n. avail, profit, behalf, service.

benevolence, n. beneficence, bounty, charity.

bent, a. crooked, flexed, hooked; determined.

benumb, v. stupefy, blunt.

bequeath, v. devise, will.

berate, v. upbraid, rate.

beseech, v. entreat, implore.

beset, v. besiege, obsess, environ, encompass; perplex.

besiege, v. obsess, environ, beset, encompass.

betoken, v. foreshadow, portend, foreshow, indicate.

betray, v. seduce, mislead, delude, beguile, reveal, disclose.

betroth, v. affiance.

better, n. upper hand, domination, advantage, control, superiority.

betterment, n. improvement, promotion, reformation.

between, prep. betwixt.

bevy, n. [of birds] flock, covey; [of deer] herd.

bewail, v. deplore, lament, wail over, bemoan.

bewilder, v. confuse, perplex, confound, mystify, embarrass.

bewitch, v. charm, fascinate, captivate, enamor. *Antonyms:* disillusionize, repel.

bias, n. bent, proneness.

Bible, n. the Scriptures, the Word of God; [Catholic] Douay Bible, Vulgate; [Islamic] Koran.

bibulous, a. absorbent; intemperate, bibacious.

bickering, n. contention, wrangling, sparring, quarrel.

bid, v. offer, proffer; order, direct, enjoin, command; invite, ask; wish, greet.

big, a. large, huge, bulky, massive, immense, gross, voluminous, capacious.

bigamy, n. polygamy, polygyny.

bigot, n. fanatic, zealot.

bile, n. choler, bitterness, anger, spleen, rancor.

bill, n. circular, placard, dodger, poster; statement; beak, nib, mandible.

bin, n. crib, bunker.

bind, v. tie, fasten, secure, gird, confine, restrict, retrain; bandage. *Antonyms:* unbind, loose.

bird, n. [young] fledgling, nestling; annotine; squab; [rare bird]

bird-catcher, n. fowler.

birr, n. whirring.

birth, n. nativity; origin, beginning, genesis; extraction, lineage; regeneration.

birthright, n. inheritance.

bishop, n. diocesan, prelate; suffragan, metropolitan.

bit, n. morsel, fragment, scrap, crumb; mite, ace, particle, whit.

bit by bit. piecemeal.

bite, v. champ, nibble, chew; sting, smart, tingle; take hold of, adhere; nip, blast.

bitter, a. poignant, intense; calamitous distressing, virulent.

bizarre, a. fantastic, whimsical, grotesque.

blab, n. babbler, telltale.

black, a. sable, ebony, inky, lowering, murky; negro.

blacken, v. darken, denigrate; begrime, tarnish, discolor; defame, malign.

blackguard, n. scoundrel, rascal, villain.

blackhearted, a. villainous, abandoned, reprobate, base.

blacklead. graphite.

blackness, n. black, nigritude; atrocity, heinousness.

blacksmith, n. ironsmith, farrier, horseshoer.

blade, n. leaf [of a plant], spire [of grass]; buck, gallant, dandy.

blamable, a. culpable, censurable, blameworthy

blame, v. censure, reproach.

bland, a. suave, mollifying, affable, complaisant; soothing, emollient.

blank, a. void, empty, unfilled; expressionless, vacant, nonplused, astounded.

blarney, n. palaver, blandishment, cajolery.

blarney, v. flatter, cajole, palaver, wheedle, blandish.

blasphemy, n. sacrilege, profanity.

blast, n. squall, gust; peal, blare, clang; explosion.

blatant, a. brawling, clamorous, bawling, braying.

blaze, n. flame.

bleach, f. whiten, blanch.

bleak, a. windswept, cheerless, raw, penetrating, desolate, dreary.

bleeding, n. hemorrhage; bloodletting venesection.

blemish, v. deface, mar, disfigure, sully.

blench, v. flinch, recoil.

blend, v. intermingle, fuse, merge, combine, mix.

blessing, n. benediction, benison, beatitude; God send.

blight, v. blast; ruin, frustrate, thwart.

blind, a. unseeing, sightless, purblind; oblivious, undiscriminating, unmindful; unintelligible, obscure.

blink, v. wink; disregard.

bliss, n. felicity, transport, rapture, beatitude, ecstasy.

blister, n. vesicle, pustule, bleb; vesicatory, pustulant.

bloat, v. inflate, distend.

block, f. obstruct, blockade.

blood, n. lifeblood; gore.

bloodsucker, n. leech.

bloodthirsty, a. truculent, ferocious, cruel.

blood vessel. artery; vein; capillary.

bloom, n. blossom, blow; prime, vigor, flush; fuzz.

blossom, n. flower, florescence, bloom, blow.

blot, n. stain, blemish, smutch, smooch, reproach.

blotch, n. eruption, blain, pustule, bleb; smutch, blot.

blow, n. blossom, bloom; whack, knock, rap, thump, assault, stroke.

blower, n. braggart, boaster, vaunter.

blow out. extinguish

blue, a. azure, cerulean, sapphire, amethystine, turquoise, ultramarine, sky-colored.

bluff, a. abrupt, brusque; gruff, surly; precipitous, steep.

blunt, a. dull, obtuse; abrupt, brusque, uncivil, ungracious, discourteous; stupid.

blur, v. dim, obscure; sully, blemish; mackle, macule.

bluster, n. swaggering, boasting; wind, storm.

boar, n. male hog; barrow

[castrated]; hogget.

boast, v. brag, vapor. *Antonyms:* belittle, disparage.

boat, n. water craft, launch, rowboat, canoe, gondola, yacht, ship.

bob, n. pendant, float.

bode, v. forebode, foreshadow, presage, betoken.

bodiless, a. disembodied.

boding, a. ominous.

boding, n. omen, sign, foreboding, auspice, portent.

body, n. the physical person; torso, trunk; physique; bulk, mass; axis.

bodyguard, n. lifeguard.

boggle, v. hesitate, stickle.

bogus, a. counterfeit, fictitious, sham, fraudulent, forged, mock, false.

boil, v. seethe, simmer.

boil away, v. evaporate.

boisterous, a. noisy, turbulent, unrestrained, rude.

bold, a. daring, brave; forward, immodest, rude, brazen, saucy, insolent. *Antonyms:* modest, coy, bashful, shy, timid.

boldness, n. impudence, presumption, impertinence.

bolster, v. prop up, support, maintain. n. cushion, pad.

bolt, v. sift; leave suddenly; gulp.

bomb, n. shell.

bona fide. in good faith, real, actual, really.

bond, n. band, tie; pl. shackles, constraint.

bondage, n. servitude, slavery, captivity, bond service, durance.

bondsman, n. bondman, slave, villain, serf; surety.

bone formation. ostosis, ectostosis, osteogeny.

bonelike, a. osseous, bony, ossified.

bonnet, n. headdress, chapeau.

bonus, n. premium.

book, n. volume; tome; manual; publication; biography; anthology.

bookkeeper, n. accountant, countercaster.

bookkeeping, n. accountancy.

booklet, n. pamphlet, brochure, tract.

book lore. bibliology.

bookman, n. scholar, student.

bookseller, n. bookmerchant, bibliopole.

book worship, bibliolatry.

boom, v. resound, roar.

boor, n. peasant, rustic [rude]; lout, churl, gawk.

boot, n. premium, bonus.

border, n. verge, edge, margin, brink, marge, skirt, rim, brim.

bore, n. perforation; caliber; tiresome person, proser.

boring, n. perforation; transformation.

bosh, n. nonsense, forth, moonshine, balderdash.

boss, n. superintendent, director, employer, foreman, overseer.

botanist, n. phytologist.

botany, n. phytology.

botch, n. bungle, fiasco.

bother, v. trouble, annoy, discommode, inconvenience, worry, molest.

bothersome, a. troublesome, perplexing, annoying.

bottle, n. vial, cruet, flask, decanter, cruse, siphon, tankard, carafe.

bottom, n. foot, base; nadir; foundation, groundwork, basis, base, pedestal.

bough, n. branch, limb.

bounce, v. spring, bound; rebound, recoil, dismiss.

bound, v. limit, inclose, terminate; leap, spring, bounce; rebound.

boundary, n. circumference; bound, limit, border, term, confines, precinct.

bounteous, a. bountiful, generous, liberal.

bouquet, n. nosegay; boutonniere.

bourne, n. destination, goal; stream, rivulet; boundary, bound.

bout, n. round, turn; contest, set-to, conflict.

bower, n. arbor.

bow-legged, a. bandy-legged.

bowman, n. archer.

bow-shaped, a. arcuate.

box, n. receptacle, chest, case, coffer, carton, casket.

boxing, n. sparring.

boyhood, n. youth, juvenility, juniority, minority.

boy-servant, n. page, footboy; groom, hostler.

brace, v. prop, support, fortify, buttress, stay, shore; strengthen.

bracket, n. console, corbel, strut, cantilever.

brag, v. boast, vaunt, vapor. *Antonyms:* disparage, decry, belittle.

braid, n. plain; queue, pigtail. v. plait, plat, entwine, interlace.

brain, n. cerebrum;cerebellum; encephalon.

brain action. cerebration.

brake, n. thicket.

branch, n. bough, limb; shoot, sprout, sprig, spray, twig, tiller.

brand, v. stigmatize.

brash, a. quick-tempered, irascible; brittle, crisp.

brassy, a. brazen; bold, impudent, forward.

bravado, n. brag; blustering, threat.

brawl, n. quarrel, dispute, rumpus, uproar.

brawny, a. muscular, sinewy, robust, strong.

breach, n. breaking, rupture; infraction, violation, trespass, nonobservance.

breadth, n. width, latitude; liberality, tolerance.

breakdown, n. downfall, collapse, crash.

breaking, n. fracture, rupture, breach, infraction.

breaking out. eruption, rash, efflorescence, exanthema.

breakup, n. disruption, disorganization.

breast, v. stem, struggle with, withstand, resist.

breathe, v. respire, inhale and exhale; infuse; sneeze, suspire, sigh, gasp, pant.

breech, n. buttocks.

breed, v. generate, procreate, engender, conceive and bear; nurture, train; occasion.

breeze, n. disturbance, quarrel, breezy, a. airy, windy.

brew, v. foment, concoct, hatch, plot.

bribe, n. hush-money, boodle.

bribery, n. subornation.

brick, n. adobe.

bridal, a. nuptial, conjugal.

bridge, n. trestlework, culvert, pons, pontoon, bridge.

bridle, n. restraint, curb, check. - v. restrain, curb, check, control.

brief, a. short-lived, transient, transitory; terse.

brigand, n. highwayman, bandit, outlaw, robber.

bright, a. luminous, gleaming, lustrous, radiant, intelligent, apt, acute, clever. *Antonyms:* dull, lackluster, obscure, dim, opaque, murky, tarnished.

brilliant, a. sparkling, glittering, dazzling, gleaming, flashing; splendid, glorious.

brim, n. rim, border, margin, edge, brink, bank, marge.

bring, v. fetch.

brink, n. edge, border, verge.

brisk, a. lively, spirited, spry, agile, rapid.

brittle, a. frangible, crisp.

broad, a. wide; extensive, extended, vast, wide-reaching, comprehensive; liberal.

broil, v. grill.

broken, a. fractured, splintered, shattered, interrupted; impaired, shattered; subdued. *Antonyms:* inviolate, intact, whole.

broker, a. agent, factor, middleman, go-between.

brood, v. incubate, sit; meditate.

brook, n. rivulet, runlet, rill, creek, streamlet.

broom, n. besom; whisk [small broom].

brothel, n. house of prostitution, bawdy-house.

brotherhood, n. fraternity, fellowship.

brow, n. forehead.

brown, a. dusky, tawny, dun.

bruise, v. contuse, ecchymose.

brush, n. brushwood; thicket, underbrush; grazing.

brutal, a. inhuman, cruel, fell, ruthless, unfeeling; beastly, bestial, brutish.

brute, n. beast; fiend, monster, ruffian.

buck, n. ram; beau, fop, blade, dandy.

bud, v. pullulate, germinate.

budding, n. gemmification, gemmation.

buffalo, n. bison; caribou, [water buffalo].

build, v. erect, construct, raise.

building, n. erection, construction; edifice, structure, pile, architecture.

businesslike, a. pragmatical.

bulging, a. protuberant, convex, gibbous.

bulldoze, v. intimidate, browbeat.

bullhead, n. dolt, lout, lubber, dunderhead.

bully, n. blusterer, swaggerer, roisterer, rowdy, rough.

bulwark, n. rampart, fortification; defense.

bump, v. jolt, jounce, thump.

bundle, n. parcel, package, bale, pack, budget, packet.

bung, n. stopper, tampoon, spigot, stopple; bunghole.

bunker, n. bin, receptacle, crib.

burden, n. load, cargo; incubus, encumbrance, weight, impediment, trial.

burial, n. interment, inhumation, sepulture *Antonyms:* disinterment, exhumation.

burlesque, n. travesty, farce.

burn, v. scorch, scald, singe, char, sear, cauterize, brand, consume.

burnable, a. combustion, incineration; cauterization, cautery; pyrography; arson; smoldering.

bury, n. inter, inhume, entomb, sepulcher; hide, secrete, conceal. *Antonyms:* disinter, exhume.

burying-ground, n. cemetery.

bush, n. shrub; thicket, jungle, underwood, boscage.

bushwacker, n. bushranger, guerrilla.

business, n. vocation, calling, pursuit; craft, trade, occupation, profession; avocation.

bustle, n. stir, agitation, ado, commotion; bishop, tournure, pannier.

busy, a. occupied, engaged, employed, engrossed; diligent, industrious, active.

butcher, v. slaughter.

buttock, n. rump, fundament.

buttress, n. support, stay.

buy, v. purchase.

buzz, n. hum, murmur, bombinate; whiz.

bystander, n. spectator, onlooker, witness.

A
B

C

cabbage, n. savoy; colwort; broccoli; collards; brussels sprouts.

cabbage, v. steal, pilfer, filch.

cabin, n, hut, hovel, shanty, cot, shack, cottage.

cage, n. mew. -v confine, coop up, encage, mew.

cajole, v. beguile, wheedle, blandish, flatter.

cajolery, n. wheedling, blandishment, beguilement.

cake, v. concrete, harden, solidify, coagulate.

calamitous, a. disastrous, deplorable, baleful, ill-fated, untoward, dire.

calamity, n. disaster, catastrophe, misfortune, adversity, mischance.

calculate, v. compute, reckon, estimate; forecast.

calendar, n. almanac; list, schedule, register, docket.

calf, n. Associated words: vellum, parchment, fatling, slink, calve, steer.

calico, n. print.

call, v. summon, bid, evoke, invite; convoke, assemble, convene.

call, n. summons, invocation, entreaty, appeal, invitation; signal; requirement, demand.

callous, a. unfeeling, insensible, hardened.

callow, a. unfledged, unfeathered; immature, green.

call to account. impeach, accuse.

calm, n. lull, tranquillity, quiet, placidity.

calm, a. still, serene, motionless, undisturbed, unruffled, pacific, placid, tranquil. *Antonyms:* excited, stormy, agitated, ruffled, perturbed.

calm, v. lull, allay, hush, becalm, still, compose, quiet, appease.

camel, n. dromedary, deloul.

cameo, n. anaglyph. *Antonyms:* intaglio.

camouflage, n. disguise, blind, deception, illusion.

camouflage, v. disguise, blind, deceive, hide, conceal, veil, dissemble, mask.

camp, n. encampment; bivouac; cantonment, quarters.

camp, v. encamp.

canal, n. channel.

cancel, v. annul, abrogate, rescind, nullify, abolish. *Antonyms:* confirm, approve, enforce, maintain.

cancellation, n. annulment, abrogation, rescission, nullification.

cancer, n. carcinoma, carcinosis.

candid, a. impartial, unbiased, fair; frank, ingenuous, unreserved. *Antonyms:* disingenuous, reserved, subtle.

candidate, n. nominee, postulant, office-seeker.

candle, n. taper, rushlight, serge; pl. chandlery.

candlestick, n. candelabrum, lustre.

candor, n. impartiality, disinterestedness; frankness, openness.

candy, n. confectionery, bonbon, confection, lollipop, caramel, fudge, fondant, praline.

candy maker, confectioner.

can sugar, sucrose.

canker, n. corrosion, erosion.

cannibal, n. anthropophagite. a. anthropophagous. cannibalism, n. anthropophagy; exophagy.

cannon, n. Associated words: ordnance, cannonade, calibre, bore, breech, chase, muzzle, rimbase, chamber, mortar.

canny, a. cunning, crafty, wary, shrewd, prudent.

C
D

canoe, n. piroque [dugout];
   pitpan [Cen. Amer.]; kayak.
canon, n. law, regulation.
canopy, n. covering, awning, tilt,
   tester, pavilion.
cant, n. slope, tilt, turn; bias,
   impulse; prating: idioms,
   vocabulary; affected piety,
   hypocrisy; slang.
cant, v. tilt, tip, incline.
cantankerous, a. perverse,
   contentious, contrary.
canvas, n. tarpaulin.
canyon, n. gorge, ravine.
cap, n. biggin, biggonnet, busby,
   berreta, barret, caul, callote,
   turban.
capability, n. ability, capacity,
   qualification, proficiency,
   efficiency.
capable, a. able, qualified,
   competent, efficient.
cape, n. promontory, headland.
caper, n. dido, trick, prank, leap,
   gambol, curlycue.
caper, v. gambol, frisk, cavort,
   leap, skip, prance.
capital, a. principal, leading,
   chief, cardinal.
capital letter, n. majuscule.
capitation, n. poll tax.
caprice, n. fancy, whim, notion,
   freak, crotchet, quirk, whimsy,
   fickleness.
capricious, a. fanciful, whimsical, vagarious, inconstant,
   fickle
cap-shaped, a. pileate, pileated.
capsize, v. upset, overturn.
captain, n. commander, chieftain, leader, chief: skipper;
   colonel; master, foreman.
captious, a. critical, carping,
   censorious.
captivate, v. enchant, subdue,
   bewitch, fascinate, entrance,
   infatuate.
captivity, n. bondage, servitude,
   vassalage, slavery.
capture, v. seize, catch, appre-

hend, arrest, corral.
capture, n. prey, prize; apprehension, arrest, seizure
   catching.
car, n. cart, vehicle, chariot,
   caboose, tender, cage, coach,
   tram, truck.
carbolic acid. phenol, phenic
   acid, cardinal, a. principal,
   chief, superior.
cardinal virtues, n. prudence,
   temperance, justice, fortitude.
care, n. concern, anxiety, worry,
   apprehension; oversight,
   charge, management, custody.
careful, a. cautious, watchful,
   provident, attentive, considerate, prudent, wary, mindful.
careless, a. negligent, unconcerned, indifferent, inattentive,
   regardless, lax, remiss.
cargo, n. freight, load, burden,
   lading, last.
caricature, n. exaggeration,
   burlesque, take-off, travesty.
carking, a. harassing, worrying,
   distressing.
carnal, a. sensual, fleshly, bodily;
   lustful.
carousal, n. revel, wassail,
   orgies, jamboree.
carouser, a. reveler, roysterer,
   debauchee.
carp, v. cavil, censure.
carpenter, n. joiner.
carriage, n. carrying, bearing,
   behavior, deportment; air,
   demeanor.
carriage, n. vehicle, coach, gig,
   buggy, sulky, surrey, chaise,
   sedan.
carrier, n. messenger, conveyer;
   porter, bearer.
carry, v. convey, transport, bear,
   carry out, complete.
cart, n. vehicle, wagon, carriage;
   lorrie, truck.
carte, n. menu, bill of fare.
cartilage, n. gristle.
carve, v. sculpture, chisel,

engrave, fashion.

case, n. sheath, covering, capsule, quiver, chest; event, happening, instance.

case-hardened, a. seared.

cash, n. coin, currency.

cashier, n. treasurer, purser.

cask, n. pipe, butt.

casket, n. gemmary; coffin.

cassock, n. soutane.

cast, v. fling, hurl, throw, pitch, sling; direct, deposit, place.

cast, n. throw, fling; ejection, secretion.

castaway, n. outcast, pariah, derelict.

castigate, v. chastise.

castiron, a. unyielding, hardy.

castle, n. fortress, citadel, fastness, mansion, chateau.

cast off, v. discard, reject.

cast-off, a. discarded, rejected.

castrate, v. alter; emasculate.

casual, a. chance, accidental.

cat, n. feline, tabby, puss, kitten, kitty.

catacomb, n. grotto, crypt.

catalogue, n. list, register, schedule, index.

cataract, n. waterfall, fall, cascade.

catastrophe, n. disaster, calamity.

catch, v. seize, grasp, clutch, gripe, nab; apprehend; arrest.

catch, n. capture, seizure, arrest, hook, clasp.

catchword, n. cue.

category, n. class, state, condition, division.

cater, v. purvey.

cathartic, n. purgative, physic, purge.

catholic, a. universal, general, tolerant; Roman Catholic, Roman. *Antonyms:* uncatholic, local, narrow.

catkin, n. ament.

cattle, n. kine; Bos: Bovine quadrupeds; Taurus.

cattle-plague, n. rinderpest, murrain.

cattle-stealing, n. abigeat

cause, n. origin, source; motive, incitement, incentive.

cause, v. occasion, induce, effect, originate.

caustic, a. burning, virulent, cutting, satirical.

caution, n. wariness, forethought; advice, warning.

caution, v. forewarn, admonish, warn, advise.

cautious, a. circumspect, prudent, wary. *Antonyms:* incautious, unwary)

cave, n. cavern, grotto, den, catacomb, crypt.

cave-dweller, n. troglodyte.

cavil, v. carp, criticize, -n objection, criticism.

Cayenne pepper. capsicum.

cease, v. discontinue, stop.

cede, v. surrender, grant.

celebrate, v. commemorate, observe.

celebration, n. commemoration, observance, solemnization.

celebrity, n. fame, renown.

cellar, n. basement

celluloid, n. zylonite.

cement, n. adhesive, glue.

cemetery, n. necropolis, God's acre, graveyard, mortuary.

censer, n. thurible, incensory.

censor, n. inspector, reviewer, critic; caviler.

censorious, a. carping, captious, critical.

censurable, a. reprehensible, blamable, reproachable.

censure, n. reprehension, blame, reprimand.

censure, v. reprove, rebuke, reprehend, chide.

centenary, n. centennial, century.

centennial, n. centenary.

center, n. middle, midst. [circumference, perimeter].

centerpiece, n. epergne.

central, a. middle, centric.

century, n. centenary.

ceremonious, a. formal, precise. *Antonyms:* informal, free and easy.

ceremony, n. rite, form, ceremonial, solemnity; formality.

certain, a. sure, assured, confident, convinced, satisfied, undoubting; undeniable, irrefutable. *Antonyms:* indefinite, uncertain.

certainty, n. sureness, confidence, assurance, fact, truth. *Antonyms:* uncertainty.

certificate, n. testimonial, credential, voucher.

certify, v. assure, attest, testify to, vouch for.

chafe, v. rub, gall, irritate; fret, fume, rage.

chaff, n. glumes, hulls.

chaffy, a. acerose, palaceous, stramineous.

chagrin, n. mortification, abashment, vexation, confusion, discomposure.

chagrin, v. mortify, abash, vex, confuse, humiliate.

chain, n. concatenation, series, congeries, catenate, necklace, gorget, links.

chain, v. fetter, restrain, shackle, enslave, trammel.

chain wheel, n. sprocket wheel.

chair, n. seat; professorship.

chalice, n. grail.

chalkstone, n. tophus.

chalky, a. cretaceous.

challenge, v. defy, dare, brave. - n. defiance; objection.

champion, n. defender, vindicator, protector, paladin; winner, hero.

chance, v. befall' risk, venture.

chance, n. fate, fortune, luck, fortuity, hap, casualty, accident; possibility.

chancery, n. equity.

change, n. variation, alteration, transition, mutation, conversion, innovation. *Antonyms:* continuation, stability, conservatism, permanence, monotony, continuance.

change, v. alter, transmute, shift, modulate, reverse, reform, vary. *Antonyms:* continue, persist.

changeable, a. mutable, variable, inconstant, unstable, unsteadfast, reversible.

changeless, a. permanent, immutable, inexorable, invariable, undeviating, unvarying.

changeling, n. oaf; waverer.

change of life. climacteric; menopause.

channel, n. water-course, canal, aqueduct, gutter, runway, conduit, duct.

chant, v. intone, cantillate.

chant, n. intonation; introit.

chaos, n. confusion, disorder.

chap, n. lad, youth.

chapel, n. oratory, chantry, bethel.

chapped, a. kibed.

chaps, n.pl. jaws, chops.

chapter, n. branch.

character, n. personality, nature, individuality.

characteristic, n. trait, feature, attribute, idiosyncrasy.

characterize, v. distinguish.

charge, n. accusation, complaint, allegation, indictment, imputation, crimination.

charge, v. impose, load, encumber; exhort, enjoin, instruct; commit, intrust.

chargeable, a. imputable, attributable, referrible.

charitable, a. benevolent, benign, beneficent, magnanimous; liberal, tolerant. *Antonyms:* uncharitable, intolerant.

charity, n. benevolence, good will, love, benignity, bounty,

C
D

philanthropy, tolerance.

charlatan, n. pretender, quack, impostor, fraud, cheat.

charlatanic, a. pretentious, empirical, quackish.

charlatanry, n. quackery, pretension, empiricism.

charm, n. spell, incantation, enchantment, amulet, talisman; glamour, attraction, illusion. *Antonyms:* disenchantment, repellence.

charmer, n. enchanter, magician, sorcerer; siren.

charming, a. bewitching, captivating, enchanting, enrapturing, magical. *Antonyms:* charmless, repellent.

charnel house, n. ossuary, tomb, carnary.

chart, n. map

chary, a. frugal, careful, saving, cautious.

chase, v. track, hunt, pursue; scatter, expel, dispel.

chase, n. hunting, field-sport, hunt, —v. chevy; pursuit.

chasm, n. abyss, gap.

chaste, a. virtuous, pure, continent, inviolated, innocent; classic, pure. *Antonyms:* unchaste.

chasten, v. discipline, correct, punish; refine, purify.

chastise, v. castigate, chasten, punish, whip.

chastisement, n. castigation

chastening, n. punishment.

chastity, n. purity, virtue.

chat, n. confabulation, talk, conversation.

cheap, a. inexpensive, low-priced; inferior, mean, mediocre, of small value.

cheapen, v. depreciate; belittle, lower.

cheat, n. fraud, trick, finesse, imposition, imposture, swindle, humbug.

cheat, v. swindle, defraud, trick,

hoax, hocus, beguile.

check, n. obstacle, restraint, curb, bridle, damper, barrier, repulse, delay.

check, v. restrain, impede, curb, bridle, checkmate.

checker, v. variegate, diversify.

checkered, a. diversified, variegated, plaid, mosaic.

checkers, n. draughts.

checking, a. repressive, restraining, curbing.

checkmate, v. defeat, vanquish, conquer, baffle.

cheek, n. jowl.

cheeky, a. audacious, bold, impudent, unabashed.

cheer, v. inspirit, elate, exhilarate, encourage, console, revive; applaud.

cheerful, a. cheery, buoyant, sunny, vivacious, optimistic, sanguine, elated, jubilant.

cheerfulness, n. cheeriness, elation, exhilaration, lightheartedness, optimism.

cheering, n. applause, plaudit; ovation.

cheerless, a. dismal, sombre, dreary, gloomy, desolate, sad, hopeless, despairing.

cheery, a. cheerful, pleasant, sunny, blithe, jovial.

cheesy, a. caseous.

chemise, n. shirt, smock, shift, chemisette.

cherish, v. treasure.

cherry-colored, a. cerise.

chest, n. box, case, trunk, hutch, receptacle.

chest, n. thorax, breast.

chew, v. masticate, munch; crunch, champ.

chewing, n. mastication; rumination, remastication.

chic, a. in good taste, neat. -n good form, style.

chicanery, n. trickery, chicane.

chicken, n. fowl; hen; rooster; pullet; capon.

chicken-hearted, a. timid, fearful, cowardly.

chicken pox, n. varicella.

chide, v. admonish, censure, upbraid, scold.

chief, n. head, leader, captain, commander, chieftain.

chief, a. leading, supreme, main, head, principal, prime, major, foremost.

child, n. progeny, offspring, issue; infant, babe, baby, tot.

childbirth, n. parturition, childbed, lying-in, labor.

childhood, n. nonage, infancy, minority, pupilage.

childish, a. juvenile, infantile, immature.

childishness, n. juvenility, immaturity.

children, n. offspring, progeny, issue, posterity.

chill, n. chilliness, shiver.

chilly, a. cool, chill, raw.

chime, v. accord, agree.

chime, n. unison, harmony.

chimera, n. delusion, phantom.

chimney, n. flue, smoke jack.

china ware, n. china, porcelain.

chink, n. crack, cranny.

chipper, a. lively, vivacious.

chirp, v. chirrup, cheep, pue.

chivalrous, a. gallant, knightly, valiant.

chivalry, n. knighthood, gallantry.

choice, n. selection, option, election, preference, preferment, volition. *Antonyms:* compulsion, indiscrimination.

choice, a. select, rare, careful, sparing. *Antonyms:* indiscriminate, common.

choir-leader, n. chorister, choirmaster.

choir vestments, cotta; cassock.

choke, v. strangle, throttle, stifle, suppress.

choleric, a. irritable, testy.

choose, v. select, elect, prefer, pick out.

chop, v. hack, mince, hash.

chop, n. stroke, chopping.

chosen, a. selected.

Christmas, n. Yule, Yuletide.

chronic, a. habitual, lingering, inveterate.

chronicle, n. record, account, diary, history.

chrysalis, n. aurelia, cocoon.

chum, n. roommate; companion, intimate, associate, friend.

church, n. temple, sanctuary, cathedral; chapel, minster, bethel, tabernacle, chantry.

church dignitary, n. prelate, primate, elder, deacon, dean.

churchly, a. ecclesiastical.

church officer. vestryman, warden, trustee.

churl, n. rustic, hind, lout.

churlish, a. boorish, rude.

cigar, n. stogie; tobie; cheroot.

cinch, n. tight grip.

cipher, n. zero, naught, nothing; nobody; device.

cipher writing, n. cryptography, crytograph, steganography.

circle, n. ring; circumference, periphery; circuit; clique, set, class.

circle, v. encircle.

circuitous, a. roundabout, devious, indirect.

circulate, v. disseminate, promulgate, diffuse.

circulation, n. dissemination, diffusion, propagation.

circumference, n. periphery, circumscription, girth.

cistern, n. reservoir; impluvium.

cite, v. quote; specify, mention, name, refer to.

citizen, n. resident.

city, n. municipality.

civil, a. civic, political, municipal; courteous, obliging, polite. *Antonyms:* uncivil.

civility, n. courtesy, politeness. *Antonyms:* incivility, discourtesy.

C
D

claim, v. demand, pretend.

claim, n. pretension, demand.

claimant, n. claimer, pretender.

clamor, n. uproar, racket.

clamorous, a. noisy, uproarious, bawling.

clandestine, a. hidden, stealthy, surreptitious.

clannish, a. narrow, exclusive.

clap, n. gonorrhea.

clapboards, n. pl. siding, weatherboarding.

claptrap, a. humbug, stage trick.

clarity, n. clearness.

clash, v. collide, hurtle, crash together; contend, disagree; clatter.

clasp, v. grasp, grapple, clutch, seize; embrace, hug.

class, v. classify, dispose.

classification, n. grouping, disposition; taxonomy.

clause, n. article, stipulation, provision.

claw, n. talon; dewclaw.

claw, v. scratch, lacerate.

clay, n. argillaceous earth; pug, argil, bole, kaolin.

clayey, a. argillaceous, luteous, cledgy.

clean, a. unsoiled, unsullied, immaculate, cleanly, neat; chaste, pure, virtuous.

clean, adv. wholly, perfectly, completely, quite, entirely.

clean, v. cleanse.

cleanse, v. purify, deterge, absterge, wash, disinfect.

cleanser, n. abstergent, detergent, purifier.

cleansing, a. detergent, abstergent, detersive.

cleansing, n. purification, detersion, purgation, lustration, expurgation.

clear, a. transparent, diaphanous, relucent, lucid, crystal; plain, evident, obvious.

clear, v. clarify; explain, interpret, acquit, absolve, vindicate; disengage, disperse.

clearer, n. clarifier.

clearing, n. clarification, clearance, dispersion; interpretation, explanation, acquittal.

clearness, n. clarity, distinctness; transparency, lucidity, perspicuity, translucency. *Antonyms:* opacity, ambiguity, vagueness.

cleave, v. adhere, cling, be loyal; split, rive.

cleft, a. riven, split, divided.

clergy, n. ministers, the cloth, ecclesiastics, clergymen. *Antonyms:* laity.

clergyman, n. minister, divine, ecclesiastic, priest, pastor, parson, preacher, rector. *Antonyms:* layman.

clergyman's residence, n. parsonage, rectory, manse.

clerk, n. salesman, saleslady; accountant, recorder, registrar, bookkeeper.

clever, a. adroit, skillful, expert, ingenious, deft.

clients, n.pl. clientele

cliff, n. crag, bluff.

climax, n. culmination.

climb, v. clamber, scale.

climbing, a. scandent, scansorial.

cling, v. adhere, cleave, hold fast.

clip, v. shear, snip, nip trim, prune, curtail.

clique, n. coterie, circle.

cloak, n. mantle, coat, dolman, pelisse; pretext, blind, mask.

cloak, v. conceal, mask, hide.

clock, n. timepiece, timekeeper, horometer; scarab, beetle.

clockmaker, n. horologist.

clodhopper, n. bumpkin, boor, hind, clown.

clog, v. impede, hamper, encumber, restrain.

clog, n. shackle, dragweight, encumbrance; sabot.

cloister, n. monastery, nunnery,

C
D

convent, abbey.
cloisterer, n. recluse.
cloistral, a. monastic, recluse.
close, a. oppressive, uncomfortable, muggy, unventilated; narrow, cramped; secretive, reserved.
close, v. shut, stop occlude; conclude, finish, end, terminate.
close, n. conclusion, end; peroration; grapple; court, area, enclosure, yard.
close-mouthed, a. wary, secretive, reserved.
closeness, n. nearness, proximity, adjacency; density; intimacy.
closet, n. private room; clothespress, ambry.
closing, a. concluding, final.
closing, n. stopping up, obstruction, blockade.
clot, n. coagulation.
cloth, n. fabric, material, drapery, textile, texture.
clothe, v. dress, attire.
clothes, n.pl. dress, clothing, garments, vesture, attire, drapery, costume, garb.
clothing, n. clothes, raiment.
cloud, n. nebulosity, rack; cirrus, cat's tail, cumulus, stratus, nimbus; storm scud.
cloud, v. overcast, becloud, obscure, shade, tarnish.
cloudy, a. overcast, lowering, murky, over clouded, obscure, sullen, hazy, dim, blurred.
cloven, a. bisulcate.
clover, n. trefoil; alsike.
clown, n. jester, merry-andrew, zany, harlequin, droll, punch, mime.
clownish, a. boorish, ungainly, awkward, churlish.
cloy, v. satiate, glut, pall.
club, n. cudgel, truncheon, bat, mace, staff, waddy, bandy; society, association.

club, v. cudgel, beat, pommel; club together, combine.
club-bearer, n. claviger.
clubfoot, n. talipes.
clubfooted, a. taliped.
club-shaped, a. clavate.
clue, n. intimation, hint.
clump, n. cluster, tuft, bunch, thicket.
clumsy, a. ungraceful, lumbering, unhandy, inapt.
cluster, n. bunch, clump, tuft; racemation, raceme, panicle; bevy, crowd.
clustered, a. aciniform.
clutch, v. seize, grasp, grip, clench, grab, snatch.
clutch, n. grasp, seizure.
clutter, n. litter, disorder.
cluttered, a. disordered, littered, jumbled.
coach, n. stage coach, diligence; trainer.
coachman, n. postilion, coach-driver, coachee .
coal, n. anthracite; bituminous; charcoal; culm.
coal-mine, n. colliery.
coal-miner, n. collier.
coal oil, n. kerosene, petroleum.
coarse, a. crass, gross, unrefined, rude, unpolished, indelicate, homespun, vulgar .
coast, n seashore, seaboard, shore, strand, beach.
coat, n. sack, jacket, frock, tuxedo, cutaway, ulster, capote, toga.
coat of arms, n. armorial bearings, arms, crest.
coax, v. wheedle, cajole, entice, cog, tweedle.
cob, n. spike, axis; sea mew.
cock, n. rooster, chanticleer; capon; weather-cock, vane; chief, leader; faucet.
cockade, n. rosette.
cockahoop, a. boastful, defiant, blustering.
cockatrice, n. basilisk.

cocker, v. fondle, indulge, pamper, pet, humor, coddle.

cockfighting, n. cockmatch.

cocky, a. pert, saucy.

coddle, v. parboil; pamper, fondle, humor, indulge.

coequal, a. coordinate.

coerce, v. constrain, compel.

coercion, n. compulsion, restraint, force, constraint.

coffee-house, n. cafe.

coffin, n. casket.

cog, n. cam, catch; trick.

cogent, a. convincing, conclusive, forcible.

coheir, n. parcener.

coheirship, n. parcenary.

coherent, n. consistent.

coil, n. convolution, intervolution; toil, mesh.

coil, v. convolve, intervolve.

coin, n. quoin, corner, coigne, wedge, plug, key.

coin, n. specie, cash; medallion.

coin, v. mint; neology.

coinage, n. minting; neologize; fabricate, invent.

coincide, v. concur, correspond, agree, tally.

coincidence, n. concurrence, agreement.

coincident, a. concurrent, contemporaneous.

coiner, n. minter; neologist.

cold, a. cool, chilly; frigid, gelid, icy; nipping, bleak, raw.

cold, n. coldness, frigidity, chilliness, algidity.

cold-blooded, a. poikilothermal; deliberate.

colic, n. gripe, enteralgia.

collar, n. neckband, carcanet, ruff, collet, rabat, piccadilly, dickey.

collar-bone, n. clavicle.

collect, v. assemble, accumulate.

collection, n. assemblage, accumulation, aggregation, heap; offering, offertory; anthology.

collision, n. clashing, concussion, interference.

colloquial, a. conversational, familiar, informal.

colony, n. settlement, dependency.

color, n. hue, shade, tinge, tincture, tint; pigment, paint, dye, stain.

color, n. ruddiness, redness, flush, blush, rosiness; semblance, pretext; variety.

color, v. dye, tinge, stain, imbue, tint, tincture, falsify, pervert.

colorable, a. specious, plausible, palliated.

color-blindness, n. Daltonism, achromatopsy.

colored, a. tinged, dyed, tinted, stained, discolored.

colorific, a. tinctorial.

coloring, n. dyeing, staining, intinction, tinting, tinction.

colorless, a. uncolored, faded; pale, pallid; neutral.

colossal, a. enormous, gigantic, huge, prodigious.

colt, n. filly [female]; foal [male]; hogget.

coltish, a. frisky, sportive, wanton, playful.

column, n. pillar, post, shaft; file, line, row.

comb, n. crest, caruncle.

combat, n. contest, bout, struggle, contention, fight.

combatant, n. contestant, fighter.

combative, a. pugnacious, contentious, bellicose.

combination, n. union, alliance, federation, confederacy, syndicate, league, merger.

combine, v. unite, incorporate, merge, blend.

combine, n. combination.

combined, a. united, confederated, federated.

combing, n. pectination.

comblike, a. pectinal, pectinate, pectinated.

come, v. arrive, approach; come from, issue, proceed, ensue, flow, originate.

come after, v. follow, succeed. *Antonyms:* precede, antecede.

come again, v. return, recur.

come and go, v. alternate.

come between, v. intervene, interpose, interfere; cause estrangement, disaffect.

come down, v. descend, alight.

comely, a. good-looking, handsome. *Antonyms:* uncomely, plain.

come near, v. approach.

come round, v. recur; change, relent; circumvent.

come short, v. be deficient.

come to, v. revive, recover; consent, yield, accede; arrive at, reach; amount to.

come to a head, v. mature; culminate.

comfort, v. console, solace.

comforter, n. consoler, cheerer; comfortable.

comfortless, a. disconsolate, desolate, distressed.

comical, a. funny

coming, n. approach, arrival.

coming between, n. intervention, interference, contravention.

comity, n. politeness, courtesy, civility.

command, v. order, direct.

command, n. order, mandate, charge, injunction, requisition, direction; authority.

commanding, a. authoritative, mandatory, imperative.

commandments, n.pl. The Decalogue.

commence, v. begin.

commend, v. commit, consign, intrust; praise, recommend.

commendable, a. praiseworthy. *Antonyms:* unpraiseworthy, illaudable.

commendatory, a. laudatory.

comment, v. remark, descant.

comment, n. remark, observation; commentary.

commentator, n. annotator, scholiast, glossarist.

commerce, n. traffic, barter, business, trading; course.

commercial, a. mercantile.

commit, v. intrust, consign; perpetrate, do.

common, a. public, general; customary, usual, ordinary, commonplace, inconspicuous.

commonalty, n. populace, proletariate, proletariat, varle try, rank and file.

commonly, adv. ordinarily.

common man, n. commoner, proletary, plebeian.

commonplace, a. ordinary, banal, trite, prosaic.

commotion, n. agitation, tumult, turmoil, riot.

communion, n. participation, sharing, fellowship.

communion, n. eucharist, Lord's Supper, sacrament.

communism, n. socialism, humanitarianism.

compact, a. close, solid, dense, crowded, impenetrable.

compact, n. covenant, pact, agreement, treaty.

companion, n. associate, comrade, intimate, consort, partner, fellow, mate, chum.

companionable, a. affable.

companionship, n. association, intimacy, fellowship, society.

company, n. guest, visitor; fellowship, companionship, association, society. *Antonyms:* seclusion, loneliness, host.

compare, v. collate, liken.

comparison, n. collation; illustration, simile.

compass, n. extent, reach.

compassion, n. pity, sympathy, commiseration, mercy.

compel, v. force, make, drive, oblige, overpower, coerce.

C
D

compelling, a. forcible, coercive, imperative. *Antonyms:* elective, optional.

compendium, n. epitome.

competency, n. fitness, ability, efficiency, proficiency, capability.

competent, a. qualified, capable, efficient, proficient. *Antonyms:* incompetent.

competition, n. emulation, rivalry, contention, strife.

competitor, n. rival, contestant, opponent.

complain, v. murmur, repine, grumble, croak.

complaining, a. murmuring, repining, discontented.

complaint, n. murmur, lamentation; ailment, disease; allegation, information.

complete, v. finish, perfect.

complete, a. entire, whole, integral, unabridged, intact.

completion, n. consummation, integration, elaboration, finishing, realization.

complex, a. composite, compound, mixed; complicated, intricate. *Antonyms:* incomplex, simple.

complexity, n. intricacy, entanglement, complication.

compliance, n. yielding, obedience, submission.

compliant, a. yielding, obedient, tractable.

complicated, a. complex, intricate, involved.

complication, n. intricacy, entanglement, involution, snarl, *Antonyms:* disentanglement.

composure, n. self-possession, calmness, sedateness.

compound, n. combination, mixture, concoction, intermixture, conglomeration, medley.

comprehend, v. understand, fathom, grasp; embrace, contain.

comprehension, n. understanding. *Antonyms:* incomprehension.

comprise, v. comprehend, include, embrace, involve.

compulsion, n. constraint, coercion, obligation, coaction. *Antonyms:* discretion, volition, election.

compulsory, a. constraining, coercive, obligatory. *Antonyms:* optional, elective.

compunction, n. qualm, contrition, remorse, regret.

compute, v. reckon, calculate, rate, estimate.

comrade, n. associate, companion, mate.

comradeship, n. association.

concave, a. rounded. *Antonyms:* convex.

concealed, a. hidden, latent, secreted, disguised.

concealment, n. secretion, hiding; secrecy, privacy, seclusion; suppression.

conceit, n. idea, conception, fancy; whim, caprice, freak; vanity, egotism.

conceited, a. egotistical, vain, bumptious, self-conceited.

concept, n. conception, notion, idea.

conception, n. imagination; idea, concept, notion.

concern, n. business, affair; moment, importance, interest, weight; solicitude, anxiety. *Antonyms:* unconcern.

concerned, a. solicitous, worried, anxious, troubled. *Antonyms:* unconcerned, indifferent.

concerning, prep. regarding, about, respecting, touching.

concert, n. accordance, harmony, musicale.

concise, a. epigrammatic, succinct, pithy. *Antonyms:* diffuse.

conclude, v. decide, determine, resolve; close; infer; effect.

conclusion, n. decision, determination; inference, deduction, illation; close, end, finale.

concoct, v. compound, mix; devise, contrive, invent.

concrete, a. solidified; specific, special.

concretion, n. solidification, stone; clot.

concubine, n. paramour.

condemn, v. denounce, curse, execrate, reprobate, doom, ban. *Antonyms:* exonerate, vindicate, absolve, justify.

condemnation, n. denunciation, execration, ban.

condemnatory, a. denunciatory.

condense, v. abridge, epitomize; reduce; compress.

condescend, v. deign.

condition, n. state, plight, category, predicament, situation; stipulation, term.

conditional, a. contingent, subject, provisory.

conduce, v. lead, tend, contribute, subserve.

conduct, v. lead, pilot, escort, guide, attend, convey.

conduct, n. guidance, management, leadership, administration; behavior.

confederate, a. confederated, federated, allied, leagued.

confederation, n. coalition, federation, league, union.

confess, v. acknowledge, own, admit, avow; divulge, reveal.

confession, n. acknowledgment, admission; shrift.

confidence, n. reliance, trust, faith dependence; certainty. *Antonyms:* doubt.

confidence game. swindle.

confident, a. sure, reliant, undoubting, undaunted.

confine, n. boundary, border.

confine, v. restrain, limit, restrict, circumscribe, inclose, bound; immure.

confinement, n. restraint, imprisonment, durance, duress, incarceration, limbo.

confines, n.pl. boundaries, borders, precincts, outskirts.

confirm, v. ratify, verify, corroborate. *Antonyms:* abrogate.

confirmation, n. ratification, substantiation.

conflict, n. clashing, encounter.

conflict, v. clash, interfere, collide, be contradictory.

conflicting, a. contending, contrary, opposing.

confound, v. confuse, disconcert, abash, nonplus.

confounded, a. confused, disconcerted, abashed.

confuse, v. disconcert, perplex, abash, fluster, embarrass, chagrin, pose, bewilder.

confusion, n. disorder, turmoil, disarray, jumble, chaos; babel, pandemonium, commotion.

confutation, n. disproof.

confute, v. refute, disprove.

congenial, a. kindred; suited, suitable, agreeable, genial.

congratulate, v. felicitate.

congratulation, n. felicitation.

conjecture, n. surmise, supposition. -v. surmise, guess, speculate.

conjuration, n. incantation, enchantment, spell, sorcery.

conjurer, n. sorcerer, wizard, diviner, exorcist.

connect, v. join, link, couple, attach, unite.

connected, a. joined, coupled, linked, affiliated, related.

connection, n. union, alliance, relationship, junction, affiliation, association. *Antonyms:* disconnection, isolation, incoherence.

conquer, v. defeat, overpower, down, vanquish, triumph,

C
D

subdue, overthrow.

conqueror, n. subjugator, subduer, victor.

conquest, n. subjection, victory, mastery, triumph, reduction, overthrow.

conscientious, a. scrupulous, just, upright, high-minded.

conscionable, a. reasonable.

conscious, a. cognizant, aware, sensible; sentient, knowing. *Antonyms:* unconscious.

consecrate, v. dedicate, hallow.

consent, v. agree, accord, concur, yield, assent, comply, permit. *Antonyms:* dissent, disagree.

consent, n. concurrence, compliance, approval.

consequence, n. result, effect, issue, event, sequel, outcome, upshot; pursuance. *Antonyms:* inconsequence.

conservation, n. preservation, keeping.

conserve, v. save, preserve.

consider, v. meditate on, ponder, contemplate; regard.

considerate, a. thoughtful, heedful. *Antonyms:* inconsiderate.

consideration, n. deliberation, advisement, contemplation; motive.

console, v. comfort, cheer, condole with, solace.

consolidate, v. solidify, compress;unify, merge.

consolidation, n. unification, union, combination.

conspicuous, a. salient, noticeable, prominent. *Antonyms:* inconspicuous.

conspiracy, n. plot, intrigue.

conspirator, n. conspirer, plotter, intriguer.

conspire, v. plot, intrigue.

constancy, n. steadfastness, stability, resolution, loyalty, fidelity.

constant, a. permanent, unchanging; unwavering, unshaken, steadfast, loyal, faithful. *Antonyms:* inconstant.

consternation, n. dismay, terror, alarm, panic.

constipated, a. bound.

constitution, n. structure, physique, temperament.

constitutional, a. inborn, innate, organic, inbred.

constrained, a. involuntary, forced, unnatural.

constraint, n. compulsion, force, pressure, restraint.

constrictor, n. sphincter.

consultation, n. conference, council, advisement.

consummate, a. perfect, supreme, complete.

consummation, n. fulfillment, perfection, realization.

consumption, n. consuming.

contact, n. touching, tangency, impact, contiguity.

contagion, n. virus, infection.

contagious, a. communicable, infectious. *Antonyms:* incommunicable.

contain, v. comprise, embody, include, hold, restrain.

container, n. receptacle.

contaminate, v. corrupt, pollute, defile, infect, taint, vitiate, debase.

contamination, n. corruption, pollution, defilement, taint.

contemporaneous, a. contemporary, synchronal.

contemporary, a. contemporaneous, coeval.

contempt, n. disdain, scorn, derision, detestation.

contemptible, a. despicable, abject.

contemptuous, a. disdainful, scornful, insolent, cynical.

contend, v. struggle, wrestle, combat, dispute, argue.

content, v. satisfy, gratify.

contented, a. content, satisfied.

contention, n. controversy, dissension, quarrel.

contentious, a. litigious, quarrelsome; dissentious.

contest, n. rivalry, match, tourney, competition; dispute, controversy, dissension.

continual, a. ceaseless, incessant, constant.

continuance, n. endurance, persistence, constancy.

continuation, n. protraction, continuance, perpetuation.

continued, a. prolonged, extended; serial.

continuous, a. ceaseless, uninterrupted, unceasing, continual, constant. *Antonyms:* intermittent, occasional.

contraband, a. prohibited, forbidden, unlawful.

contract, v. reduce, narrow; incur, acquire; agree; shrivel, shrink; syncopate.

contract, n. agreement, compact, pact, treaty, convention, stipulation.

contracting, a. astringent.

contraction, n. astriction, stricture, syncopation.

contradict, v. gainsay, controvert, dispute.

contradiction, n. gainsaying, opposition, antagonism.

contradictory, a. inconsistent, irreconcilable, opposing, contradicting.

contrariety, n. antagonism, disagreement, inconsistency.

contradictory, a. inconsistent, irreconcilable, opposing.

contrariety, n. antagonism, disagreement, inconsistency.

contrary, a. opposite, adverse, counter, opposed; repugnant, incompatible, contradictory, retroactive.

contrast, n. comparison; opposition, unlikeness.

contravene, v. thwart, oppose, counteract, transgress.

contravention, n. opposition, counteraction, violation.

contrite, a. penitent, repentant. *Antonyms:* impenitent.

contrite person. penitent.

contrition, n. penitence, remorse, self-reproach.

contrivance, n. contriving, devising; device, scheme.

contrive, v. devise, concoct, invent, scheme, plan.

control, v. restrain, regulate, govern, manage, repress, direct, bridle.

control, n. restraint, repression, hindrance; domination, regulation, governance. *Antonyms:* unrestraint, abandon.

controller, n. governor, regulator, ruler.

controversial, a. disputatious.

controversy, n. dispute, contention, disputation.

convalescence, n. revalescence.

convene, v. assemble.

convenient, a. handy, advantageous; seasonable, timely, suitable.

convent, n. nunnery, monastery, cloister, abbey.

convention, n. custom, usage; assembly congress, diet.

conversation, n. converse, colloquy, parley, chat, conference, interview.

conversational, a. colloquial.

converse, v. talk, chat, commune, parley.

converse, n. intercourse, communion, conversation.

conversion, n. transmutation, transformation; regeneration; appropriation, application.

convert, v. transform; regenerate; appropriate.

convex, a. protuberant, bulging, *Antonyms:* concave.

convexity, n. protuberance. *Antonyms:* concavity.

conveyance, n. carriage, transmission; transfer, alienation, demise.

convict, n. felon, prisoner, criminal, culprit.

convincing, a, persuasive.

convivial, a. festive, social.

convocation, n. convention, congress, diet, council.

convoy, n. protection, escort; guard, escort.

convulsion, n. spasm, paroxysm; agitation, upheaval.

cook, n. chef.

cook, v. stew, seethe, gratinate.

cookable, a. coctible.

cooking, n. cuisine.

cool, v. chill, refrigerate; moderate, allay.

cool, a. deliberate, self-possessed, unexcited, dispassionate, indifferent, nonchalant, unconcerned, composed.

cooler, n. refrigerator.

cooling, n. refrigeration; gelation.

coolness, n. dispassion, nonchalance.

coon, n. raccoon.

coop, n. pen, cote, mew, hutch.

coop, v. confine, shut up, imprison, incage, mew.

cooperate, v. concur, unite, work together.

cooperating, a. cooperative, auxiliary.

cooperation, n. concurrence, working together; collusion; synergy. *Antonyms:* antagonism.

copier, n. copyist, transcriber; imitator. *Antonyms:* originator.

copious, a. plentiful, abundant, overflowing, ample.

copper, n. cuprum; cauldron.

copperas, n. green vitriol, suphate of iron.

coppice, n. copse.

copse, n. thicket, brushwood.

copulation, n. union, conjunction; sexual union, coition.

copy, n. transcript, reproduction, transcription, replica, facsimile, duplicate, counterpart.

copy, v. transcribe, reproduce, trace, duplicate; imitate, follow.

copyist, n. transcriber, copier; imitator.

coquette, n. flirt.

coral, n. madrepora.

cord, n. string, twine.

cordial, a. hearty, sincere, affectionate; invigorating.

cordiality, n. sincerity, heartiness, ardor.

cork, n. stopper, stopple.

corn, n, maize, Indian corn.

corner, n. angle, cusp, bight, coin, nook, recess, niche.

corner, v. nonplus, pose.

cornerwise, adv. diagonally.

cornhouse, n. granary.

corporal, a. bodily, material.

corpse, n. remains, relics, cadaver; carcass; mummy.

correct, a. accurate, right, exact, precise. *Antonyms:* incorrect.

correct, v. rectify, amend, emend, right; reprove, modify.

correctible, a. rectifiable.

correction, n. rectification, amendment, discipline.

corrective, a. rectifying, reformatory, correctory.

correctness, n. accuracy, exactness, precision. *Antonyms:* incorrectness, inexactness.

correspond, v. accord, comport, tally, correlate.

correspondence, n. adaptation, agreement, congruity, homology.

correspondent, a. conformable.

corrode, v. erode, canker; consume, wear away.

corrosion, n. erosion.

corrosive, a. erosive, eroding, corroding; vexing.

corrupt, a. spoiled, tainted, addled, rotten, decaying; depraved, dissolute.

corrupt, v. rot, spoil, deprave, pervert, debase, demoralize, defile, infect.

corruption, n. putrefaction, decay; pollution; improbity, depravity, dishonesty, bribery. *Antonyms:* incorruption.

cortege, n. procession.

cosmopolitan, n. cosmopolite.

cost, n. charge, expense, price, outlay; detriment.

costiveness, n. constipation.

costly, a. expensive, dear, high-priced; rich

cot, n. cottage, hut; pen, coop, cote; cradle, crib.

coterie, n. clique, set.

cottage, n. cot, cabin, lodge, casino. bungalow, chalet, croft, shack, shanty.

couch, n. lounge, sofa, bed.

council, n. aldermen, cabinet; assembly.

council-chamber, n. audience-room, divan.

counsel, n. consultation; prudence, deliberation, forethought; advice, admonition.

counsel, v. advise, admonish.

counselor, n. adviser, mentor, monitor, lawyer, attorney.

count, v. enumerate, number; esteem, consider, reckon.

count, n. numbering.

countenance, n. face, visage, features; support, good will.

counter, a. contrary, opposite.

counteract, v. defeat, frustrate, neutralize.

counteraction, n. frustration, contravention.

counterbalance, v. counterpoise, countervail, balance.

counterfeit, a. false, fraudulent, fictitious, sham.

countermand, v. revoke, cancel, recall. -n. revocation, rescission.

counterpoint, n. polyphony.

counterpoise, v. counterbalance, balance.

countersign, n. watchword, password, consigne.

counterterm, n. antonym.

counting frame, n. abacus.

count out, v. exclude.

countrified, a. rude, uncourtly, rustic, rural.

country, n. region, territory; nation; rural parts, farming region.

country, a. rural, rustic.

countryman, n. compatriot, fellow-citizen; farmer, granger, husbandman, rustic.

county, n. shire.

couple, n. two, pair, brace, span, team.

couple, v. join, link, connect.

couplet, n. distich.

courage, n. intrepidity, heroism, bravery, gallantry, hardihood, fortitude, valor. *Antonyms:* cowardice, fear.

courageous, a. intrepid, brave, heroic, gallant, hardy, bold, fearless, valiant.

courier, n. messenger, runner.

course, n. progress, passage; direction, bearing; bout; procedure; sequence.

court, n. tribunal, judicatory, judicature, judiciary, forum, mall; courtyard, cortile.

court, v. woo, spark; solicit, seek, allure, invite.

courteous, a. deferential, polite, debonair, gracious, urbane, civil, respectful.

courtesan, n. prostitute, harlot.

courtesy, n. politeness, urbanity, civility, favor.

courtly, a. elegant, polite.

courtyard, n. court, area, yard, cortile; patio.

cove, n. bay, recess, inlet.

C
D

covenant, n. compact, agreement, pact.

cover, v. overspread, overlay, thatch, hide, conceal, comprise, embrace, embody.

cover, n. lid, covering, case, canopy, awning, tilt, roof, casing.

covered, a. covert, screened, protected, hidden.

covering, n. cover, sheath.

covert, a. secret, hidden, disguised, stealthy.

covert, n. shelter, refuge, retreat; underwood, jungle.

cow, n. female of bovine animals; heifer, maverick.

cow, v. overawe, daunt, scare.

coward, n. craven, poltroon.

cowardice, n. pusillanimity, dastardly, recreancy, timidity.

cowardly, a. craven, dastard, dastardly, recreant, timorous.

cowboy, n. cattle herder, drover, herdsman.

cowcatcher, n. pilot.

cower, v. crouch, squat.

cowlike, a. bovine.

coworker, n. colleague, collaborator, associate.

cowpox, n. vaccinia, cowpock.

coxcomb, n. fop, dandy, dude.

coy, a. shy, modest, retiring.

cozy, a. snug; talkative.

crab, n. crustacean, mollusk.

crabs, n. pl. Cancer, Crustcea, Mollusca.

crack, n. chink, crevice, cranny, rift, rent, cleft; rupture, fláw.

crack, v. break, chop, split.

crack, a. first-rate, excellent, fine, capital.

cracked. a. crotchety, crazy.

crackle, v. crepitate.

crackling, a. crepitant.

cracksman, n. burglar.

cradle, n. baby's bed, trundle-bed; solen.

craft, n. dexterity, skill; trade; guild; cunning.

craftiness, n. artfulness, craft, cunning.

craftsman, n. artificer, mechanic, skilled workman.

crafty, a. shrewd, artful, wily, tricky, cunning, sly, deceitful. *Antonyms:* guileless, artless.

cragged, a. jagged, broken.

cram, v. compress, crowd, press, squeeze.

cramp, v. restrain, confine, hinder, restrict, obstruct.

cranium, n. skull.

crank, n. winch, turning-handle; bend, turn, twist.

cranky, a. crotchety, capricious, unreasonable, cross, perverse, unsteady.

cranny, n. crevice, chink.

crash, n. ruin, smash, failure.

crass, a. coarse, unrefined.

crave, v. long for, yearn for, hanker after; beseech, entreat.

craven, a. cowardly.

craving, n, longing, yearning, hankering, hungering; entreaty.

crawler, n. creeper, reptile.

craze, v. madden, distract.

craziness, n. insanity, lunacy, delirium; monomania; paranoia.

crazy, a. demented, deranged, insane, delirious, demented, mad, lunatic. *Antonyms:* sane, rational.

crazy person, n. madman, maniac, lunatic; paranoiac.

cream, n. best part; cremor.

crease, n. ruck, wrinkle.

creation, n. origination, making, invention; universe, cosmos, world.

creative, a. demiurgic, inventive, omnific.

creature, n. being.

credence, n. belief, credit.

credit, n. belief, faith; confidence; esteem, honor; prestige; trust. *Antonyms:* discredit, unbelief.

credulous, a. unsuspecting,

gullible. *Antonyms:* incredulous.

creek, n. brook, race, streamlet, burp; cove.

creepers, n.pl. Reptilia.

creephole, n. retreat; subterfuge, expedient.

creeping, a. crawling, reptile;truckling.

creeping, n. reputation; formication.

creepingly, adv. insidiously.

cremate, v. incremate.

cremation, n. incremation, incineration.

crest, n. tuft; helmet; top, ridge, crown; device.

crested, a. cristate.

crestfallen, a. dejected, discouraged, down cast.

crevice, n. cleft, rent, cranny, crack.

crew, n. assemblage, gang, mob, band, crowd.

crib, n. manger, rack; bin, bunker, box.

crime, n. felony, outrage, enormity; offense misdemeanor, dereliction, malefaction.

criminal, a. felonious.

criminal, n. felon, culprit.

criminate, v. incriminate, accuse.

crimination, n. incrimination.

crimp, v. curl, crisp, frizz.

crimpy, a. frizzly, wavy.

crincum, n. twist, turn, freak, caprice, fancy.

cringe, v. truckle, fawn, crouch.

cringing, a. truckling, servile, slavish, fawning.

crinkle, v. curl, wrinkle.

crinkly, a. wavy, wrinkly.

cripple, v. maim, lame, disable; hough, hamstring.

crippled, a. maimed, lame, disabled, deformed, halt.

crisis, n. critical juncture; climacteric, emergency, strait.

crisp, a. brittle, friable, short;

crackling, lively.

critic, n. censor, reviewer, judge, inspector; carper.

critical, a. discriminating; carping, censorious, captious, caviling; crucial, decisive.

criticism, n. critique, censure, stricture, cavil.

croak, v. forebode, decry.

croaker, n. grumbler, alarmist, pessimist.

crock, n. jar, pot; soot.

crony, n. bosom friend, intimate, chum.

crook, n. bend, turn, curve, curvature; crosier; artifice, trick, subterfuge.

crook, v. bend, curve, incurvate.

crooked, a. twisted, bent, devious, deformed, tortuous, winding, flexuous, curved.

crookedness, n. tortuousness, sinuosity, curvature, deformity, curvity, wryness.

crop, n. harvest, fruit, product.

crop, v. clip, lop, cut off; gather, reap, harvest; browse.

cross, n. crucifix, rood, gibbet; rebated cross, gammadion, saltire.

cross, n. hybrid, mongrel.

cross, a. athwart, transverse, intersecting; adverse, contrary; petulant, cynical.

cross, v. intersect; traverse; run counter to, thwart, frustrate, foil; interbreed.

crossbars, n.pl. lattice, grille.

crossbeam, n. girder, stringer.

crossbow, n. arbalest.

crossbreed, n. hybrid, mongrel.

crossbreeding, n. hybridization.

crossbred, a. hybrid.

crosscut, v. intersect.

cross-examination, n. cross-questioning, inquisition.

cross-eye, n. strabismus.

cross-fertilization, n. allogamy.

crossgrained, a. intractable, contrary, perverse, stubborn.

crossing, n. hybridization.

crossing, n. intersection, cancellation; traversing; junction; crosswalk; frustration, interference.

crossness, n. petulance, cynicism, anamiability, irritability, ill-nature, inaffiability.

crosswise, adv. across, transversely.

crotch, n. fork, crotchet.

crotchet, n. whim, fancy, caprice, freak.

crotchety, a. whimsical, fanciful, vagarious.

crouch, v. squat, couch, stoop; cringe, fawn.

croup, n. cynanche.

crowd, n. concourse, crush, multitude, number, mass, horde, host, troop.

crowded, a. congested, serried, dense, compact. *Antonyms:* incompact.

crowding, n. congestion.

crown, n. diadem, coronet, corona; tiara; wreath, garland, laurel; royalty.

crown, v. consummate.

crowning, a. consummating.

crowning, n. coronation.

crucial, a. cruciform, cross-shaped; severe, trying.

crude, a. undeveloped, uncouth, inartistic.

cruel, a. pitiless, merciless, inhuman, unmerciful, fell, relentless, ruthless, brutal.

cruelty, n. inhumanity, implacability, severity.

crumble, v. disintegrate, decay.

crumbly, a. friable.

crumple, v. rumple, wrinkle, crush together.

crush, v. overpower, vanquish, quell, subdue, conquer, suppress; squeeze, press.

crush, n. compression; pressure, crowd.

crushing, a. overwhelming.

crust, n. incrustation.

crusty, a. cross, unamiable.

crux, n. puzzle, riddle.

cry, v. weep, sob, wail, bawl, squall, whimper, blubber, bewail.

cry, n. exclamation, acclamation, outcry, clamor, scream, shriek, howl, yell.

cry down. decry, disparage, traduce.

crying, n. weeping, sobbing, wailing, wail, bawling.

crying, a. weeping, sobbing, clamant; flagrant, heinous.

cry out upon, v. denounce, censure.

crypt, n. catacomb.

cryptic, a. hidden, secret, occult.

cry to, v. pray to, implore, beseech.

cube, n. hexahedron.

cucumber, n. gherkin.

cud, n. rumen; quid.

cuddle, v. nestle, snuggle.

cudgel, n. club, bludgeon.

cue, n. catchword; pigtail; hint, suggestion.

cuff, n. box, slap, buffet.

cuff, v. box, slap, smite, strike.

cull, n. cully, dupe, gull.

culprit, n. offender, delinquent, criminal, sinner.

cultivable, a. tillable.

cultivate, v. till.

cultivation, n. tillage.

culture, n. cultivation, tillage; refinement, education.

cultured, a. refined, educated.

cumbersome, a. burdensome, troublesome, unwieldy.

cunning, a. artful, crafty, sly, wily, arch, designing, deceitful; curious; skillful.

cunning, n. craft, deceit, craftiness, subtlety, wiliness.

cup, n. mug, noggin, nipperkin, beaker, bumper, tankard.

cupboard, n. locker, buffet, ambry.

cupidity, n. covetousness.
cupola, n. dome; lantern.
curable, a. remediable *Antonyms:* incurable.
curative, a. remedial, sanatory.
curator, n. custodian, keeper, trustee.
curb, v. check, restrain, control.
curdle, v. coagulate, thicken, curd.
curdled, a. coagulated, thickened.
cure, n. spiritual charge, curacy; medical treatment, therapy; antidote, remedy.
cure, v. heal, remedy.
cure-all, n. panacea.
curiosity, n. inquisitiveness; curio, freak, rarity. *Antonyms:* incuriosity.
curious, a. inquisitive; strange, rare, unusual. *Antonyms:* incurious.
curl, n. ringlet, kink.
curl, v. crisp, crimp; writhe, wreathe, twist, wind.
curling, n. crispation.
curly, a. curling, curled, crinkled, crinkly, wavy, kinky.
curlycue, n. flourish, paraph, caper.
current, a. present, instant; circulating.
curse, n. denunciation, anathema, ban, execration, imprecation, fulmination.
curse, v. execrate, fulminated, condemn.
cursed, a. accursed, abominable.
curtail, v. shorten, reduce.
curtain, n. hanging, drapery, valance.
curvature, n. curve, flexure, sinuosity.
curve, v. bend, crook, turn, inflect, deviate, wind.
cushion, n. pad, bolster, pillow; pouf.
cussedness, n. perversity, doggedness.
custodian, n. curator, guardian, keeper.
custody, n. safe-keeping, care; imprisonment.
custom, n. usage, practice; patronage; impost, duty.
customary, a. usual, wonted, habitual, conventional.
customer, n. patron.
cut, v. gash, slash, hew, crop, reap, mow, lop, prune, clip.
cut, n. incision, gash, slash, slit, wound; slight; sarcasm; notch.
cut down, v. fell; retrench, curtail, reduce.
cute, a. clever, sharp, cunning, shrewd.
cut off, v. amputate, sever; interrupt, stop.
cut out, v. exscind, excise, remove; supplant; exclude.
cutting, a. incisive, sharp, keen; penetrating, biting; sarcastic, caustic.
cutting, n. incision, felling, amputation, cleavage, curtailment, dissection, slashing.
cutting out, v. excision.
cut to pieces, v. dissect, mutilate, dismember.
cut up, v. afflict, grieve, distress; play pranks, play tricks, cut capers, misbehave.
cylone, n. tornado.

D

dabbler, n. superficialist, smatterer.
dabblingly, adv. superficially.
dabster, n. expert, adept, master-hand.
dagger, n. stiletto, bowie knife, dirk.
daily, a. diurnal, quotidian.
dainty, n. delicacy, tidbit, treat, rarebit.
dainty, a. fastidious, squeamish, finical; delicate.

dale, n. glen, dell, dingle.
dalliance, n. fondling, endearments; delay, procrastination.
dally, v. dawdle, trifle; fondle, wanton; delay.
dam, n. barrier, weir.
dam, v. restrain, obstruct.
damage, v. injure, hurt, harm, scathe, deface, impair, disfigure.
damage, n. injury, detriment, impairment, harm, hurt.
damages, n.pl. indemnity, satisfaction, reparation.
damn, v. condemn, curse, reprobate, denounce.
damnable, a. accursed, atrocious, execrable.
damnation, n. condemnation, reprobation, perdition.
damning, a. condemnatory, damnatory.
damp, a. moist, wet, humid.
dampen, v. moisten, damp; check, repress, restrain.
damper, n. check, setback, set blanket, discouragement.
dampness, n. moisture, humidity.
dance, n. ballet, cotillion, waltz, reel, fandango, polka, two-step, minuet.
dancing-mania, n. epidemic chorea, choromania.
dandified, a. foppish. *Antonyms:* slovenly, careless, seedy.
dandy, n. fop, exquisite, dude, incroyable, *Antonyms:* sloven.
danger, n. jeopardy, hazard, peril, insecurity, risk, exposure. *Antonyms:* safety, immunity, security, shelter, protection.
dangerous, a. perilous, hazardous, risky, unsafe, critical, imminent. *Antonyms:* safe.
dapper, a. spruce, trim, spry.
dappled, a. spotted, mottled.
dare, v. venture, presume; defy, challenge, stump.
date, n. defiance, provocation.
dare-devil, a. reckless, rash,

inconsiderate.
dark, a. unilluminated, sunless, dusky, rayless, pitchy, murk, dingy, shadowy.
darken, v. shade, obscure, shadow, becloud; perplex, confuse; tarnish, discolor.
darkness, n. obscurity, shadow, dimness, gloom, infuscation.
dart, v. hurl, launch; spring, dodge, bolt.
dash, n. collision, allision, crash; abashment; infusion, smack, tincture.
dashboard, n. splashboard.
dashing, a. spirited, bold, brilliant, gay, roaring.
dastard, n. coward, craven.
daub, v. smear, besmear, soil.
daunt, v. cow, intimidate, frighten, alarm.
dauntless, a. intrepid, daring, fearless.
dawn, n. daybreak, dayspring, sunrise.
day, n. daytime; time, age, generation.
day-dream, n. revery.
dazzle, v. daze, blind; bewilder, astonish.
dazzling, a. brilliant, intense, glaring.
dead, a. lifeless, deceased, inanimate, defunct, extinct; inert, obtuse, impassive.
deadborn, a. stillborn.
deaden, v. blunt, benumb, hebetate, moderate; devitalize, subdue.
dead-house, n. morgue; charnel-house, mortuary.
deadly, a. fatal, mortal, lethal, internecine; implacable.
deal, v. distribute, apportion, dispense, allot; trade, traffic.
dealer, n. trader, dispenser, retailer, shopkeeper, merchant, vender, tradesman.
dealing, n. distribution, apportionment; traffic, intercourse,

barter, business.

dear, a. costly, expensive, high-priced; beloved, darling. *Antonyms:* cheap, inexpensive.

dearth, n. scarcity, lack, deficiency, paucity, want. *Antonyms:* plenty.

death, n. decease, demise, dissolution, dying, mortality, expiration, mort.

deathless, a. immortal, imperishable, undying.

death notice, n. obituary.

debar, v. preclude, exclude.

debase, v. degrade, deteriorate, abase, corrupt, alloy, humiliate.

debasement, n. degradation, abasement, deterioration.

debatable, a. contestable, disputable. *Antonyms:* incontestable, indisputable.

debate, v. argue, discuss, contend, controvert.

debate, n. discussion, argument, dispute, controversy, forensic.

debauch, v. vitiate, deprave, corrupt, ravish, rape.

debauch, n. debauchery, abandon, drunkenness, orgies, lechery; rape. *Antonyms:* temperance, moderation.

debauched, a. dissolute, dissipated, corrupt.

debauchee, n. libertine, lecher, rake, drunkard.

debauchery, n. lechery, libertinism, sensuality.

debonair, a. suave, courteous, urbane, gracious.

debt, n. liability, due, obligation, debit. *Antonyms:* asset)

decadent, a. deteriorating.

decay, v. decline, retrograde; rot, decompose, putrefy.

decease, n. demise, death.

deceased person. decedent.

deceit, n. deception, imposition, trickery, artifice, delusion, guile, duplicity.

deceive, v. delude, beguile,

mislead, gull, impose upon, circumvent. *Antonyms:* undeceive, disabuse.

decency, n. propriety, seemliness, decorum. *Antonyms:* indecency.

decent, a. suitable, modest, seemly. *Antonyms:* indecent.

deception, n. imposition, craft, duplicity, deceit, fallacy, ruse, imposture. *Antonyms:* guilelessness, candor, disillusionment, fair dealing.

deceptive, a. delusive, deceitful, specious, sophistical. *Antonyms:* guileless, candid, sincere, open.

decharm, v. disillusionize, disenchant, disabuse.

decide, v. determine, settle, conclude, resolve.

decided, a. unequivocal, determined, pronounced, unwavering, positive.

decision, n. determination, settlement, conclusion, verdict, inference; firmness, resolution, constancy. *Antonyms:* indecision, irresolution.

decisive, a. conclusive, final, summary.

deck, v. bedeck, array.

declaration, n. assertion, affirmation, predication.

declare, v. affirm, assert, state, predicate.

decline, v. lean, incline, bend; languish, sink, diminish, decrease; deviate.

decline, n. deterioration, diminution, degeneracy, declination, decay; progressive emaciation, *Antonyms:* progress, advancement.

decolor, v. decolorate.

decorate, v. embellish, adorn, beautify, ornament, garnish, trim, bedeck.

decorated, a. embellished, ornate, trimmed. *Antonyms:*

C
D

plain.

decorative, a. ornamental, embellishing, adorning.

decoy, v. entice, lure, allure, entrap.

decrease, n. decrement, diminution, reduction, decline, abatement.

decrease, v. diminish, reduce, dwindle, subside, abate.

decrease of motion. retardation.

decree, n. edict, fiat, mandate, decretal, enact, ordain, enjoin.

decrial, n. condemnation, disparagement, dispraise, detraction, belittling.

decry, v. disparage, belittle.

dedicate, v. consecrate.

dedication, n. consecration.

deduct, v. subtract, rebate.

deduction, n, subtraction, discount; inference, conclusion, illation.

deed, n. exploit, act, feat, perpetration, performance.

deep, a. profound, intricate, inexplicable, unfathomable, recondite, abstruse; sagacious, cunning. *Antonyms:* superficial, shallow.

deepen, v. intensify.

deer, n. Cervidae; reindeer; buck, doe, roe; stag.

deerhound, n. staghound.

deface, v. mar, disfigure.

defacement, n. disfigurement, mutilation, marring.

defamation, n. calumny, libel, lampoon, traducement.

defamatory, a. slanderous, libellous, vituperative.

defame, v. calumniate, malign, vilify, lampoon, slander.

defaulter, n. delinquent, peculator, defalcator.

defeat, n. repulse, overthrow, foil, rout, frustration.

defeat, v. conquer, vanquish, repulse, discomfit, checkmate, outwit, balk, frustrate.

defect, n. blemish, flaw, imperfection, failing, shortcoming, infirmity.

defend, v. guard, protect, shield, secure, screen, shelter, fortify, preserve.

defender, n. defendant, vindicator, advocate, champion, upholder, guardian.

defense, n. protection, defending, maintenance, protection, bulwark, fortification, shield. *Antonyms:* betrayal, exposure, surrender.

defiance, n. challenge, provocation; opposition, insubmission, comtempt, mutiny, rebellion.

defiant, a. disobedient, insubmissive, rebellious, refractory, mutinous. *Antonyms:* obedient, submissive.

deficiency, n. inadequacy, insufficiency, shortage.

deficient, a. defective, imperfect, scanty, inadequate.

defile, v. contaminate, pollute, soil, vitiate, taint, corrupt, sully.

definite, a. positive, specific, explicit, specified, precise. *Antonyms:* indefinite.

deformed, a. misshapen, disfigured.

deformity, n. malformation, disfigurement, distortion.

defraud, v. see cheat.

deft, a. dexterous, expert, skillful, clever.

defy, v. challenge, dare; spurn, scorn.

degeneracy, n. decline, degeneration, retrogression.

degenerate, v. deteriorate, decline.

degradation, n. abasement, disgrace, humiliation.

degrade, v. abase, disgrace, pervert, dishonor.

deification, n. apotheosis.

deify, v. apotheosize.

deign, v. condescend.

C
D

delay, n. deferring, procrastination, postponement, respite,
reprieve; retardation. *Ant-*
onyms: dispatch, promptness,
haste.
delegate, v. depute, commission.
deleterious, a. hurtful, pernicious.
deliberate, a. intentional,
prepense, done on purpose.
Antonyms: accidental, unpremeditated.
delicacy, n. daintiness, fineness,
refinement, discrimination;
dainty, tidbit. *Antonyms:*
indelicacy, coarseness.
delicate, a. graceful, fine,
minute, slender; refined,
sensitive, dainty; critical.
Antonyms: indelicate.
delicious, a. luscious, palatable,
savory, delightful. *Antonyms:*
unpalatable, distasteful,
fulsome.
delightful, a. charming, enchanting, rapturous, ravishing,
delectable, delicious, enjoyable.
delirious, a. irrational. *Antonyms:*
rational, lucid, sane.
deliverance, n. rescue, salvation, redemption.
delivery, n. rescue, release,
liberation, extrication; surrender, transfer.
delusion, n, illusion, deception,
hallucination, ruse. *Antonyms:*
disillusionment, reality, fact.
demand, n. exaction, requirement, order.
demeanor, n. deportment,
carriage, bearing.
demerit, n. fault, misconduct.
demon, n. devil, fiend.
demon worship, demonolatry.
demoralize, v. deprave, corrupt.
demure, a. sedate, staid.
den, n. cavern, cave, retreat.
denial, n. negation, rejection,
disclaimer, controverting,

refusal, renunciation. *Ant-*
onyms: affirmation, acceptance.
denote, v. signify, imply.
denouncing, n. denunciation.
dent, n. indentation.
denunciation, n. condemnation,
accusation, malediction.
denunciatory, a. condemnatory.
deny, v. gainsay, contradict;
disown, renounce.
department, n. division, section,
part, category; district, precinct,
branch; station.
departure, n. deviation; withdrawal.
depend, v. lean, rely, trust.
dependable, a. trustworthy,
reliable. *Antonyms:* untrustworthy.
dependant, n. retainer, minion,
feudatory, adherent; consequence.
dependence, n. suspension,
dependency; reliance, trust;
support/
dependent, a. conditioned.
Antonyms: independent.
depict, v. portray, describe.
depiction, n. portrayal, description.
deplore, v. lament, regret.
deportment, n. behavior,
demeanor.
deposit, n. deposition, precipitate, alluvion.
depositary, n. trustee, guardian.
depository, n. storehouse,
magazine, depot, warehouse.
depot, n. depository; station.
depredation, n. pillage, sacking,
spoliation, plunder.
depredator, n. plunderer,
despoiler, robber.
depressed, a. dejected.
depression, n. cavity, hollow,
concavity; dejection, discouragement, despondency.
deprive, v. dispossess, strip.
depth, n. profundity; extent,

intensity; deep; astuteness, discernment.

derelict, a. abandoned, forsaken; lost, adrift; careless, negligent, remiss.

deride, v. ridicule, mock, taunt, jeer.

derision, n. ridicule, jeering.

derogatory, a. disparaging.

descendants, n.pl. posterity.

descent, n. descension; incursion, raid, foray; derivation, extraction, birth; slope.

describe, v. delineate, depict.

desription, n. delineation, depiction, portrayal; class, species, sort.

desecrate, v. profane, pollute.

desecration, n. profanation.

desert, n. merit, meed, due.

desert, a. waste, unproductive, barren, desolate. *Antonyms:* fertile.

desert, v. forsake, abandon, leave, run away from.

deserted, a. forsaken, desolate, derelict.

deserter, n. renegade, turncoat, delinquent, backslider, rat, traitor.

desertion, n. abandonment.

desert wind, n. sirocco, simoon.

deserve, v. merit.

deserved, a. merited, condign. *Antonyms:* undeserved.

deserving, a. meritorious, worthy. *Antonyms:* undeserving.

design, n. sketch, draught, outline, plan; scheme, intention, purpose, project, intent.

designing, n. artful, wily, crafty, subtle, politic.

desire, n. longing, craving, will, aspiration, hankering, cupidity, impulse. *Antonyms:* apathy, aversion.

desire, v. want, crave, long for, lust, covet, yearn, aspire, request.

desolate, a. dreary, waste; broken-hearted, solitary.

despair, n. hopelessness, desperation.

desperate, a. irretrievable, hopeless, incurable, remediless; outrageous, monstrous.

desperation, n. despair, hopelessness.

despicable, a. contemptible.

despise, v. contemn.

despiteful, a. malicious, spiteful.

despondency, n. melancholy, depression.

despondent, a. disheartened, discouraged, dejected.

despot, n. tyrant, autocrat.

despotic, a. autocratic, tyrannical, absolute.

despotism, n. absolutism, tyranny.

destine, v. doom, preordain, appoint.

destiny, n. fate, doom, lot.

destitute, a. devoid, deficient, lacking; needy.

destroy, v. annihilate, undo, demolish, raze, desolate, sack, dismantle. *Antonyms:* conserve, preserve, spare.

destroyer, n. iconoclast, vandal, hun, destructionist.

destruction, n. annihilation, demolition, ruin, perdition, havoc, vandalism, desolation. *Antonyms:* conservation, preservation.

destructive, a. ruinous, vandal, internecine, pernicious.

desultory, a. fitful, irregular, unsystematic.

detach, v. disconnect, disjoin, disunite, isolate.

detachment, n. disconnection, separation, isolation.

detail, v. particularize.

detention, n. restraint, custody, arrest.

deter, v. hinder, prevent, restrain.

C
D

deteriorate, v. decline, degenerate; corrupt, debase.

detest, v. loathe, despise, abhor, hate, execrate.

destable, a. abominable, execrable.

detestation, n. abomination, loathing, antipathy.

deuced, a. devilish, excessive, extreme.

devastate, v. desolate, sack, ravage, plunder.

devastation, n. desolation, sacking, ravage, havoc.

develop, v. mature, evolve; unfold, disentangle, unravel. *Antonyms:* atrophy, blast, blight.

development, n. unfoldment, progression, evolution. *Antonyms:* atrophy, undevelopment, embryo.

deviate, v. swerve, deflect, digress, stray, wander. *Antonyms:* continue.

deviation, n. swerving, digression.

device, n. invention, expedient, wile, artifice, trickery; symbol, legend.

devil, n. Satan, Lucifer, demon, fiend.

devilish, a. demoniac, diabolical, fiendish, infernal.

devil-may-care, a. reckless, defiant.

deviltry, n. devilry, diablerie, devilment, fiendishness.

devious, a. wandering, circuitous, winding, tortuous; sinful.

devise, v. contrive, invent, scheme, concoct, bequeath.

devoted person. devotee.

devotion, n. consecration, dedication; zeal, allegiance, love; worship, adoration.

devour, v. consume.

devout, a. pious, reverent, devotional, godly, holy, religious. *Antonyms:* irreverent, impious, unholy.

dexterity, n. expertness, skill, aptitude, readiness.

dexterous, a. expert, skillful.

dialing, n. gnomonics.

dialogue, n. colloquy, duologue, interlocutory, collocution.

diarrhea, n. flux; lientery; scour.

diatribe, n. philippic, tirade, invective.

dice, n. die, cube.

dicker, v. trade, barter, negotiate, exchange.

dictate, n. command, admonition, impulse.

dictator, n. despot, autocrat.

dictatorial, a. dogmatical, overbearing.

diction, n. language.

dictionary, n. lexicon, vocabulary, wordbook, glossary; gradus, thesaurus.

dido, n. trick, antic, caper.

die, v. expire, perish, decease; wither, fade, vanish, recede, subside.

die, n. dice; stamp.

differ, v. be unlike; disagree. *Antonyms:* agree, concur.

difference, n. dissimilarity, unlikeness, variation, discrepancy, disparity, dissimilitude. *Antonyms:* uniformity, agreement, correspondence, promiscuity.

different, a. dissimilar, unlike, contrary, opposity, variant, manifold, diverse. *Antonyms:* similar, like, same.

differentiate, v. discriminate.

difficult, a. complicated, intricate, hard; uncompliant, perverse, exacting. *Antonyms:* light, easy.

difficulty, n. obstacle, impediment, obstruction; hardness; controversy, disagreement. *Antonyms:* ease, facility, release.

diffidence, n. timidity.

diffident, a. bashful, timid.

diffuse, a. copious, full.

dig, v. delve, excavate; thrust, poke, jab; exhume.

dig, n. thrust, punch, poke.

digest, v. systematize, classify.

digest, n. summary, code, system.

digestion, n. eupepsia. *Antonyms:* indigestion.

digging, n. excavation; uxhumation.

diggings, n. pl. region, locality.

dignified, a. stately, majestic, imposing.

dignify, v. exalt, grace, honor, elevate.

dignity, n. exaltation, eminence; stateliness; honor.

digress, v. deviate, depart.

digression, n. deviation, deivergence; episode.

dike, n. levee.

dilapidated, a. ramshackle.

dilate, v. expand, distend.

dilation, n. expansion, distention.

dilemma, n. predicament, difficulty, strait. *Antonyms:* extrication, release.

diligence, n. assiduity, sedulousness, perseverance.

diligent, a. sedulous, assiduous, persevering. *Antonyms:* lazy)

dillydally, v. dawdle, dally, fritter, loiter.

dilute, v. attenuate, thin, weaken.

diluter, n. diluent.

dim, a. obscure, indistinct, faint, blurred. *Antonyms:* bright, vivid.

diminish, v. decrease, reduce, lessen, curtail.

diminution, n. reduction, decrease, decrement.

dim-sighted, a. purblind.

din, n. clamor, noise, racket, clangor.

dint, n. indentation, dent.

dip, v. plunge, immerse, souse, douse, dive.

direct, a. straight, undeviating. *Antonyms:* indirect, roundabout.

direction, n. guidance, government, administration, superintendence, oversight; instruction.

directly, adv. diametrically.

dirge, n. requiem, trental.

dirt, n. earth, soil; filth, muck, foulness.

dirt-eater, n. geophagist.

dirt-eating, n. geophagism, chthonophagia, pica.

dirty, a. defiled, unclean, nasty, filthy, soiled, begrimed, uncleanly, loathsome.

dirty, v. soil, befoul, begrime, sully, tarnish, defile.

disable, v. incapacitate, disqualify, cripple, maim.

disadvantage, n. invonvenience, detriment, hindrance, drawback.

disagree, v. be at variance, differ, dissent, contradict, quarrel, contend.

disagreeable, a. unpleasant, distasteful, offensive, contrary, inconformable.

disagreeing, a. incompatible.

disagreement, n. difference; quarrel, bickering, dispute, squabble, controversy.

disappear, v. vanish, recede, be lost to view.

disappearance, n. vanishing, evanescence.

disappoint, v. dissatisfy, frustrate, balk, foil, defeat.

disapproval, n. disapprobation, dislike.

disaster, n. calamity, mishap, casualty.

disastrous, a. calamitous, deplorable, unfortunate.

disband, v. demobilize, disorganize.

discern, v. perceive, discriminate.

discernible, a. perceptible, visible, discoverable, apparent, manifest.

discerning, a. acute, sharp-sighted, shrewd.

discernment, n. insight, penetration, judgment.

discharge, v. absolve, acquit, release, exonerate, free; dismiss, remove; excrete. *Antonyms:* retain, hold.

discharge, n. firing, burst, volley; acquittance, release; fulfillment, performance.

discharged, a. dismissed, acquitted; emeritus.

disciple, n. adherent, follower.

disciplinarian, n. martinet.

discipline, n. correction, chastisement, submission, regulation. *Antonyms:* laxity, unrestraint.

disclaim, v. disown, deny, renounce.

discomfiture, n. disconcertion, confusion, frustration, defeat.

discommode, v. inconvenience, trouble.

discomposure, n. agitation, perturbation, confusion.

discommode, v. inconvenience, trouble.

discomposure, n. agitation, confusion.

disconnect, v. detach, dissever, disjoin.

disconnected, a. detached, separate, isolated.

disconnection, n. detachment, disunion, incoherence.

disconsolate, a. inconsolable.

discontent, n. dissatisfaction. *Antonyms:* contentment.

discontented, a. dissatisfied, restless, disgruntled.

discord, n. dissonance, inharmony, variance. *Antonyms:* harmony, agreement, consonance.

discordant, a. inharmonious,

dissonant, jarring, strident; at variance, contradictory, absonant.

discount, n. deduction, allowance, rebate.

discourage, v. dishearten, dispirit, deptress, dampen, unnerve, oppose.

discouragement, n. depression, dejaction; opposition, intimidation, determent, damper, difficulty.

discouraging, a. depressing, disheartening, dissuasive.

discourse, n. dissertation, address, oration, harangue, speech.

discourteous, a. uncivil, rude, disrespectful, abrupt, unmannerly.

discourtesy, n. rudeness, incivility, impoliteness.

discover, v. ascertain, detect, descry, discern, disclose.

discovery, n. ascertainment, unearthing, disclosure.

discredit, n. disesteem, disrepute.

discreet, a. prudent, wary.

discretion, n. prudence, circumspection, wariness; choice, liberty. *Antonyms:* indiscretion, impurdence, constraint.

discretional, a. optional, discretionary, elective. *Antonyms:* compulsory.

discriminating, a. distinguishing, differential.

discrimination, n. difference, distinction, discernment. *Antonyms:* indiscrimination, promiscuity.

discuss, v. debate, argue, canvass, agitate, deliberate.

discussion, n. debate, argument, canvass, agitation, consideration.

disdain, n. scorn, contumely, contempt.

disdainful, a. contemptuous,

C
D

scornful, supercilious.

disease, n. ailment, disorder, malady, complaint, affection, distemper; plague. *Antonyms:* health, vigor.

diseased, a. morbid, unhealthful.

disembowel, v. eviscerate, gut.

disembowelment, n. evisceration.

disengage, v. extricate, disembarrass, disentangle, detach, dissociate.

disfavor, n. disapproval.

disfigure, v. deface, mar.

disfigurement, n. disfiguration, defacement; blemish.

disgrace, n. reproach, discredit, dishonor, shame, infamy, desrepute, scandal.

disgrace, v. dishonor, humiliate, degrade, discredit, tarnish.

disgraceful, a. ignominious, shameful, dishonorable, scandalous, disreputable.

disgruntled, a. dissatisfied.

disguise, v. mask, dissemble, cloak, masquerade.

disguise, n. mask, blind, cloak.

disguised, a. veiled, masked, incognito.

disgust, n. aversion, repulstion.

disgust, v. revolt, offend.

disgusting, a. revolting, loathsome, repulsive, nauseating, sickening, repugnant.

dish, n. vessel, utensil.

dished, a. ruined, spoiled, undone; upset, disappointed.

disheveled, a. disarranged, disorderly, frowzy.

dishonest, a. unscrupulous, deceitful.

dishonesty, n. improbity, fraudulence, cheating.

dishonor, n. disrepute, descredit.

dishonorable, a. discreditable, disgraceful.

disillusionize, v. disenchant, decharm.

disinterested, a. impartial,

indifferent, neutral, unselfish.

disjoint, v. dislocate, disarticulate.

disjointed, a. incoherent, desultory, loose.

dislike, v. disapprove, disrelish.

dislike, n. aversion, disrelish, disapproval, hatred.

dislocate, v. disjoint.

dislocation, n. luxation.

disloyal, a. perfidious, unfaithful, false, trasonable, traitorous.

disloyalty, n. perfidy, unfaithfulness, treason, faithlessness.

dismal, a. dreary, gloomy, cheerless, joyless, sombre.

dismantle, v. raze, demolish.

dismay, n. consternation.

dismember, v. mutilate, dislimb.

dismemberment, n. mutilation.

dismiss, v. discharge, cashier; banish.

dismissal, n. discharge, dismission, removal.

disobedience, n. contumacy, undutifulness, defiance, noncompliance, insubordination.

disobedient, a. contumacious, insubmissive, undutiful, defiant, remiss, derelict.

disobey, v. transgress, violate, disregard, defy, infringe.

disorder, n. confusion, disarray, disarrangement, disorganization, chaos, litter, disturbance.

disorder, v. disarrange, confuse, jumble, disorganize, derange, discompose.

disordered, a. deranged, confused, jumbled. littered.

disorderly, a. immethodical, confused; chaotic, lawless.

disorganization, n. disorder, demobilization, dissolution.

disorganize, v. dissolve, disband, disorder, disarrange.

disown, v. repudiate, deny, disclaim, disavow, reject.

disowning, n. denial, disclaimer,

disavow, renounce.

disparage, v. belittle, decry, depreciate. *Antonyms:* laud, commend, praise.

disparagement, n. detraction, decrial, defamation, dispraise.

disparaging, a. derogatory, unfavorable, detractory.

dispatch, n. haste, speed, expedition; message.

dispense, v. deal out, apportion, distribute; execute.

disperse, v. dissipate, dispel, scatter.

displace, v. remove, disarrange; supplant.

display, n. exhibition, parade, show.

display, v. exhibit, evince, expose, parade, flourish.

displease, v. offend, anger.

displeasure, n. disapprobation, dislike, disapproval, resentment, dissatisfaction.

disposed, a. inclined, minded, willing.

disposition, n. temperament, mood, nature; willingness, readiness, inclination. *Antonyms:* indisposition, unwillingness.

dispossess, v. dislodge, oust, eject, dispropriate, remove.

dispossession, n. dislodgment, ejection, ousting, divestiture, ouster.

disproof, n. confutation.

disprove, v. confute, refute.

disputable, a. controvertible. *Antonyms:* indisputable, incontrovertible.

disputant, n. controversialist, controvertist, dissenter, disputer, arguer.

disputatious, a. contentious, polemical, quarrelsome.

dispute, v. contend, argue, controvert, wrangle, bicker, squabble.

dispute, n. disputation, contro-

versy, argument, debate, squabble, contention.

disregard, n. indifference, slight, neglect, disesteem.

disregard, v. ignore, slight, overlook.

disrepute, n. disesteem, disgrace.

disrespect, n. discourtesy, disesteem, rudeness, irreverence.

disrespectful, a. discourteous, uncivil, rude, irreverent, insolent, saucy.

dissatisfaction, n. discontent, disapproval, displeasure.

dissatisfied, a. discontented, displeased, restless, impatient.

dissection, n. anatomy; analysis, examination; vivisection, sentisection.

dissector, n. anatomist, prosector.

dissent, n. dissension, disagreement, fariance; nonconformity.

dissenter, n. nonconformist, sectary, dissident, separatist, rescuant.

dissertation, n. discourse, disquisition.

dissipated, a. profligate, dissolute, fast.

dissipation, n. dispersion, scattering; dissoluteness.

dissolute, a. debauched, dissipated, abandoned.

dissolution, n. dissolving, analysis; solution, ; decomposition, resolution.

dissolvable, a. dissoluble, soluble, fusible. *Antonyms:* indissoluble, indissolvable.

dissolve, v. melt, liquefy, macerate, fuse, disorganize, disband, disperse; disunite.

dissolvent, n. menstruum, solvent.

dissuade, v. deter, divert.

dissuasion, n. dehortation.

distance, n. interval, intervening

C
D

space; remoteness; reserve,
ceremoniousness.

distance, v. outstrip, outdo,
surpass.

distant, a. remote, far-off,
uncordial, reserved, cold.

distate, n. aversion, dislike,
disrelish. *Antonyms:* taste,
liking, relish.

distasteful, a. unpleasant,
offensive, repugnant, unpalatable, unsavory.

distill, v. trickle, drop, drip.

distillation, n. trickling; rectification.

distinction, n. discrimination;
eminence, celebrity, renown,
fame, repute. *Antonyms:*
indistinction, promiscuity,
obscurity.

distinctive, a. discriminative,
distinguishing.

distinguish, v. characterize;
discriminate, discern, recognize.

distinguished, a. marked,
special; eminent, illustrious,
famous, renowned, noted.
Antonyms: undistinguished,
obscure, humble.

distinguishing, a. distinctive,
peculiar, characteristic.

distort, v. deform, twist; pervert,
falsify.

distortion, n. defomity; perversion; falsification.

distracted, a. frantic, frenzied,
raving. *Antonyms:* calm.

distraction, n. diversion,
amusement; confusion,
bewilderment; commotion,
despair.

distress, n. anguish, torture,
sorrow, grief; misery, affliction,
adversity, disaster.

distress, v. pain, grieve, afflict,
wound.

distribute, v. apportion, allot,
deal out, dispense; classify.

distribution, n. apportionment,

allotment, dispensing, division;
disposition, grouping.

district, n. region, precinct,
circuit, locality, ward.

distrust, n. doubt, suspicion.

distrustful, a. suspicious.

disturb, v. molest, perturb,
annoy, agitate, disarrange,
derange, unsettle.

disuse, n. desuetude, discontinu-
ance, obsoletness.

ditch, n. trench, moat, channel.

dive, v. plunge.

divergence, n. radiation;
disagreement, variance;
divarication.

divergent, a. diverging; variant,
different.

divers, a. several, various, many,
numerous.

diverse, a. different, heterogeneous, diversified.

diversion, n. turning aside;
amusement, sport, recreation.

diversity, n. difference, dissimilarity; variety.

divide, v. sunder, split, cleave,
disunite, part, separate, sever,
detach.

divine, a. Godlike; religious, holy;
heavenly, angelic, seraphic,
transcendent.

divine, v. foresee, foreknow,
surmise, forebode, foretell.

diving bell. nautilus.

divisible, a. separable, dividable,
partible.

division, n. separation, partition,
dimidiation; section, part,
portion, category, group.

dizziness, n. vertigo.

dizzy, a. vertiginous, giddy.

do, v. effect, accomplish,
produce, achieve, consum-
mate, perform; perpetrate,
commit.

do-all, n. factotum.

do away with. abolish.

docile, a. tractable, teachable,
gentle, submissive.

dock, v. curtail; deduct from.

dock, n. wharf, pier, jetty.

dockhand, stevedore.

doctor, n. physician, edical practitioner, leech; homeopath; interne; externe.

doctor, v. repair, treat, falsify, adulterate.

doctrine, n. tenet, dogma, belief, principle.

doddering, a. shaking, trembling, infirm.

dodge, v. duck, evade, parry; shift, evade, parry.

dodger, n. prevaricator; handbill, circular.

dog, n. canine; pup, puppy, whelp; cur, mongrel.

dog, v. follow, worry, hound.

dog days. canicular days.

dogged, a. stubborn, obstinate, mulish, headstrong.

doggish, a. surly, sullen, cynical, morose.

dog house. kennel.

dogma, n. doctrine, tenet.

dogmatic, a. positive, magisterial, dicatorial, imperious, overbearing.

doings, n.pl. actions, proceedings, deeds, acts, performances.

dole, n. pittnce, alms; distribution, share, portion; grief, sorrow.

doleful, a. sorrowful, plaintive, piteous, lugubrious.

domain, n. dominion, sovereignty; realm, territory; province, department.

dome, n. cuola.

domestic, a. home, household, family; intestine; domesticated, tame; fond of home.

dominant, a. predominant, prevailing, paramount.

dominate, v. predominate, sway, rule, govern, control.

domineer, v. tyrannize, lord it; swagger, vapor.

dominion, n. sovereignty, sway, supremacy; realm.

donation, n. gift, present.

donkey, n. ass, buro, Neddy.

do-nothing, a. inactive, idle.

doom, n. jucicial sentence, judgment; destiny.

door, n. entrance, portal, gate; postern; porch, portico.

doorkeeper, n. porter, concierge, ostiary.

doorsill, n. threshold.

dormancy, n. abeyance, inactivity, lethargy.

dormant, a. quiescent, latent, inert, inactive, torpid.

dose, n. draught, potion.

dot, n. period, point; speck.

dotage, n. senility, anility; fondness, affection.

double, a. twofold, duplex, befold, deceitful, insincere.

double, v. duplicate; fold.

double, n. duplicate, counterpart; plait; circuit, shift, artifice.

double-dealing, n. duplicity, trickery.

double-faced, a. Janus-faced, deceitful.

double-minded, a. irresolute, vacillating, unsettled.

doubling, n. duplication, reduplication; fold, double.

doubt, v. waver, hesitate, question; distruct, supect. *Antonyms:* believe, trust, rely upon.

doubtful, a. unsettled, undetermined, dubious, precarious; questionable, involved. *Antonyms:* certain, implicit, sure.

doughty, a. redoubtable, valiant, bold, fearless.

dour, a. hard, obstinate.

douse, v. duck, immerse, dip, plunge, souse, submerge.

dove, n. pigeon.

dovelike, a. columbine.

dowdy, a. vulgar-looking,

C

D

slovenly, untidy. *Antonyms:*
neat.
do without. dispense with.
down, adv. downward, below.
down, v. overthrow, subdue.
down, a. descending, sloping.
down, n. pubescence; pl.
depression.
downcast, a. despondent,
dejected, gloomy.
downcome, n. downfall.
downfall, n. downcome, descent,
reverse, humiliation.
downhearted, a. dejected,
despondent.
downhill, n. descent, declivity,
slope.
downright, a. lunt, direct,
positive, absolute, unmixed,
straightforward.
downy, a. pubescent.
draft, n. drawing, draught; bill of
exchange; sketch, current of
air.
drag, v. haul, tril, tug, pull; break.
drag, n. dragging; dragnet;
harrow; skid; obstacle.
drain, n. channel, gutter, trench,
ditch.
drain, v. empty, exhaust.
draw, v. haul, drag, tug, tow;
attract; entice, allure, induce.
Antonyms: repel, repulse,
reject, alienate.
drawback, n. disadvantage,
hindrance, imperfection;
rebate, discount.
draw back. retract; shrink, recoil,
withdraw, wince.
drawer, n. till.
drawing, n. traction, pulling;
graphics, delineation; sketch,
diagram, picture.
dread, n. apprehension, fear.
dread, v. fear, apprehend.
dreadful, a. fearful, dread,
terrible, formidable, awful
dream, n. vision; illusion, wild
conceit, revery, fantasy.
Antonyms: fact, actuality,

reality.
dreamer, n. visionary, enthusiast.
dreamy, a. visionary, unreal.
Antonyms: practical, real .
dreary, a. dismal, drear, lone-
some, wearisome, dull.
dregs, n.pl. refuse, sediment,
draff; riffraff.
dress, n. gown, toilett, robe;
raiment, clothes, clothing,
garments. *Antonyms:* undress.
dress, v. clothe, deck, apparel,
robe array, attire; adjust, align.
Antonyms: undress, disrobe,
strip.
dressmaker, n. modiste.
dribble, v. drip, trickle.
dribble, n. trickling.
drier, n. desiccator, desiccative,
exsiccant.
drift, n. course, direction,
bearing, tendency, aim,
intention, desigh, meaning.
drill, v. perforate, pierce; train,
exercise.
drink, v. quaff, sip, imbibe; tipple,
guzzle, booze; absorb.
drink, n. beverage, potation;
draught, drench.
drinkable, a. potable. *Antonyms:*
undrinkable.
drinking, n. potation; tippling,
drunkenness, guzzling.
Antonyms: temperance,
abstinence.
drip, v. drop, trickle.
dripping, n. trickling.
drive, v. impel, force, compel;
propel, send; rush, press;
conduct.
drive at. aim, intend.
drive away. dispel, disperse.
drive back, repulse, repel.
drivel, n. driveling; nonsense.
drivel, v. drool.
driveler, n. drooler; imbecile,
fool, idiot.
driver, n. coachman, charioteer,
whip.
driving, a. violent, forcible;

impelling, impulsive.

driving, n. guiding by reins; propulsion, compulsion.

driving back. repulse, rebuff, repulsion, recussion.

driving out. expulsion

drizzle, n. mizzle, misle, mist.

droll, n. jester, buffoon, zany, comedy, farce.

droll, a. ludicrous, comical, facetious, funny.

drollery, n. waggery, pleasantry, facetiousness.

drone, n. sluggard, idler.

drool, v. drivel, slaver.

drooler, n. driveler, slaverer.

droop, v. languish, faint, grow faint, sink; bend, drop, hang; clouch; fade, wilt.

drop, n. globule, minim, blob; descent, fall.

drop, v. distill, dribble, trickle; drip; fall; lower, sink, depress.

drop by drop. stillatitious.

droplight, n. pendant.

dropping, n. distillation, trickling, dribbling, falling.

droppings, n.pl. excrement.

drop-shaped, a. globular, guttiform, stilliform.

dross, n. refuse, scum, recrement, draff, dregs, waste.

drought, n. aridity, dryness; scarcity, dearth.

drove, n. herd, flock; crown.

drown, v. overwhelm, submerge, flood, inundate.

drowning, n. demersion, inundation; noyade.

drowsiness, n. sleepiness.

drowsy, a. sleepy, dozy.

drudge, n. menial, hack, slave, scullion.

drug, v. deaden, dull, stupefy; surfeit; hocus.

druggist, n. pharmacist, apothecary.

drum, n. snare-drum; base-drum; kettle-drum.

drum, v. thrum, strum.

drumstick, n. tibiotarsus.

drunk, a. intoxicated, drunken, tipsy, boozy. *Antonyms:* sober, unintoxicated.

drunkard, n. inebriate, toper, tippler, carouser, wine-bibber, debauchee. *Antonyms:* abstainer, ascetic, teetotaler.

drunken, a. intoxicated, drunk; maudlin, mellow, gorggy.

drunkenness, n. intoxication, inebriety, inebriation, debauch; excitement, frenzy. *Antonyms:* sobriety, temperance.

dry, a. desiccated, dried, evaporated; anhydrous; barren, uninteresting, vapid, prosaic.

dry, v. evaporate, desiccate, insolate, torrefy.

dry goods. textile fabrics.

drying, n. desiccation, evaporation, torrefaction.

dryness, n. aridity, dessiccation, drought.

dubious, a. undetermined, undecided, doubtful; questionable, vague.

duck, v. souse, dip, plunge, immerse; dive; dodge, cringe.

duck, n. drake; teal.

duct, n. tube, canal, pipe.

dude, n. dandy, fop, coscomb, swell, exquisite. *Antonyms:* sloven, guy.

dudgeon, n. resentment, anger.

dudish, a. foppish, dandified. *Antonyms:* slovenly, seedy.

duds, n.pl. frippery [old clothes]; clothes, effects, things.

due, a. payable, unpaid; appropriate, becoming, proper, regular, appointed; owing.

due, n. debt; duty, right.

duel, n. monomachia, monomachy.

duelist, n. monomachist.

dugout, n. excavation.

dull, a. unintelligent, obtuse, stolid, inapt, blockish, sluggish; apathetic, unfeeling.

C
D

dull, v. blunt, rebate, benumb, stupefy, deaden; tarnish, obscure, dim.

dumb, a. mute, speechless.

dubness, n. muteness, obmutescence, speechlessness.

dub show. pantomime.

dumfound, v. astound, amaze, astonish.

dumpish, a. dull, moody, moping, dejected, gloomy.

dumps, n.pl. melancholy, depression.

dunce, n. dullard, numskull, witling, blockhead, coot, ninny, oaf, nincompoop.

duncical, a. doltish, witless.

dung, n. ordure, excrement, faeces, dejections, muck; puer, fumet.

dupe, n. gull, cully, gudgeon, dotterel, citim.

duplicate, a. double, twofold, duplex.

dusk, n. twilight, evening.

dust, n. powder; detritus; stive [in flour mills].

dust storm, somoon; [in India] shaitan, devil, dust whirl.

dusty, a. powdery, pulverulent, pulverous.

dutiful, a. obedient, duteous, submissive, deferential.

duty, n. responsibility, incumbency, accountability; service, business, work, function.

dwarf, n. pygmy, gnome, manikin, dandiprat, midget, runt, homunculus.

dwarf, v. stunt, atrophy.

dwarfish, a. diminutive, undersized, pygmy, runty, stunted, undeveloped, tiny.

dweller, n. denizen, resident, inhabitant.

dwelling, n. denizen, resident, sojourner, inhabitant, habitant.

dwelling, n. residence, domicile, house, abode.

dwindle, v. decrease, diminish, shrink.

dwindling, n. decrease, diminution, shrinkage.

dye, v. color, stain, tinge.

dying, a. moribund; expiring, last; mortal, perishable.

E

eager, a. ardent, avid, zealous, intent, impatient, athirst, impassioned. *Antonyms:* indifferent, apathetic, dispassionate, unconcerned, unmoved, stolid.

eagle, n. Aquila, bird of Jove; eaglet.

ear, n. [of grain] spike.

ear, n. [external] auricle, pinna, concha; [inner] labyrinth.

earache, n. otalgia, otalgy.

eardrum, n. tympanum.

earlier, a. antecedent.

early, a. seasonable, timely, forehanded.

earnest, a. unfeigned, ardent, sincere, impassioned, intent.

earnest, n. sincerity, seriousness, good faith; pledge, token. *Antonyms:* jest.

earring, n. eardrop, pendant.

ear-shaped, a. auriform.

earth, n. world, terra firma, globe; land, soil, ground.

earthborn, a. terrigenous, human; groveling, base.

earthenware, n. crockery, pottery, stoneware, porcelain.

earthling, n. mortal, tellurian.

earthly, a. worldly, carnal, groveling, sordid; terrestrial; temporal.

earthly-minded, a. worldly-minded, sensual, groveling.

earthquake, n. earthshock, earth tremor.

earthwork, n. fortification.

earthworm, n. angleworm,

dewworm, lumbric.

earthy, a. terrestrial, terrene, earthly; gross, carnal, groveling, low.

ear-trumpet, n. sonifer, otophone, auricle.

earwax, n. cerumen.

ease, n. facility, easiness; repose, comfort, contentment, peace, serenity. *Antonyms:* constraint, discomfort, uneasiness.

ease, v. facilitate, mitigate, appease, allay, soothe, alleviate, release, relax.

easiness, n. ease, facility.

eastern, a. oriental, orient.

easy, a. facile, slight; comfortable, untroubled, quiet, tranquil.

easy-going, a. mild-tempered, ease-loving, unenterprising.

eat, v. feed, devour; bolt, gulp, gorge. *Antonyms:* abstain, fast, diet, starve, famish.

eat, v. consume, aorrode, erode, fret.

eatable, a. edible, comestible, esculent. *Antonyms:* inedible.

eaten away. eroded, erose.

eating, n. feeding, repast; gluttony, bolting, gulping, browsing.

eating, n. corrosion, erosion.

eating-room, n. dining-room, refectory.

eating together. commensalism.

ebb, n. reflux, refluence; decline, deterioration.

ebb, v. recede, return, retire; decline, wante decay.

ebbing, a. receding, refluent.

eccentric, a. whimsical, erratic, irregular, odd.

eccentricity, n. whimsicality, oddness, freakishness, irregularity.

echo, n. reverberation.

echo, v. resound, reverberate.

eclipse, n. occultation;

obscuration, extinction, concealment.

eclipse, v. obscure, outshine, surpass, outrival.

economical, a. frugal, saving, thrifty, provident. *Antonyms:* extravagant.

economize, v. save, retrench, husband.

economy, n. thrift, frugality, thriftiness, retrenchment; management, system.

eczema, n. tetter, milk crust.

eddy, n. vortex, whirlpool.

edge, n. verge, brink, border, margin, rim, sharpmess, intensity.

edge, v. sharpen, fringe, border, rim; hitch along.

edgy, a. touchy, sharp, irritable, excitable.

edible, a. eatable, comestible. *Antonyms:* inedible.

edict, n. mandate, decree, rescript, manifesto, ordinance.

educate, v. teach, instruct, school, nurture, edify.

educated, a. learned, versed, erudite, scholarly, enlightened, schooled, literate.

education, n. culture, learning, schooling, tuition, scholarship, enlightenment, literacy.

efface, v. expunge, obliterate, erase, eradicate.

effect, n. result, outcome, issue; validity, force; execution, performance.

effect, v. effectuate, accomplish, realize, achieve, consummate, compass.

effective, a. effectual, efficient, cogent, productive.

effectual, a. efficacious, effective, availing, successful. *Antonyms:* ineffectual.

effeminate, a. womanish, unmanly, cockney.

effervescence, n. ebullition. *Antonyms:* ineffervescence, defervescence.

effete, a. exhausted, infecund, unfruitful, wasted, barren.

efficacious, a. potent, effectual, effective. *Antonyms:* inefficacious.

efficacy, n. petency, effectiveness, productiveness. *Antonyms:* inefficacy, impotency.

efficient, a. competent, capable, proficient, potent.

effort, n. attempt, endeavor, trial, essay, strain, struggle.

egg, n. ovum, germ, cell; spawn.

egg, v. urge on, instigate.

egg-shaped, a. oval, ovoid.

egotism, n. self-conceit, vanity, egoism.

egotistical, a. conceited, overweening, vain, self-important, opinionated.

eight-angled, a. octangular.

eightfold, a. octuple.

eight-sided, a. octagonal, octahedral, octangular.

eight-sided figure. octagon.

eight-sided solid. octahedron.

eight years. octennium.

eject, v. void, discharge; oust, evict, dislodge.

ejection, n. voiding, disharge; ousting.

elastic, a. resilient, springy, ductile, rebounding.

elasticity, n. resiliency, springiness, ductility. *Antonyms:* inelasticity, irresilience.

elated, a. elate, exhilerated, overjoyed, jubilant.

electric, a. stimulating, inspiriting, magnetic.

elegance, n. beauty, grace, richness, sumpuousness.

elegant, a. courtly, sumptuous, luxurious, rich.

element, n. constituent, ingredient.

elemental, a. rudimental, elementary.

elementary, a. rudimental,

elemental, constituent, primary; simple.

elevate, v. lift, raise; promote, advance; ennoble.

elevation, n. promotion, exaltation, dignity, advancement; eminence, hill.

elf, n. sprite, fairy, imp, fay, gnome.

elfish, n. mischievous, impish, elvish, prankish.

embankment, n. levee, dike.

embarrass, v. disconcert, discompose, morify, abash, pose, perplex.

embarrassment, n. discomposure, chagrin, mortification, disconcertion.

embillish, v. decorate, beautify, garnish, ornament.

embellishment, n. adornment, decoration, beautification; ornament, garnish, trimming.

embezzle, v. peculate, defalcate.

embezzlement, n. peculation.

embezzler, n. defalcator.

embroidery frame, tabouret.

embryo, a. undeveloped.

emery, n. abradant.

emigrant, n. emigrator, immigrant.

emigrate, v. migrate.

emigration, n. migration, exodus.

eminent, a. distinguished, renowned, illustrious, famous.

emphasis, n. accentuation.

emphasize, v. accentuate.

empire, n. sovereignty, sway, dominion, domain, kingdom.

emptiness, n. vacancy, inantion; hollowness, mockery; space, vacuum, void; triviality.

empty, a. depleted, vacant, inane; unoccupied, void, unfilled, blank.

empty, v. deplete, exhaust, unburden, evacuate; disembogue, deflate.

enchant, v. bewitch, charm,

enrapture, transport, delight.

enchantment, n. charm, witchery, glamour; sorcery, witchcraft, spell. *Antonyms:* disenchantment, disillusionment.

enchantress, n. siren, charmer, sorceress.

encircle, v. environ, surround, gird, enfold.

encounter, n. meeting, collision, rencounter; battle, conflick, attack.

encourage, v. enhearten, reassure, inspirit, stimulate, rally, countenance, incite.

encouragement, n. enheartenment, incentive, stiulus, fomentation, patronage.

encouraging, a. reassuring, inspiriting, assuring.

encroach, v. trespass, intrench, infringe, invade.

encroachment, n. trespass, intrenchemnt, invasion.

end, n. termination, terminal, extremity, limit; close, finale, finis.

end, v. terminate, conclude, discontinue, close.

endable, a. terminable.

endanger, v. imperil.

ending, n. termination, conclusion.

endless, a. interminable, limitless, boundless; continuous, uninterrupted, continual.

endowment, n. dotation, bounty, gequest, talent, faculty, dower.

endurable, a. sufferable, tolerable. *Antonyms:* unendurable.

endurance, n. permanence, continuance, persistence, continuation; sufferance, patience.

endure, v. suffer, experience, undergo; stand, brook, submit to; sustain. *Antonyms:* succumb, falter, yield.

enduring, a. lasting, durable,

permanent, imperishable

enemy, n. foe, adversary, opponent, rival, hostile.

energetic, a. forcible, potent, cogent, active, strenuous.

energizing, a. potent, vitalizing, invigorating.

energy, n. power, force, vigor, zeal, strength.

engage, v. pledge, bind, commit; betroth, plight; engross, busy, occupy.

engagement, n. betrothal, affiance; contract, pledge, promise; encounter, combat.

engine, n. locomotive, traction engine.

England, n. Albion [Ancient name].

English, a. British, Anglican.

Englishism, a. Anglicism, Briticism.

English legislature. Parliament.

Englishman, n. Britisher, Briton.

engrave, v. chisel, carve, cut; imprint, infix, impress.

engraving, n. celature, graving, chiseling, carving; print, plate.

enjoyment, n. pleasure, delight, delectation, felicity.

enlarge, v. magnify, amplify, expand, develop, increase, extend; dilate, descant.

enlargement, n. augmentation, extension, expansion, dilation, growth, increase.

enmity, n. hostility, unfriendliness, opposition, antagonism, malignity, hatred.

enormity, n. atrocity, heinousness, flagrancy.

enormous, a. colossal, gigantic, mammoth, huge; atrocious, flagrant, flagitious.

enough, n. sufficiency, plenty, abundance, adequacy. *Antonyms:* deficiency, surplus.

enrich, v. fertilize; embellish, adorn, beautify.

enrichment, n. fertilization;

endowment; embillishment, decoration.

enroll, v. enlist, register, list, record.

enrollment, n. registration, enlistment, register, record, roster.

enslave, v. enthrall, overcome.

enslavement, n. enthrallment, subjection, bondage, slavery.

entangle, v. interweave, complicate, tangle, snarl; insnare, puzzle, involve.

entanglement, n. complication, intricacy, snarl, tangle, embarrassment.

enter, v. penetrate, pierce, perforate; embark in, enlist in; insert.

enterprise, n. project, undertaking; activity.

enterprising, a. active, stirring, energetic.

entertain, v. divert, amuse, please, junket, cheer; harbor, hold, lodge.

entertaining, a. diverting, amusing, interesting.

entertainment, n. diversion, amusement, recreation, pastime, play; banquet, junket.

enthusiasm, n. eagerness, intensity, ardor, fervency, verve, unction. *Antonyms:* indifference, wariness, caution, calmness.

enthusiast, n. zealot, fanatic, devotee.

enthusiastic, a. eager, zealous, fanatical, fervent.

entice, v. seduce, allure, persuade, tempt.

enticement, n. seduction, allurement, temptation, decoy.

enticing, a. seductive, alluring, tempting.

entire, a. complete, undivided.

entirety, n. completeness, integrity, totality.

entrance, n. ingress, access;

entry, portal, inlet, gate.

entrap, v. insnare, entangle, decoy, entice.

entry, n. entrance, access; hall, vestibule; minute, record.

envelop, v. surround, inwrap, inclose, encircle, encompass.

envelope, n. wrapper, inclosure, capsule, case.

enveloping, a. surrounding, enfolding, encircling.

environment, n. conditions.

epicure, n. gourmand, gourmet; sensualist; sybarite.

epicurean, a. sensual, voluptuous, luxurious.

epicurism, n. hedonism, epicureanism, sensuality, gastronomy.

epitome, n. compendium, abstract, digest.

equal, a. coordinate, tantamount, equivalent, identical, commensurate, adequate.

equal, n. peer, mate, compeer, match. *Antonyms:* inferior, subordinate.

equality, n. coordination, uniformity, parity, agreement.

equilibrium, n. equipoise.

equip, v. accouter, furnish, fit out, gird.

equipage, n. equipment; carriage, turnout; suite, train.

equipment, n. apparatus, accouterments, rigging, gear.

equipoise, n. equilibrium.

equivalent, a. tantamount, equal; interchangeable.

eradicate, v. extirpate.

eradication, n. extirpation.

erase, v. expunge, rub out, efface, obliterate, delete.

erasure, n. expunging, erasion.

erect, v. build, raise.

erect, a. upright, vertical, raised; undaunted, bold, undismayed. *Antonyms:* horizontal, redumbent, inverted, oblique.

erection, n. building, raising.

erosion, n. corrosion, eroding.

err, v. misjudge, mistake, blunder; deviate, sin.

errand, n. mission, commission.

erratic, a. nomadic, wandering; eccentric.

erring, a. peccable, sinful, fallible, weak. *Antonyms:* impeccable, inerrable.

erroneous, a. false, incorrect, untrue, mistaken.

error, n. mistake, inaccuracy, blunder, falsity.

errors, n. pl. errata; sing. erratum.

erudition, n. learning, scholarship.

eruption, n. outburst, outbreak; exanthema, rash.

erysipelas, n. Saint Anthony's fire, rose.

excort, n. guard, convoy, usher.

Eskimo, n. Husky.

Eskimo house, Topek, igloo.

Eskimo language, Husky.

especial, a. special, particular, specific.

essay, n. dissertation, article, disquisition, thesis; attempt, effort, trial.

essential, a. indispensable, necessary, requisite. *Antonyms:* nonessential, superfluous.

establish, v. found, organize, institute; verify, ratify.

establishment, n. organization, founding, verification.

esteem, v. respect, value, honor, revere; rate, reckon.

esteem, n. respect, honor, regard; opinion, judgment. *Antonyms:* disesteem, aversion, antipathy.

estimable, a. computable, calculable; worthy, excellent. *Antonyms:* inestimable, incalculable.

estimate, v. appraise, value, rate, prize; calculate.

estimation, n. esteem, respect, honor; appraisement, estimate.

estrange, v. alienate, disaffect.

estranged, a. alienate.

estrangement, n. alienation, disaffection.

eternal, a. self-existent, infinite; endless.

eulogist, n. encomiast, praiser.

eulogize, v. laud, praise, extol.

eulogy, n. encomium, panegyric, laudation, praise.

evade, v. shun, avoid; elude, parry, foil, baffle; prevaricate, dodge, quibble.

evaporate, v. vaporize, evanesce.

evaporation, n. vaporization, evanescence; exhalation.

evasion, n. evading, eluding, escape; baffling, foiling; prevarication, sophistry.

evasive, a. equivocal, indefinite, elusive.

even, a. plane, level, flush, flat, smooth; uniform.

evening, n. dusk, twilight, nightfall, eventide, even.

evening prayer. compline.

evening service. vespers; evensong.

evenness, n. uniformity, smoothness, equableness.

event, n. occurrence, affair, incident, happening; result, outcome.

evergreen, a. indeciduous.

everlasting, a. continual, perpetual, interminable, eternal, endless, never-ending.

everlasting, n. eternity; immortelle.

every-day, a. commonplace, common, customary.

every now and then. occasionally, repeatedly.

evident, a. manifest, obvious, clear, patent.

evil, a. sinful, immoral, unrighteous, vicious.

evil, n. wickedness, depravity,

E

F

sin, iniquity, unrighteousness;
disaster, misfortune.

evil-doer, n. sinner, cuprit,
offender, delinquent.

evil-minded, a. malicious,
wicked, depraved.

evolution, n. development,
evolement, unfolding.

exact, a. precise, accurate, true,
undeviating; methodical, rigid,
severe, rigorous.

exact, v. demand, extort.

exacting, a. severe, harsh,
oppressive.

exaction, n. extortion, oppression.

exactness, n. precision, accuracy, strictness, scrupulous-
ness.

exaggerate, v. overstate.

exalt, v. elevate; dignify, ennoble;
magnify, apotheosize.

exaltation, n. elevation, loftiness,
apotheosis.

exalted, a. sublime, elevated,
lofty, grand, dignified.

examination, n. inquiry, autopsy,
scrutiny, inspection, audit,
inquest, inquisition.

examine, v. inspect, scrutinize,
question, audit, heckle, review,
search, probe.

examiner, n. inspector, inquirer,
questioner, auditor, consor,
reviewer, inquisitor.

example, n. sample, specimen,
exemplification; model, pattern,
prototype, copy.

exasperate, v. provoke, irritate,
incense, anger; aggravate,
imbitter.

exceed, v. surpass, tanscend;
outvie, excell, outdo; preponderate.

exceeding, a. surpassing.

excel, v. outrival, outstrip,
surpass, eclipse, outdo, outvie,
exceed.

excellence, n. preeminence;
superiority, eminence; integrity,

probity, goodness, worth.

excellent, a. estimable, meritorious, good, worthy, choice.

excess, n. superabundance,
superfluity, redundancy,
redundance; overplus, surplus,
residue.

excessive, a. superfluous,
exuberant, disproportionate;
outrageous, unreasonable,
exorbitant.

exchange, v. trade, barter, traffic,
commute, interchange, bandy,
permute.

exchange, n. traffic, trade,
barter, commutation, interchange, reciprocity.

excitable, a. susceptible,
sensitive, emotional, impressible, mobile; irritable. *Antonyms:* unexcitable, imperturbable, calm.

excite, v. stimulate, arouse,
inflame, incite, provoke;
perturb, agitate.

excitement, n. perturbation,
agitation, commotion, inquietude, tumult, turmoil. *Antonyms:* imperturbation,
calmness, serenity.

exciting, a. stirring, rousing,
stimulating.

exclaim, v. ejaculate, shout.

exclamation, n. ejaculation,
outcry; interjection.

exclamation point. ecphoneme.

exclude, v. debar, preclude;
except, omit; eject.

exclusion, n. debarment,
preclusion; exception, ejection,
expulsion.

excrement, n. faeces, stools,
dejections; dung, ordure.

excusable, a. venial, pardonable, justifiable. *Antonyms:*
inexcusable.

excuse, v. absolve, forgive,
pardon, exonerate, justify,
acquit, release.

excuse, n. justification, apology,

plea, palliation, pardon; evasion, makeshift.

execute, v. effectuate, perform, accomplish, consummate, achieve; behead, hang.

execution, n. performance, consummation, perpetration.

executioner, n. hangman.

exercise, n. performance, application, practice, employment, use; activity; training.

exercise, v. employ, apply, busy, exert; practice, discipline, drill, train.

exertion, n. effort, struggle, attempt.

exhaust, v. drain deplete; prostrate, enervate.

exhaustion, n. consuption, depletion, draining; lassitude, collapse, weariness.

exhaustless, a. inexhaustible.

exhibit, v. display, show.

exhibition, n. display, show.

exhumation, n. disinterment.

exhume, v. disinter, disentomb.

exile, n. banishment, proscription.

exile, v. banish, expatriate.

exiled person. exile, expatriate.

exorbitant, a. unreasonable, inordinate, excessive.

expand, v. dilate, distend, enlarge.

expansion, n. dilation, distension.

expatiate, v. descant.

expect, v. anticipate.

expectation, n. expectancy, anticipation.

expel, v. eject, drive out; ostracize, banish, exile; excommunicate; discharge.

expelling, n. expulstion, ejectment, dismissal; exile, ostracism.

expend, v. disburse.

expenditure, n. disbursement.

expense, n. outlay, cost, charge.

expensive, a. costly, dear, high-priced. *Antonyms:* inexpensive.

experienced, a. practiced, veteran. *Antonyms:* inexperienced.

experiment, n. test, trial.

experimental, a. empirical, tentative.

expert, a. skilled, proficient, adroit. *Antonyms:* inexpert.

expert, n. adept, master, dabster, connoisseur. *Antonyms:* tyro, bungler.

explain, v. expound, educidate, unfold.

explainable, a. explicable, solvable. *Antonyms:* unexplainable.

explainer, n. expositor, interpretator, exegetist.

explanation, n. elucidation, explication; solution, deduction.

explanatory, a. expository, elucidative, interpretative.

explode, v. burst; detonate, detonize.

exploint, v. develop, utilize.

exploitation, n. utilization, exploiture.

explosion, n. detonation; bursting; outburst.

explosive, n. dynamite, notroglycerine, tonite, fulgurite.

expose, v. exhibit, show, display; uncover, unveil, emperil, subject. *Antonyms:* conceal, suppress, dissemble, hide.

exposition, n. display, exposure; commentary, fair.

expostulate, v. remonstrate.

expostulation, n. remonstration.

exposure, n. exposing, disclosure, divulgement, revelation; subjection, jeapordy.

express, a. explicity, definite, specific. *Antonyms:* vague, tacit, implied, indefinite.

express, v. say, utter; represent, indicate, denote, mean.

expression, n. assertion, statement, declaration;

E
F

indication; phrase, term, word.

expulsion, n. expelling, ejection, debarment.

exquisite, a. beautiful, rare, choice; fastidious; keen, acute, poignant.

extend, v. lengthen, protract; jut, project; enlarge.

extensible, a. extendible, ductile, tensible. *Antonyms:* inextensible, rigid.

extension, n. enlargement, expansion, projection.

extent, n. magnitude, size, volume; reach.

exterminate, v. eradicate, extirpate.

extermination, n. eradication, uprooting.

external, a. outward, exterior, extrinsic.

extol, v. eulogize, praise, exalt.

extortion, n. exaction, over-charge, rapacity.

extortionate, a. oppressive, exacting.

extortioner, n. harpy.

extra, a. supplemental, additional, supernumerary.

extract, n. essence, quintessence; excerpt, quotation, citation.

extraordinary, a. uncommon, unuasual, remarkable, phenomenal, signal.

extravagance, n. improvidence, prodigality, waste, preposterousness. *Antonyms:* economy, thrift, frugality.

extravagant, a. wasteful, unthrifty, prodigal, lavish; wild, preposterous. *Antonyms:* thrifty.

extreme, a. outermost, utmost, farthest; last, final; ultra, radical, fanatical.

extreme, n. extremity, acme.

extremist, n. radical.

exuberance, n. superabundance, rampancy, excess, luxuriance.

exuberant, a. overflowing, copious, excessive, wanton, rank, luxuriant.

exultant, a. triumphant, jubilant, joyous.

eye, n. optic.

eyebrows, n. pl. supercilium.

eye doctor, oculist.

eye-glasses, n. pl. pince-nex, monocle, lorgnette, spectacles, goggles.

eyelashes, n. pl. cilia.

eyelid, n. palpebra; pl. palpebrae.

eyesore, n. blemish, defect.

eyewater, n. collyrium.

F

fable, n. apologue; fiction, fabrication, myth.

fabier, n. fabulist.

fabulous, a. fictitious, feigned, unverified; inordinate.

face, n. countenance, visage, features; front, exterior; obverse; facet.

face, v. confront, meet; bully, bluff; plane, dress.

face guard, n. mask, beaver.

facsimile, n. duplicate, copy, likeness, counterpart.

fact, n. reality, actuality.

faction, n. dissension, sedition, rebellion, division.

factious, a. turbulent, rebellious, refractory, insubordinate.

factor, n. broker, middleman, commission, merchant, agent; element.

factory, n. manufactory, shop, plant, mill.

facts, n. pl. data.

faculty, n. endowment, capability, talent, ability, knack, gift; dexterity.

fade, v. decay, decline, droop, evanesce, disappear.

fadeless, a. unfading, permanent, fast.

fading, a. fugitive, evanescent, declining.

faeces, n. pl, excrement, stools.

fail, v. default, lack; deteriorate, decline, disappoint, desert; miscarry, foil.

failing, n. shortcoming, deficiency, imperfection, fault, defect, fallibility, decline, deterioration.

failure, n. failing, shortcoming, lack; omission, pretermission, default, nonperformance, neglect.

faint, a. weak, exhausted, feeble; indistinct, dim, faded, dull; faint-hearted.

faint, v. swoon.

faint-hearted, a. timorous, diffident, fearful.

faint-heartedness, n. timidity, diffidence.

fainting, n. swoon, syncope.

fair, a. impartial, equitable, unbiased, just, honorable, ingenuous; average, tolerable.

fair, adv. clear, openly, honestly, favorably, impartially.

fair, n. bazaar; exposition.

fair and square. equitably, impartially, fairly.

fairly, adv. impartially, equitably, openly, favorably.

fair play. justice, equity.

fair-spoken, a. plausible, bland, civil, suave.

fairy, n. fay, elf, pixy, sprite, sylph.

faith, n. credence, belief, trust, dependence, credit, confidence; tenet, creed. *Antonyms:* doubt, incredulity, unbelief.

faithful, a. true, constant, stanch, unwavering, devoted; trustworthy, reliable, exact.

faithfulness, n. constancy, devotion, loyalty, fidelity, fealty, allegiance; exactness, accuracy.

faithless, a. unbelieving, skeptical, incredulous, doubting, disloyal, false.

faithlessness, n. unbelief, incredulity, doubt; disloyalty.

fake, n. trick, swindle, imposture, fraud, imposition.

fake, v. cheat, swindle, bumbug, defraud, manipulate fraudulently.

faker, n. trickster, swindler.

fall, v. descend, drop, gravitate; collapse, founder, slump, tumble, topple.

fall, n. descent, collapse, tumble, drop; decrease, decline, slump; cadence.

fallacious, a. sophistical, misleading, illusive.

fallacy, n. deception, delusion; sophism, sophistry.

fall away, v. emaciate; renounce, rebel; backslide; decline.

fall back, v. recede, retreat, retire, withdraw.

fallen, a. dropped, prostrate, degraded, debased.

fallibility, n. errancy. *Antonyms:* infallibility.

fallible, a. errable, erring. *Antonyms:* infallible.

fall in, v. collapse, cave in.

falling away, v. emaciation, pining; desertion, revolt; apostasy, defection, decline, declension.

falling back, v. recession, retreat, retirement, withdrawal.

falling down, v. prostration, collapse.

falling off, v. dropping; withdrawal, separation, detachment; defection; depreciation.

falling short, v. deficiency, inadequacy, deficit, shortcoming.

falling star, n. meteor.

falling to pieces, v. disintegration, dilapidation.

fall off, v. drop; withdraw,

E
F

separate; apostatize, depreciate, deteriorate.

fallow, a. uncultivated, untilled;
dormant.

fall short, v. be deficient, be
inadequate.

fall to pieces, v. disintegrate.

false, a. spurious, forged,
counterfeit, sham, unauthentic,
bogus, feigned, fallacious.

false friend, n. traitor, betrayer,
Judas.

falsehood, n. inveracity, untruth-
fulness; lie, fiction, untruth,
fabrication, canard.

false name, n. pseudonym.

false swearing, n. perjury.

false writing, n. forgery.

falsification, n. forgery, counterfeiting, n. falsifying; distortion.

falsify, v. misstate, garble,
misrepresent, distort, pervert;
refute. disprove.

falter, v. hesitate, tremble, waver,
vacillate.

faltering, a. wavering.

faltering, n. hesitation, wavering,
vacillation.

fame, n. celebrity, note, eminence, renown, glory, repute.
Antonyms: obscurity, oblivion.

familiar, a. intimate, close,
cordial, near, friendly; informal,
unconstrained, easy. *Antonyms:* unfamiliar, shy, distant.

familiarity, n. intimacy,
conversance; informality,
freedom, disrespect,
unreserve. *Antonyms:* unfamil-
iarity, strangeness.

family, n. household; genealogy,
lineage, ancestry.

family way, a. pregnancy.

famous, a. renowned, famed,
noted, eminent, distinguished.
Antonyms: obscure, inglorious,
unknown.

fan, n. flabellum.

fan, v. winnow; cool, ventilate;
stimulate, rouse, provoke,

encourage.

fanatic, n. extremist, zealot.

fanatical, a. fanatic, rabid,
overzealous.

fancied, a. imaginary.

fanciful, a. whimsical, visionary,
unpractical; fantastic, illusive,
phantasmic, bizarre, erratic.

fancy, n. imagination, conception, conceit, idea, impression,
opinion, notion; caprice.

fancy, a. ornate, elaborate;
fanciful, fabulous.

fancy, v. believe, imagine,
conjecture, conceive; like.

fandangle, a. fantastic,
highfalutin.

fang, n. tusk.

fan-shaped, a. plicate, flagellate.

fantastic, a. fanciful; unreal,
spectral, illusive; whimsical,
erratic; grotesque, odd,
baroque, bizarre.

fantod, n. worry, excitement,
fuss; indisposition, sulks.

far, a. distant, remote; alienated,
estranged.

farce, n. burlesque, caricature,
sham, take-off.

farcical, a. burlesque, ludicrous,
absurd.

farewell, n. adieu, leave-taking,
good-bye, valedictory.

farewell, n. parting, valedictory,
final.

far-fetched, a. forced, strained,
catachrestic.

farm, n. grange; plantation; croft;
hacienda.

farmer, n. agriculturist, granger.

farming, n. agriculture, hus-
bandry.

far-off, a. remote, distant.

far-sighted, a. hypermetropic,
presbyopic; long-sighted.

far-sightedness, n.
hypermetropia, hyperopia;
long-sightedness.

far-sighted person, n.
presbyope.

fascinate, v. bewitch, enchant, charm, captivate, enamor, infatuate, entrance, enrapture. *Antonyms:* disillusionize, decharm.

fascination, n. enchantment, witchcraft, sorcery, magic, captivation, charm. *Antonyms:* disenchantment.

fashion, n. vogue, style.

fast, a. immovable, firm, rigid; strong, invincible, fortified; steadfast, faithful.

fast, adv. swiftly, rapidly, quickly, with celerity, posthaste, speedily; fixedly, firmly.

fast and loose. inconstant.

fasten, v. secure, fix, lock, find, tie, attach, rivet, cement.

fastidious, a. critical, punctilious. *Antonyms:* careless, slovenly.

fastness, n. fixedness, immovability, firmness, security; fortress, stronghold, swiftness.

fat, a. fleshy, plump, obese, portly, burly, pampered, gross, stout.

fatal, a. mortal, deadly.

fatality, n. fatalness, fate, destiny; mortality; calamity.

fate, n. destiny, lot, doom; chance, fortune; karma; kismet.

fated, a. destined, doomed, predestined.

fateful, a. ominous.

father, n. pater familias, procreator, sire, founder, originator, author.

father, v. beget, engender.

fatherhood, n. paternity.

fatherly, a. paternal.

fatigue, n. weariness, languor, exhaustion.

fatigue, v. weary, tire, exhaust, bore.

fatness, n. corpulency, obesity, plumpness, fleshiness, stoutness, pudginess; fertility.

fatten, v. batten.

fatty, a. greasy, unctuous.

fatty tumor. lipoma.

fault, n. defect, imperfection, failing, shortcoming, flaw; dereliction, offense, lapse. *Antonyms:* merit, perfection, beauty.

fault-finder, n. critic, grumbler, censurer, censor.

fault-finding, a. captious, critical, dissatisfied, grumbling, discontented, carping.

faultiness, n. defectiveness, imperfection, peccability.

faultless, a. perfect, blameless, impeccable.

faulty, a. imperfect, defective; peccable, erring.

faun, n. satyr, sylvan.

favor, n. countenance, regard, good-will, kindness; support, promotion, befriending. *Antonyms:* disfavor, opposition.

favor, v. support, countenance, encourage.

favorable, a. propitious, conducive, beneficial, partial. *Antonyms:* unfavorable, unpropitious.

favoring, a. partial, approving.

favoritism, n. partiality. *Antonyms:* impartiality.

fawn, v. truckle, curry favor, court.

fawner, n. bootlicker, footlicker.

fawning, a. obsequious, servile.

fear, n. apprehension, anxiety, solicitude, alarm, dread, panic, dismay, terror.

fear, v. apprehend, dread, be afraid of; reverence, stand in awe of.

fearful, a. apprehensive, alarmed, afraid, frightened; timid, faint-hearted, cowardly, craven.

fearless, a. intrepid, courageous, bold, undaunted, unafraid, unflinching.

feasibility, n. practicability.

feasible, a. practicable.

E
F

feast, n. banquet, repast, regale, junket.

feast, v. banquet, junket; delight, gratify.

feastful, a. festive.

feat, n. exploit, stunt, act, deed.

feather, n. plume, quill.

feather, v. fledge.

feathered, a. fledged.

feathers, n.pl. plumage; panache, remiges [quill feathers]; down [soft under feathers]; coverts; retrices.

feathery, a. plumy, pennaceous.

feature, n. aspect, appearance; lineament; trait, characteristic, peculiarity.

federation, n. confederation, league, union.

fee, n. retainer, tip, honorarium, perquisite.

feeble, a. infirm, doddering.

feeble-minded, a. half-witted, defective, imbecile.

feeble-minded person, n. defective, imbecile.

feed, v. bait, regale.

feed, n. provender, fodder.

feel, v. touch, handle; grope, grabble; experience, suffer.

feeler, n. antenna, tentacle, horn, palpus; pl. antennae, palpi.

feeling, a. susceptible, sensitive, sympathetic. *Antonyms:* insentient, unfeeling, stoic.

feeling, n. sensibility, sensation; emotion. *Antonyms:* insensibility, numbness.

feign, v. pretend, dissemble, affect, assume.

feigned, a. pretended, simulate, counterfeit, assumed. *Antonyms:* real, sincere, unfeigned.

feigning, n. simulation, dissembling.

feint, n. pretense, blind.

felicitate, v. congratulate.

felicitation, n. congratulate.

fellow-countryman, n. compa-

triot.

fellowship, n. companionship, communion, converse.

felon, n. criminal, convict.

felonious, a. heinous, atrocious, flagitious, infamous.

female, a. feminine.

female warrior, n. Amazon.

fence, n. pale, palings, stockade, hurdle, raddle, defense, enclosure.

fence, v. defend, fortify, protect; evade, parry, shift.

fencing, n. swordsmanship, gladiature, swordplay.

fend, v. ward off, avoid.

fender, n. protection, defense, screen, guard.

ferment, n. barm, leaven, yeast; enzyme, syme.

fern, n. brake, maiden hair, Venus hair, polypody.

ferns, n.pl. Felices.

ferocious, a. rapacious, ravenous, fell, savage.

ferocity, n. rapacity, fierceness.

ferrotype, n. tintype.

fertile, a. fruitful, fecund; pistillate. *Antonyms:* infertile, barren.

fertility, n. fruitfulness, fecundity, richness. *Antonyms:* infertility, barrenness.

fertilization, n. enriching; impregnation.

fertilize, v. enrich, manure; impregnate.

fertilizer, n. manure, phosphate of lime, compost.

fervency, n. See ardor.

fester, v. suppurate, maturate, ulcerate.

fester, n. sore, pustule, festering, abscess.

festering, n. suppuration, maturation; fester.

festering, a. suppurating, maturating; rankling.

festival, n. fete, banquet, feast, holiday.

festive, a. festal, convivial.
festoon, n. garland.
fetid, a. malodorous, stinking.
fetter, n. shackle, bond, hamper, restraint.
fetter, v. shackle, manacle, hamper; restrain, impede.
feverish, a. febrile.
fever spots. petechiae.
fewness, n. paucity.
fiat, n. order, decree, mandate, edict.
fib, n. falsehood, untruth.
fiber, n. staple, thread.
fickle, a. vacillating, volatile, irresolute, fitful, unstable, variable, wavering. *Antonyms:* constant, steadfast.
fickleness, n. vacillation, irresolution, volatility.
fiddle, n. violin; kit.
fiddler, n. violinist.
fidelity, n. loyalty, fealty, faithfulness; truth. *Antonyms:* infidelity.
fidgets, n.pl.restlessness.
field, n. meadow, lea; campaign, croft; scope, range, room, province.
fiend, n. demon.
fiendish, a. diabolical, infernal.
fierce, a. violent, unrestrained, furious, impetuous, passionate, fiery. *Antonyms:* tame, gentle, docile.
fiery, a. igneous; vehement, impetuous, passionate, irritable.
fig, n. fico, snap, fillip.
fight, n. combat, battle, engagement, struggle, fray, scrimmage; pugnacity.
fight, v. battle, combat, militate, cope with.
fighter, n. warrior, champion, combatant, gladiator.
fight shy, a. avoid, elude.
figment, n. fabrication.
figurative, a. typical, representative; metaphorical.

figure, n. shape, form, outline, image, statue, bust, likeness; numeral, digit.
figure, v. compute, cipher; contrive, scheme, plan; typify, represent.
figure of speech, n. trope, metaphor.
file, n. line, row; rasp.
filing, n. limature.
fill, n. thill, shaft.
fill, n. sufficiency, plenty.
fill, v. satisfy, cloy, sate, glut, stuff; occupy, replenish; expand.
fill out, v. extend, inflate, complete, amplify.
film, n. pellicle.
filter, v. strain, clarify, percolate, exude, ooze, transude.
filtering, n. filtration; exudation, infiltration.
filth, n. squalor, foulness, corruption, muck, dirt.
filthy, a. nasty, dirty, squalid, foul; obscene, indecent, lewd.
finally, adv. ultimately, eventually.
find fault, v. object, disapprove, demur, except, criticize, repine, complain.
finding, n. discovery; verdict.
finding out, n. detection, discovery.
find out, v. discover, detect, solve, unriddle.
fine, n. amercement, penalty. -v. mulct, amerce.
fine, a. refined, nice, exquisite, excellent, elegant, admirable, choice, select. *Antonyms:* coarse, crude, stout, crass, thick.
finedrawn, a. subtle.
finery, n. ornaments, decorations, clothes.
finespun, a. subtle.
finesse, n. artifice, maneuvering, ruses.
finger, n. digit; medius [middle finger]; minimus [little finger];

E F

index [fore or index finger].

finger, v. touch, handle; strum.

finger bone, n. phalanx, internode.

finger-shaped, a. digitform.

finical, a. overparticular.

finicky, a. finical, fastidious, dainty.

finish, v. complete, elaborate.

finish, n. completion.

fire, v. ignite, kindle; dismiss; inflame, irritate, excite; animate.

fire, n. combustion, ignition, burning; conflagration, holocaust; flame, blaze.

fire-arms, n. pl. guns, gunnery.

firebug, n. incendiary.

firedog, n. andiron.

fireman, n. fire-tender, stoker.

fireproof, a. incombustible.

fireside, n. hearth, ingleside.

fire-worship, n. pyrolatry.

firm, a. fast, immovable, secure; compact, solid, dense; fixed, resolute. *Antonyms:* flaccid, soft, irresolute, yielding, facile.

first, a. earliest; foremost, leading, chief, premier; primary, primordial, primitive.

first, adv. primarily.

first principles, n. rudiment, prinsipia.

first-rate, a. excellent, first-class.

fish, n. fry, alevin; monilifer.

fish eggs, n. spawn, roe.

fisherman, n. fisher, piscator.

fishes, n.pl. Pisces; Piscifauna.

fish culture, n. pisciculture.

fish hawk, n. osprey.

fishing, n. angling, trawling, trolling, whiffing, fishing.

fishy, a. fishlike; extravagant, exaggerated.

fistic, a. pugilistic.

fisticuffs, n. pl. boxing, pugilism.

fit, n. spasm, paroxysm, convulsion; access, outburst, attack; epilepsy, humor, whim.

fit, a. meet, becoming, suitable,

proper, congruous, expedient, apposite, qualified.

fit, v. adapt, qualify, prepare, equip, shape, adjust.

fitful, a. variable, capricious, unstable, inconstant, changeable.

fitness, n. becomingness, appropriateness, competency, congruity, eligibility.

fitting, a. suitable, proper, fit.

five, n. cinque, quintuplet, quintette.

five-angled figure, n. pentagon, pentahedron.

five cents, n. nickel.

fivefold, a. quintuple.

five-sided, a. pentagonal, pentahedral.

five years, n. quinquennium, lustrum.

fix, v. mend, repair, restore, adjust; rivet, fasten; settle, fasten, implant, define.

fix, n. dilemma, predicament, plight, quandary. *Antonyms:* extrication.

fixed, a. immovable, stable, firm, unchangeable, steadfast.

fixings, n.pl. embellishments, trimmings.

fizzle, n. failure, fiasco.

flabbergast, v. astonish, amaze, surprise.

flabbergastation, n. astonishment, amazement.

flabbiness, n. flaccidity, limpness.

flabby, a. yielding, limp, soft. *Antonyms:* firm, stiff, rigid.

flag, n. colors, standard, banner, pennant, ensign, guidon, streamer; iris.

flagrant, a. glowing, flaming, ardent; heinous, wicked.

flake, n. film, flock, scale.

flame, n. blaze, fire; love.

flameless, a. aphlogistic.

flaming, a. blazine, afire, flagrant; dazzling, brilliant;

ardent.

flare, v. flicker, flutter; dazzle, blaze, glare.

flare, n. glare, flicker.

flare-up, n. passion, anger.

flash, n. gleam, glare.

flash, v. glitter, gleam, sparkle, glisten.

flash, n. instant, moment.

flashy, a. dazzling; gaudy, tawdry, showy.

flask, n. betty, matrass.

flat, a. level, even, plane, smooth; prone; stale, vapid, tasteless. *Antonyms:* convex, concave, undulating, projecting.

flat, n. lowland, champaign; floor, suite.

flatboat, n. punt.

flatfoot, n. splayfoot.

flatfooted, a. splayfooted; determined, resolute, firmfooted.

flatiron, n. sadiron.

flatnosed, a. simous.

flatter, v. blandish, cajole, wheedle.

flatterer, n. wheedler, toady, flunky.

flattering, a. wheedling, adulatory, alluring, obsequious.

flattery, n. adulation, wheedling, flummery, cajolery.

flaunting, a. ostentatious, showy.

flavor, n. savor, taste, relish, zest, gusto, race.

flavorless, a. insipid, vapid, unpalatable, savorless.

flavorous, a. sapid, savory.

flaw, n. defect, fault, blemish.

flawless, a. faultless, perfect.

flawy, a. defective, faulty.

flay, v. skin, excoriate.

fleece, v. plunder, swindle, despoil.

fleet, n. squadron, navy, armada.

fleeting, a. impermanent, transitory, ephemeral, fugitive, temporary.

flesh, n. meat, carnage; pulp; sensual appetites;.

flesh-eating, a. carnivorous.

flesh-eating animal, n. carnivore, sarcophile.

fleshiness, n. corpulence, obesity, plumpness.

fleshly, a. carnal, sensual.

fleshy, a. corpulent, fat, obese, plump.

flexibility, n. pliability, suppleness, ductility.

flexible, a. pliable, supple, pliant, lithe, limber; compliant. *Antonyms:* inflexible, incompliant.

flight, n. flying; exodus, hegira; fleeing.

flighty, a. volatile, mercurial, giddy, fickle.

flimflam, n. trick, deception.

flimsy, a. superficial, weak, feeble, shallow.

flinch, v. shrink, wince, recoil, withdraw.

flinders, n.pl. splinters.

flinty, a. unimpressible, impenetrable, unyielding.

flippant, a. voluble, glib, fluent; pert, malaper, forward.

flirt, n. coquette, jilt.

flirtation, n. coquetry.

flirtatious, a. coquettish.

float, n. raft; buoy.

floating, n. flotation, flotage.

flock, n, covey, herd, bevy, drove, pack, lot, brood.

flog, v. See whip.

flood, v. inundate, deluge.

flood-gate, n. sluice-gate.

floor, v. prostrate, fell, overthrow; embarrass.

floor, n. planching, pavement; story.

floral ornament, n. anthemion, palmette.

florid, a. flushed.

florist, n. floriculturist.

flounce, n. ruffle, furbelow.

flourish, v. thrive; wave.

E

F

flourish, n. embellishment; curlycue; fanfare, call; parade, show, display; waving.

flout, v. mock, jeer, sneer.

flow, v. circulate; proceed, issue. *Antonyms:* stagnate, ebb.

flower, n. blossom, bloom; floweret.

flowering, a. phaenogamous.

flowering plants, n. Phaenogamia.

flowerless, a. cryptogamous.

flowerless plants, n. Cryptogamia.

flowery, a. florid, ornate.

flowing, a. running, gliding, cursive. *Antonyms:* stagnant.

fluctuate, v. vacillate, waver, whiffle. *Antonyms:* continue, persist, adhere, abide, remain.

fluctuation, n. vacillation, oscillation, instability.

fluent, a. flowing, gliding.

fluid, n. liquid, liquor.

flunk, v. fail, back out.

flunky, n. lackey, footman, servant; snob.

flurried, a. agitated, excited, perturbed.

flurry, n. squall, breeze, wind; agitation, commotion.

flush, n. flush, flow; thrill; redness.

flush, a. liberal, prodigal, free; even, plane.

fluster, v. perturb, discompose, disconcert.

fluster, n. perturbation, discompose, confusion.

flustrate, v. fluster, agitate.

flustration, n. agitation, fluster, confusion.

fluted, a. chamfered, grooved.

flutter, v. tremble, palpitate; hover; fluctuate.

flutter, n. tremor, agitation, palpitation; confusion, disorder, commotion.

fly, a. wide-awake, knowing.

fly, v. wing, soar, flit, hover; decamp, flee.

flyaway, a. flighty, giddy, volatile.

flying, a. awing, volant, soaring.

flying, n. aviation, flight.

foam, n. froth, spume.

foamy, a. frothy, spumy.

fodder, n. provender, forage, stover.

foe, n. antagonist, enemy.

fog, n. haze, mist, vapor.

fog, v. befog, obscure, confuse.

foggy, a. misty, hazy, vaporous; beclouded, confused.

fogy, n. fogram, mossback.

foil, v. baffle, frustrate.

foist, v. interpolate.

fold, n. doubling, plait; sheep-pen, embrace.

fold, v. double; embrace, clasp.

foliage, n. leafage, leaves.

folks, n.pl. people, persons.

follow, v. succeed, chase, pursue, tag; result, flow, ensue; issue; pursue, practice, engage in; track.

follower, n. pursuer; attendant, retainer, disciple, advocate, adherent, imitator.

following, n. pursuance, pursuit; sequence, succession; adherents, retinue; vocation, trade, business.

following, a. succeeding, ensuing, consecutive.

folly, n. foolishness, fatuity, unwisdom, absurdity.

foment, v. encourage, nurse; stupe.

fond, a. indulgent, doting; affectionate, loving; baseless, vain.

fondle, v. caress, pet, cosset, humor.

fondness, n. indulgence, doting; affection, love; partiality, liking, propensity, appetite.

food, n. aliment, nutriment, pabulum, nutrition, fare, diet, bread, meat.

food for cattle, n. feed, fooder,

provender, forage.

fool, n. idiot, imbecile; simpleton, dunce, defective, dotterel, blockhead, ninny.

fool, v. dupe, gull, delude, deceive, trick, beguile, victimize, cully.

fooling, n. foolishness, folly; mummery, monkey-tricks, harlequinism.

foolhardy, a. daredevil, reckless.

foolish, a. idiotic, senseless, irrational, silly, imbecile, witless, insensate, half-witted.

foolishness, n. idiocy, fatuity, silliness, irrationality, imprudence, folly, absurdity.

foot, n. paw; hoof; base, bottom.

footboy, n. page, lackey.

footing, n. foothold; rank, status, grade, amount, total; tread, step.

footman, n. infantryman.

footprint, n. footmark, track.

foot-soldiers, n.pl. infantry.

footstep, n. footmark, footprint, track, trace; football, tread, step.

fop, n. coxcomb, dude, dandy, exquisite, blade. *Antonyms:* sloven, guy).

foppish, a. coxcombical, dandified, finical. *Antonyms:* slovenly, seedy.

forbear, v. refrain, stop, pause, withhold; endure.

forbearance, n. withholding; long-suffering, patience, toleration.

forbearing, a. long-suffering, patient, tolerant, lenient.

forbears, n.pl. ancestors.

forbid, v. prohibit, interdict, inhibit, restrain, preclude, proscribe.

forbidden, a. prohibited, proscribed, contraband, illicit, taboo.

forbidding, a. repellent, repulsive, offensive, odious.

forbidding, n. prohibition, interdiction, restraint, taboo.

force, v. compel, coerce, constrain, oblige, make; impel, obtrude, extort. *Antonyms:* induce, seduce, persuade.

force, n. strength, energy, power, vigor, might, potency, validity, efficacy.

forced, a. involuntary, compulsory, strained. *Antonyms:* spontaneous, voluntary.

forcible, a. energetic, potent, effective, coercive, drastic, vigorous.

forcing, n. compelling, compulsion, coercion, extortion, constraint; rape. *Antonyms:* discretion, option, election.

forearm, n. antibrachium.

forebode, v. portend, presage, augue, betoken.

foreboding, n. premonition, presentiment, prescience.

forecast, n. predetermination, premeditation.

forefather, n. ancestor, progenitor, forebear.

forego, v. quit, relinquish, surrender, yield, do without.

foregoer, n. predecessor, forefather; forerunner, herald, precursor, harbinger.

foregoing, a. previous, anterior, preceding, fore, prior, aforesaid.

forehead, n. brow, sinciput. *Antonyms:* occiput.

foreign, a. alien, extraneous, exotic; remote, adventitious.

foreigner, n. alien; extraneous, exotic; remote, adventitious.

foreigner, n. alien, emigrant, immigrant. *Antonyms:* native, indigence.

foreknowledge, n. prescience.

foreordain, v. preordain, predestinate, foredoom, predetermine.

forerun, v. precede, herald.

forerunner, n. precursor,

E
F

harbinger, herald.

foreshadow, v. presage, presignify, prefigure.

foresight, n. prescience, foreknowledge.

foreskin, n. prepuce.

forest, n. wood, woodland, timerland, woods, wildwood.

forestall, v. anticipate; preoccupy.

foretell, v. predict, prophesy, augur, portend, forebode, divine, presignify.

foretelling, a. prophetic, portentous, predictive, augurial.

foretelling, n. prediction, prophecy, prognostication, presage, foreboding, divination.

forethought, a. aforethought, prepense.

forever, adv. eternally, continually, perpetually.

forewarning, n. premonition.

forfeit, n. forfeiture, philopena; fine, mulct, penalty.

forge, n. smithy, stithy.

forger, n. fabricator, falsifier.

forgery, n. counterfeiting, falsification, counterfeit.

forgetfulness, n. amnesty, amnesia, oblivion.

forget-me-not, n. myosotis.

forgivable, a. pardonable, venial.

forgive, v. pardon, excuse, absolve, condone, connive.

forgiveness, n. pardon, remission, absolution, acquittal.

forgiving, a. compassionate, indulgent, placable. *Antonyms:* unforgiving.

forgo, v. omit, relinquish.

fork, n. fourchette; divarication, branch, crotch; prong, tine; pew.

fork, v. ramify, branch.

forked, a. furcated, crotched.

forlorn, a. deserted, lorn, disconsolate.

form, n. shape, structure, figure, conformation, cast; formula, ritual; formality.

form, v. shape, fashion.

formal, a. ceremonial, express, explicit, prim, ceremonious.

formality, n. ceremoniousness, precision, ceremony.

formative, a. plastic, creative.

former, a. antecedent, preceding, prior, bygone.

formerly, adv. heretofore.

formless, a. shapeless, amorphous.

formula, n. ritual, ceremony; rule, recipe.

formulary, n. ritual, ceremonial, rule.

forsake, v. quit, abandon, leave; renounce, reject, relinquish.

forsaken, a. abandoned, deserted, derelict.

forsaking, n. desertion.

fort, n. fortress, fortification, fastness, stronghold, redoubt.

forthwith, adv. immediately, directly.

fortunate, a. lucky, favored; favorable. *Antonyms:* unfortunate.

fortune-teller, n. chiromancer, palmist.

fortune-telling, n. chiromancy, palmistry.

forty-niner, n, Argonaut.

forum, n. tribunal.

forward, a. anterior, fore; overready, presumptuous, impertinent, intrusive; premature.

forward, v. advance, promote, accelerate, further; transmit, send, ship.

forwarding, n. transmission.

fossilist, n. paleontologist.

fossilization, n. fossilification.

fossilize, v. petrify, lapidify.

fossilized, a. petrified; antiquated.

foster, v. nourish, nurse, support; promote.

foul, a. filthy, squalid, dirty;

abusive, obscene, vituperative,
vulgar; detestable.

foul, v. defile, soil, dirty.

foul-mouthed, a. scurrilous,
abusive; profane, obscene.

found, v. establish, plant; cast
form, mould.

foundation, n. substructure,
base; founding; endowment;
grillage. *Antonyms:* superstruc-
ture.

founder, n. establisher, institutor,
planter originator; moulder.

founder, v. fall, stumble; fail.

fount, n. spring,
fountain.fountain, n. fount,
spring; source, fountainhead.

four, n. quaternion, tetrad,
quartette; quadruplets.

four cities, n. tetrapolis

fourfold, a. quadruple,
quadruplex, quadruplicate.

four-sided, a. quadrangular,
square, tetragonal, tetrahedral.

four-sided figure, n. square,
tetragon, quadrangle, rhombus.

foursquare, a. quadrangular.

fourth, n. quarter.

four years, n. quadrennium.

fox, n. Reynard, Renard, tod,
Charlie.

foxglove, n. digitalis.

foxy, a. cunning, sly, wily.

foyer, n. greenroom.

fracas, n. brawl, uproar, disturbance, quarrel.

fractious, a. unruly, perverse,
irritable, ugly.

fracture, n. rupture, breach.

fragile, a. brittle, frangible, frail.

fragility, n. brittleness, frailty.

fragment, n. remnant, chip,
scrap, piece, flitter.

fragmentary, a. disconnected,
fractional.

fragrance, n. perfume, aroma,
redolence. *Antonyms:* fetor,
stench.

fragrant, a. sweet-smelling,
redolent. aromatic, balmy.

Antonyms: fetor, stench,
inodorousness.

frail, a. fragile, brittle; feeble,
weak, infirm.

frailty, n. fragility, brittleness;
imperfection, fault.

frame, v. devise, plan, contrive;
invent, fabricate; adjust, fit.

framework, n. frame, skeleton.

frank, a. candid, outspoken,
ingenuous.

frankness, n. candor, unreserve.

frantic, a. distracted, frenzied,
crazed.

fraternal, a. brotherly.

fraternity, n. brotherhood.

fraud, n. imposture, deceit,
duplicity, imposition, wile,
circumvention, hypocrisy,
surreption.

fraudulent, a. deceptive, wily,
crafty, surreptitious.

fraught, a. laden, freighted,
charged.

fray, n. fight, battle, combat,
affray; fret.

frazzle, v. fray, tatter.

frazzle, n. tag end.freak, n. whim,
vagary, whimsey, humor.

freakish, a. whimsical, capricious, fanciful, crotchety.

freckle, n. lentigo.

freckled, a. spotted.

free, v. liberate, disenthrall,
deliver, release, disengage,
exonerate, extricate, disentangle.

free, a. exempt, immune,
unrestrained; liberated, freed,
released, delivered; unreserved. *Antonyms:* subject,
reserved, formal, coercive,
restrained, bound.

free and easy, a. informal,
unceremonious, unrestrained.

freebooter, n. buccaneer,
pillager, pirate.

freedom, n. exemption, immunity; liberty, independence,
autonomy; privileges, immuni-

E

F

ties. *Antonyms:* subjection, liability, heteronomy, reserve, constraint, repression.

freeing, n. emancipation, liberation, release, enfranchisement, extrication, discharge, exoneration.

freely, adv. bounteously, readily, abundantly, voluntarily, copiously, unreservedly.

free-thinker, n. infidel, skeptic.

free-will, a. voluntary.

freezable, a. congealable.

freeze, v. congeal.

freezing, n. congelation.

freight, n. cargo, lading.

frenzied, a. distracted, frantic.

frenzy, n. distraction, rage.

frequenter, n. habitue.

freshen, v. refresh, revive.

fresh-water, a. fresh, unsalted; raw, untrained.

fret, v. chafe, abrade, fray; gnaw, corrode; ruffle, agitate; worry, tease, irritate, fume, rankle.

fret, n. vexation, agitation, irritation; herpes, tetter, ringworm; whelk, wale.

fretful, a. irritable, petulant, peevish, captious.

friction, n. abrasion, attrition, rubbing; clashing.

friend, n. wellwisher, intimate, chum, associate; patron, adherent, supporter; ally; Quaker.

friendliness, n. comity, amity, good will.

friendly, a. amicable, favorable, kind; fraternal, neighborly, cordial; favorable, salutary. *Antonyms:* unfriendly.

friendship, n. amity, intimacy, friendliness. *Antonyms:* enmity, estrangement, disaffection, hostility.

fright, n. alarm, fear, terror, dismay; ogre, guy.

frighten, v. terrify, alarm, scare, intimidate, dismay, daunt, appall.

frightful, a. terrible, dreadful, hideous, ogreish, fearful, grewsome, grim, dire, awful, horrible.

frill, n. ruffle, gathering.

fringe, n. edging, margin, confine, border.

fringed, a. fimbriate, fimbriate.

frisk, a. frolic, gambol.

frisky, a. frolicsome, sportive, playful, gay.

frivolous, a. trivial, trifling, petty.

friz, v. curl, crisp.

frizzle, n. curl, frix.

frock, n. gown; smock-frock; cassock.

frolic, n. pran, lark, escapade, fun.

frolicsome, a. playful, prankish, frisky.

from head to foot, a. throughout, completely.

front, n. facade; obverse, face; van, front, rank.

frost, n. rime, hoarfrost; uncordiality, unsociability.

frosting, n. icing.

frosty, a. cold, icy; uncordial, distant, aloof, pruinose.

froth, n. spume, foam.

frothing, n. rant.

frothy, a. spumy, foamy, spumous; trivial, frivolous.

froward, a. refractory, unyielding, insubmissive.

frown, n. scowl, lower.

frowning, a. scowling, lowering, stern.

frugal, a. economical, saving, sparing, thrifty.

frugality, n. economy, thriftiness, thrift.

fruit, n. fruitage, fruitery.

fruitful, a. prolific, productive, fertile, bountiful.

fruitless, a. unfruitful, infecund; unavailing, useless.

fruit sugar, n. levulose.

frump, n. gossip.

frustrate, v. baffle, defeat, foil, balk, circumvent, nullify.

frustration, n. defeat, disappointment, balking, foiling.

fuddled, a. muddled, tipsy, drunk, intoxicated, groggy.

fuel, n. combustibles.

fugitive, a. fleeing; evanescent, short-lived. volatile, impermanent.

fugitive, n. runaway, runagate, renegade.

fulfill, v. accomplish, complete, realize; satisfy, fill, answer, meet; discharge.

fulfillment, n. consummation, fruition, realization; discharge, performance.

full, a. filled up, replete; copious, ample, bountiful, abundant, liberal.

full swing, a. liberty, unrestraint.

fulsome, a. offensive, nauseous, disgusting, gross, immoderate.

fume, n, exhalation, reek, smoke, steam, vapor.

fume, v. smoke, reek; storm, rage.

fun, n, merriment, mirth, gayety, frolic, jest, divertisement, amusement, relaxation.

function, n, duty, province, office, business, part; discharge, performance, execution.

fundament, n, buttocks.

fundamental, a. basal, elementary, original, essential.

fundamentally, adv. primarily, essentially, radically.

funeral, n. obsequies.

funeral director, n. undertaker.

funereal, a. exequial, mournful, solemn, sad.

fungology, n. mycology.

fungus, n. thallogen, thallophyte; proud, flesh.

funnel, n. tunnel.

funny, a. comic, comical, amusing, laughable, witty, ludicrous, burlesque, absurd, humorous.

fur, n. peltry, pelage.

furbish, v. polish, scour, clean.

furious, a. infuriated, angry, raging, violent, turbulent.

furnish, v. supply, provide, bestow, purvey, cater.

furniture, n. goods, movables.

furthermore, adv. moreover.

fury, n. wrath, rage, indignation, frenzy; termagant, shrew, vixen; agitation, excitement.

fuse, v. melt, liquefy, dissolve, smelt; commingle, blend, intermix.

fusion, n. melting, fluidity; intermingling, coalition, blending.

fuss, n. ado, bustle, to-do agitation, excitement.

fuss, v. pother, fume, fret; disturb, annoy, bothre.

fussy, a. fidgety, finical, scrupulous, overnice.

futile, a. vain, bootless, unavailing, abortive.

fuzz, n. down, pubescence.

fuzzy, a. downy, pubescent.

G

gabble, n. gibberish, babble, prate, chatter.

gabble, v. gibber, jabber, babble, prate, chatter.

gable, n. pediment.

gad, n. goad.

gag, v. silence, muzzle, muffle, hush; retch.

gag, n. muffler, muzzler, silencer.

gain, n. increase, profit, advantage, increment, acquisition, accretion, store; lucre.

gain, v. get, acquire, achieve, win, obtain, attain; persuade.

gainsay, v. contradict, dispute, deny, controvert.

gaiters, n.pl. spats,

G H

spatterdashes, legging, gramashes.

gale, n. wind, tempest; excitement, confusion.

gall, n. bile; bitterness, rancor.

gall, n. impudence, audacity, insolence.

gall, v. chafe, fret; vex, annoy.

gallant, a. polite, deferential, courtly.

gallant, n. spark, beau, philander; lover, seducer.

gallantry, n. chivalry, bravery; heroism; politeness; intrigue.

gall bladder. cholecystis.

gallery, n. balcony; corridor, passage, museum.

gallstone, n. bilestone, biliary.

galoot, n. rowdy, blusterer.

galore, n. and a. plenty, abundance, abounding.

gambler, n. gamester, cardsharper, blackleg, punter.

gambol, v. caper, frolic, play, sport, curvet.

game, n. play, amusement, pastime, fun sport; context; prey; scheme, plan.

game, a. plucky, resolute, courageous, unflinching, undaunted, crippled, lame, crooked.

gang, n. band, crew, company, group, crowd, set, party, number.

gangrene, n. mortification.

gangrene, v. mortify, sphacelate.

gap, n. hiatus, rift, rent, chasm.

gape, v. yawn; gaze, stare.

gape, n. yawn, gaping, oscitancy.

garbage, n. offal, refuse, swill, waste.

garble, v. pervert, distort, falsify, misstate, wrench.

gardener, n. horticulturist.

gardening, n. horticulture.

garland, n. wreath, chaplet, bays, laurel; rosary.

garnish, v. embellish, beautify, decorate, trim.

garniture, n. garnish, garnishment, decoration.

garret, n.attic, cockloft.

gaseous, a. aeriform, gassy, gasiform; tenuous, thin.

gash, v. slash, incise.

gash, . incision, slash.

gasp, n. pant, panting -v. pant.

gassing, n. boasting, vaunt, gasconade, vapor.

gassy, a. gaseous, aeriform; boastful, vaporous.

gate, n. entrance, portal; wicket; turnstile, postern; tollgate; sluice gate; stanch.

gather, v. congregate, assemble, convene, muster, collect; harvest, pick, glean.

gather, n. pucker, plait, ruffle.

gathering, n. collection, crowd, assembly, congregation, concourse, muster, party, company.

gaudy, a. showy, flashy, ostentatious, garish.

gaunt, a. emaciated, pinched, meager, lean.

gawk, n. gawky, booby, lout, hind.

gay, a. merry, sportive, lively, exhilarating, jolly, blithe, airy, convivial.

gayety, n. merriment, mirth, hilarity, sportiveness, joviality, elation.

gear, n. rigging, tackle, mechanism; accouterments.

geld, v. castrate.

gem, n. jewel.

general, a. indefinite, vague, ill-defined; prevalent, extensive; usual, common, regular. *Antonyms:* specific, definite.

generality, n. bulk, common run, mass, main body; universality.

generalship, n. strategy.

generate, v. procreate, beget, reproduce, originate, produce.

generation, n. procreation, reproduction, begetting;

origination, formation.

generative, a. generating, procreative, genial.

generosity, n. magnanimity, nobleness; liberality, bounty, beneficence, lavishness.

generous, a. magnanimous, noble, highminded, ingenuous; munificent, bountiful, liberal, lavish. *Antonyms:* illiberal, stingy, scant, miserly.

genial, a. generative, procreative; cheerful, pleasant, cordial, friendly.

gentle, a. well-born, genteel, high-born; docile, tame, subdued; mild, quiet. *Antonyms:* drastic, vicious, brusque, harsh, rough, severe, rigorous.

gentlemanly, a. courteous, deferential, polite, urbane, gallant.

genuine, a. authentic, veritable, sterling, unmixed, real pure; sincere, unaffected. *Antonyms:* spurious, counterfeit, false, adulterated.

germ, n. origin, first principle; embryo, bud, seed.

German, a. Teutonic.

german, a. related, allied.

German, n, Teuton.

German characteristic. Germanism, Teutonicism.

germane, a. related, allied, akin, relevant.

German measles, rubella.

German silver, packfong.

germ destroyer. germicide.

gesture, n. gesticulation, gesturing. -v. gesticulate.

get, v. procure, obtain, acquire, secure, gain, achieve, attain, realize.

get ahead. advance, prosper, flourish, thrive.

get back, return; recover, recuperate, reclaim, retrieve.

get out. extricate, release.

get over. surmount, overcome, conquer; recover from.

getting, n. acquisition, obtaining, receiving, procurement.

ghastly, a. cadaverous, ghostly, pallid, pale, horrible, repulsive.

ghost, n. shade, phantom, apparition, spectre, spook, revenant, sprite.

ghostly, a. spiritual; spectral.

ghoul, n. vampire.

giant, n. colossus, monster, Hercules, Goliath, Titan Cyclops, ogre.

gibberish, n. jargon, jabber, gabbling, babble.

gibe, v. scoff, flout, jeer, sneer, deride.

gibe, n. ridicule, sneer, sarcasm.

giddy, a. fickle, mercurial, volatile, flighty, unstable, thoughtless; light-headed, dizzy.

gift, n. gratuity, present, largess, offering, grant, donation, bounty, bequest.

gifted, a. talented.

gigantic, a. enormous, colossal, vast, prodigious, Titanic, Gargantuan.

giggle, n. snicker, snigger.

gin, n. trap, snare, springe, artifice, toils; crane; Holland gin.

gingerly, adv. carefully, cautiously, timidly.

gird, v. encircle, engird, surround prepare.

girdle, n. cestus, sash, belt, band.

girl, n. maiden, maid, lass, lassie, damsel, miss, nymph, virgin.

girth, n. belly-band; circumference.

gist, n. core, substance, pith.

give, v. confer, bestow, accord, grant, donate, contribute, impart. *Antonyms:* withhold, refuse.

G
H

give and take. exchange, interchange, alternate.

given, a. granted, assumed; disposed, inclined; stated.

giver, n. donor.

give up, v. surrender, disgorge; yield, cease, desist, quit, relinquish, waive. *Antonyms:* resist, withstand, continue, persist.

give way, v. withdraw, retire, recede; yield.

giving, n. conferring, bestowal, granting.

glad, a. pleased, delighted, happy, joyous, joyful, gratified, merry, elated. *Antonyms:* sad, sorrowful.

gladden, v. cheer, delight, please, exhilarate, gratify, elate.

gladness, n. delight, pleasure, elation, jubilation, rejoicing.

glamour, n. charm, witchery, magic, spell; illusion, glitter, glory. *Antonyms:* disillusionment, disenchantment.

glance, n. glimpse; allusion; gleam, flash.

glance, v. glimpse; allude, hint; gleam, beam.

glare, v. glitter, glisten, dazzle; frown.

glaring, a. dazzling, intense, brilliant; flagrant, notorious.

glass, n. flint glass, crystal glass; aventurine; murrhine glass; strass.

glass, n. tumbler, goblet, bumper, beaker; decanter; carafe; mirror, telescope, binocular.

glasses, n.pl. spectacles, eyeglasses, pince-nez, goggles, blinkers, barnacles.

glassy, a. vitreous, transparent, crystal.

gleam, v. glimmer, glitter, radiate, beam, sparkle.

gleam, n. beam, ray, glimmer, glance, flash; splendor, sparkle.

glee, n. merriment, joy, mirth.

gleeful, a. merry, gay, mirthful.

glib, a. smooth slippery; fluent, voluble, bland.

glimmering, n. glimmer, glimpse.

glimpse, n. glance; flash; inkling.

glisten, v. sparkle, shine, gleam, flash, glitter, glister.

glister, v. sparkle, glisten, glitter.

glitter, n. brilliancy, shine, gleam, fulgency.

glitter, v. sparkle, gleam, glisten.

glittering, a. sparkling, glistening, glistering, bright, tinsel.

globe, n. sphere, ball, orb.

gloom, n. gloominess, shadow; melancholy, dejection.

gloomy, a. dark, dismal, obscure, dim, shaded, overcast, lurid.

glorious, a. magnificent, grand, splendid, admirable, excellent; hilarious, elated.

glory, n. fame, renown, honor, celebrity; magnificence, splendor; pride. *Antonyms:* ignominy, dishonor, obscurity, shame.

glory, v. exult, boast, vaunt.

gloss, n. luster, polish, sheen, glaze, enamel; show, commentary, note, comment.

gloss, v. annotate, illustrate; glaze, polish; extenuate.

glossy, a. shining, sleek, lustrous, polished, glazed; specious.

glowing, a. ardent, warm, flushed; luminous.

glue, v. cement, glutinate. *Antonyms:* unglue, deglutinate.

glum, a. moody, dumpish, sullen, morose, sour.

glut, v. satiate, sate, cloy; overfeed, overstock.

glut, n. superfluity, overstock, excess.

glutton, n. gormandizer, bellgod, cormorant; wolverine.

gluttonous, a. voracious, gluttonish.

gluttony, a. voracity, gormandism.

gnawing, a. rodent.

go, v. operate, pass, move, advance, repair, hark, stir, resort.

go, n. fashion, vogue, mode, custom, style; animation, spirit, fire.

goad, n. gad, prick; instigation.

goad, v. urge, incite.

goal, n. bourne, end, aim.

goat, n. buck; Billy goat; Nanny goat.

goatish, a. hircine, caprine.

go back, return, recede, retreat, back, withdraw.

goblin, n. gnome, spectre.

go between, intervene, interpose.

go-between, n. middleman, agent, broker, procurer, factor, arbitrator, referee, advocate.

go beyond. surpass, transcend, exceed, overstep.

go-by, n. neglect, ignoring.

god, n. deity, divinity, idol.

God, n. the Supreme Being, the Creator, Jehovah, the Almighty.

godfather, n. sponsor.

godless, a. irreligious, impious.

godlike, a. divine.

godlessness, n. irreligion, impiety, atheism, ungodliness.

godly, a. devout, religious, pious.

godmother, n. sponsor.

going, n. traveling; departure; exit, egress.

going between, intercession, mediation, intervention, arbitration. -z. mediatorial, intercessory.

goiter, n. bronchocele.

gold, n. aurum; bullion.

golden age. Saturnian

good, a. virtuous, worthy, moral, exemplary, conscientious, sterling, saintly, altruistic.

good, n. welfare, benefit, advantage, utility, interest; virtue, worth.

good-bye, n. farewell, adieu.

good humor, amiability, affability.

good-looking, a. comely, handsome, pretty, personable.

good nature. amiability, geniality, complaisance, good humor.

good-natured, a. amiable, affable, indulgent, genial.

goods, n.pl. chattels, effects, possessions; merchandise, wares.

goose, n. gander; gosling; graylag, ganza; goslet; pl. geese; Anseres, Anseriformes.

goose, n. simpleton, gull, dupe.

gore, v. stab, pierce, penetrate. - n. blood, cruor; gusset.

gorge, n. gully, defile, ravine.

gorge, v. bolt, gulp, eat greedily; glut, stuff.

gorgeous, a. magnificent, elegant, grand, splendid.

gossip, n. tattler, tale-bearer, frump; gossipry.

go to bed. retire.

gourd, n. calabash.

gout, n. podagra, arthritis.

govern, v. direct, control, regulate, command, reign, restrain, bridle, guide.

governable, a. manageable, obedient.

government, n, governance, sway, dominion, command, regency, regulation. *Antonyms:* anarchy, license.

governor, n. chief magistrate, executive.

gown, n. dress; robe; wrapper.

grab, v. seize, snatch, clutch.

grace, n. compassion, lenity, mercy, love, comeliness; refinement, elegance, polish.

grace, v. adorn, beautify, embellish; dignify, exalt.

graceful, a. elegant, easy,

G
H

willowy, courtly, polished.
Antonyms: ungraceful.
gracious, a. merciful, lenient,
compassionate, benign, tender;
graceful.
graduate, n. alumnus; pl. alumni.
graft, v. ingraft, inarch.
grain, n. kernel, seed; cereals;
granule, pellet.
grain, n. fiber, texture; disposition, humor, temper; particle.
grainy, a. granular, granulate.
grand, a. august, imposing,
sublime, stately, splendid, lofty,
glorious, superb.
grandeur, n. splendor, magnificence, elegance, majesty.
grandfather, n. grandsire,
patriarch.
grandiose, a. impressing,
imposing; declamatory,
grandiloquent.
grandmother, n. grandam.
grant, v. convey, transfer, cede;
give, bestow, allot, deign;
admit.
grant, n. conveyance, transfer,
cession; concession; gift.
grapple, v. seize, attack, clutch,
struggle, contend.
grasp, v. seize, clutch, clinch,
clasp, gripe; wrestle; comprehend.
grasp, n. seizure, apprehension,
gripe, grip; hold, possession;
understanding.
grasping, a. avaricious, covetous.
grass, n. herbage, pasture;
sward, sod, lawn, esplanade.
grateful, a. thankful. *Antonyms:*
ungrateful.
gratification, n. satisfaction,
indulgence, enjoyment,
pleasure.
gratify, v. satisfy, indulge,
content, delight, humor.
Antonyms: deny, mortify.
grating, a. harsh, jarring,
rasping.

gratitude, n. thankfulness.
Antonyms: ingratitude.
gratuitous, a. spontaneous, free,
voluntary; unrepaid, uncalled
for, unwarranted.
grave, a. important, momentous,
serious; sober, solemn,
demure, sedate.
grave, n. tomb, sepulcher,
charnel-house, ossuary;
tumulus, barrow.
gravel, n. pebbles, grit, shingle;
arena; pebble, calculus.
graver, n. engraver, sculptor;
burin.
gray, a. hoary; slate, drab.
grease, n. lubricant, fat. -v.
lubricate.
greasy, a. sebaceous, oily,
oleaginous, fatty.
great, a. immense, enormous,
prodigious, gigantic; numerous;
superior, excellent.
greatest, a. supreme, superlative, utmost.
greediness, n. avarice, voracity,
covetousness, rapacity,
insatiableness, cupidity.
greedy, a. avaricious, grasping;
sordid, covetous; insatiable,
ravenous, gluttonous; insatiate.
Greek, a. Grecian, Hellenic.
Greek, n. Grecian, Hellene;
Romaic, Hellenic.
Greek, n. mystery.
green, a. verdant, emerald, virid;
awkward, unskilled; fresh.
Antonyms: sear, parched,
seasoned, ripe, veteran.
green horn, n. tyro novice, gull,
dupe, yahoo.
green house, n. conservatory.
greenness, n. verdancy, viridity,
verdure; rawness, immaturity,
unripeness; inexperience;
gullibility.
greet, v. address, salute, hail.
greeting, n. salutation, salute.
grief, n. anguish, sorrow,
heartbreak, regret, remorse,

misery, woe, tribulation.

grievance, n. wrong, injustice, resentment, trouble.

grieve, v. mourn, regret, lament, rue, weep, sorrow, bewail, deplore.

grievous, a. afflictive, distressing, deplorable. grill, n. gridiron, broiler.

grilling, n. broiling, grillade.

grimy, a. begrimed.

grind, v. crush, powder, pulverize, comminute, bruise, levigate; harass, persecute.

grind, n. grinding, pulverization; drudgery; dig.

grinder, n. abradant.

grinding, n. pulverization, trituration, crushing.

grinding stone. millstone, muller.

grip, n. clutch, grasp.

grip, n. gripsack, valise, satchel.

grip, v. seize, clutch, grasp.

grit, n. firmness, resolution, courage, fortitude, spirit.

gritty, a. sandy; unyielding, plucky, spirited.

groan, n. and v. moan

groom, n. valet; hostler, stableman; bridegroom.

groove, n. rut, channel, furrow; chamfret, rabbet, fluting; stria.

groove, v. channel, furrow; chamfer.

grooved, a. channeled, chamfered, fluted, striated.

gross, n. aggregate.

grotesque, a. fantastic, bizarre, outlandish.

grouchy, a. unamiable, sullen, surly, morose, cross.

ground, n. soil, earth, dirt, clod, loam, mould, clay, land.

ground hog. woodchuck.

groundless, a. unfounded, chimerical, baseless.

grounds, n.pl. settlings, sediment.

ground squirrel. chipmunk.

groundwork, n. foundation, basis.

group, n. cluster, crowd.

grovel, v. crawl, sneak, cringe.

groveling, a. debased, abject, servile.

grow, v. increase, extend, augment, wax, accrue, develop, expand, flourish. *Antonyms:* wane, atrophy, blast, stunt, stagnate.

grower, n. cultivator.

growing, a. developing, waxing.

growl, n. grumble, snarl.

growler, n. grumbler, snarler, cynic, pessimist.

growth, n. growing, development, accretion, extension, augmentation, enlargement. *Antonyms:* atrophy, decrease, blasting.

grub, v. drudge, slave, moil; root out, uproot.

grub, n. caterpillar, maggot, larva.

grudge, n. ill-will, hatred, rancor, enmity, envy.

grudge, v. begrudge, resent.

grudgingly, adv. unwillingly, reluctantly, sullenly, resentfully.

gruff, a. ungracious, surly, rude, impolite, stern.

grumble, v. murmur, repine, complain, croak.

grumbler, n. complainer, croaker, fault-finder.

grumpy, a. surly, disgruntled, grouty, sullen.

guarantee, n. warranty, security.

guard, v. protect, defend, shield, shelter, fortify. *Antonyms:* expose.

guard, n. guardsman, watch, sentinel, patrol, sentry, picket; convoy, escort.

guarded, a. cautious, wary, careful, reserved.

guardian, n. defender, guard, saint, keeper, protector, defense. *Antonyms:* ward,

G
H

protege.

guardian, a. tutelary, protecting.

guardianship, n. protection, care, watch.

guess, v. conjecture, speculate, surmise; think, suppose, presume. believe, opine.

guess, n. conjecture, surmise, speculation.

guesswork, n. conjecture.

guide, v. pilot, steer, direct.

guide, n. conductor, pilot, director; polestar; rudder; mentor, monitor, key.

guidebook, n. itinerary.

guild, n. society, fraternity, corporation.

guile, n. subtlety, cunning, deceit, artifice.

guileful, a. deceitful, crafty, artful, wily, subtle.

guilt, n. criminality, guiltiness, complicity, crime; wrong, offense. *Antonyms:* innocence, inculpability.

guiltless, a. inculpable, blameless.

guilty, a. culpable, punishable, . criminal, sinful.

gulch, n. gully, ravine.

gulf, n. abyss, chasm; vortex, rapids; bay.

gull, n. cheat, swindle, humbug, fraud; dupe, gudgeon; seamew, mew.

gullet, n. esophagus.

gullible, a. credulous.

gully, n. gulch, ravine, gorge.

gummy, a. viscous, adhesive.

gun, n. firearm, weapon, rifle, shotgun, pistol, revolver, cannon.

guns, n.pl. artillery, ordnance, cannon.

gunsmith, n. armorer, gunmanker.

gush, v. rush, pour, stream.

gushing, a. rushing, pouring; effusive, demonstrative, sentimental.

gusto, n. enjoyment, appreciation.

gut, n. intestine. -v. disembowel.

guts, n.pl. intestines, bowels.

gutter, n. eaves trough, cullis; conduit, channel, drain.

gutting, n. disembowelment.

guy, n. guy-rope, stay, shore; scarecrow, dowdy, fright.

guy, v. steady, guide, shore, stay.

gymnast, n. athlete.

gymnastic, a. athletic, calisthenic.

gymnastics, n.pl. athletics.

gypsy, a. nomadic, vagabond.

H

habit, n. wont, custom, practice, usage, addiction, way.

habitual, a. wonted, customary, regular.

habituate, v. accustom, addict, inure. *Antonyms:* disaccustom, wean.

hag, n. vixen, virago, termagant, fury, beldame.

haggard, a. gaunt, emaciated.

haggle, v. hack, hackle; chaffer.

hail, v. accost, salute, address.

hair, n. bristle; pubescence; pubes; tentaculum; lock, tress; coiffure; forelock.

hairiness, n. hirsuteness, pubescence, villosity, capillament, hypertrichosis.

hairless, a. bald, glabrous, depilous.

hairsplitting, a. subtle, fine.

hairy, a. hirsute, shaggy, bristly.

half, adv. partially, imperfectly.

half, n. moiety.

half-hearted, a. indifferent, lukewarm, perfunctory.

half-moon, n. crescent.

halfway, adv. in the middle, imperfectly, partially -a. intermediate, midway.

half-witted, a. imbecile, defective, silly, dull-witted, witless.

half-yearly, a. semi-annual, bi-annual.

hall, n. auditorium, lyceum; vestibule, entry, court; corridor, passage, lobby.

hallow, v. consecrate, venerate, reverence, sanctify, gless.

hallowed, a. holy, sacred, consecrated, dedicated, blessed, sanctified.

hallucination, n. aberration, chimers, fallacy, self-deception, delusion, phantasm, illusion.

halo, n. nimbus, glory, aureola, aureole.

haloed, a. glorified, aureoled.

haive, v. bisect, dimidiate.

halving, n. bisection, dichotomy, dimidiation.

habber, n. sledge, sledgehammer, maul, mallet, gavel.

hammer, v. beat, forege, malleate, beetle.

hamper, v. fetter, shackle, impede, restrain, hinder, encumber, embarrass.

hamper, n. hanaper; shackle, fetter, restraint.

hamstring, n. hough. -v. diable, cripple, lame, hough.

hand, n. paw, manus.

handbag, n. satchel, reticule.

handbook, n. manual, guide-book, vade mecum, hornbook, enchiridion.

handcuff, n. manacle, fetter, shackle.

hand down. transmit [in succession].

handle, n. bail; hilt, haft.

handy, a. dexterous, adroit, ready; convenient.

hang, v. suspend; dangle; execute; droop, drop; append, attach.

hang, n. connection, arrangement, plan.

hang back. hesitate, falter, be reluctant.

hanging, a. suspended, pendent, pendulous, pensile, dangling.

hanging, n. suspension; execution; drapery, valance, tapestry, dorsal, lambrequin.

hanging on. persistence, tenacity, importunity.

hangman, n. executioner.

hanker, v. long for, yearn, crave, covet, lust.

hankering, n. longing, craving.

haphazard, n. chance, accident.

happen, v. occur, befall, betide; supervene, intervene.

happiness, n. felicity, blessedness, delight, gladness, pleasure, bliss, rapture. *Antonyms:* sorrow, grief.

happy, a. joyous, light-hearted, gay, blissful, glad, delighted, elated, merry. *Antonyms:* unhappy.

happy-go-lucky, a. improvident, easy-going, unthrifty.

harangue, n. declamation, ranting, screed.

harangue, v. declaim, spout, rant.

harass, v. fatigue, tire, weary; annoy, vex, torment, perplex, distress.

harbinger, n. forerunner, precursor, herald.

harbor, n. refuge, shelter, retreat; port, haven.

hard, a. firm, solid, compact, impenetrable, unyielding, rigid, dense, insoluble.

hard case. incorrigible, reprobate, derelict, outcast.

harden, v. indurate, solidify; petrify, ossify, sear; inure, season, steel.

hardened, a. indurated; callous, ossified, obdurate, incorrigible, inveterate, case-hardened.

hard-headed, a. shrewd, astute.

hard-hearted, a. unsympathetic, inexorable, unsparing, obdurate.

G
H

hardness, n. induration, compactness, solidity, firmness.

hardship, n. privation, adversity, reverse, disaster.

hardware, n. ironmongery.

hardy, a. courageous, intrepid, brave; hearty, robust.

hare-brained, a. heedless, reckless, rash, giddy.

harem, n. concubines.

harlot, n. prostitute, courtesan.

harlotry, n. prostitution, whoredom.

harm, v. injure, hurt, damage, impair, mar, deface, abuse.

harm, n. injury, damage, scathe, mischief, misfortune.

harmful, a. injurious, detrimental, baneful, prejudicial, ruinous.

harmless, a. innocuous; inoffensive, peaceable; unscathed.

harmonious, a. symmetrical, consistent, conformable; consonant, melodious; amicable. *Antonyms:* inharmonious, discordant, incompatible.

harmonize, v. agree, chime, tally, accord, adjust.

harmony, n. concord, agreement, consonance, chime, unison; concordance, congruity, consistency.

harness, n. saddlery; armor, array, gearing, tackling, gear; caparison.

harness, v. equip, array, caparison.

harp, n. lyre.

harsh, a. inharmonious, rough, disagreeable, unpleasant; dissonant, discordant, austere, morose.

harum-scarum, a. wild, giddy, volatile, hare-brained.

harvest, n. ingathering; crop, produce, fruit.

hash, n. ragout, potpourri, olio.

haste, n. celerity, swiftness, dispatch, speed; hurry, urgency. *Antonyms:* slowness, dilatoriness.

hasten, v. accelerate, expedite, quicken, urge; hurry.

hastiness, n. haste, precipitancy, precipitance.

hasty, a. swift, rapid, quick, fast; rash, eager; hurried, superficial.

hatch, v. breed, incubate; concoct, brew, scheme.

hatchet, n. small ax; tomahawk; dolabra.

hate, v. dislike, detest, abhor, despise, loathe.

hateful, a. execrable, odious, detestable, abominable, malicious.

hatred, n. hate, aversion, animosity, malignity, spite, feud, malice, grudge.

haughtiness, n. arrogance, hauteur, disdain, contumely.

haughty, a. arrogant, disdainful, magisterial, lordly.

haunt, n. resort.

hauteur, n. arrogance, superciliousness, overweening.

haven, n. harbor, port, retreat, refuge, shelter.

havoc, n. destruction, waste, ruin, demolition, wreck.

hawk, n. falcon; kestrel.

haystack, n. rick.

hazard, n. chance, casualty; risk, random, danger, venture. *Antonyms:* safety, security, certainty.

hazard, v. venture, risk, jeopard.

hazardous, a. perilous, precarious, risky, unsafe.

haze, n. obscurity, dimness, fog, mist.

hazy, a. foggy, misty, obscure.

head, a. poll, costard, noddle.

head, n. chief, leader, commander, director; crisis, culmination; ear, spike.

head, a. principal, chief, leading, cardinal, main, premier.

headache, n. megrim, galea.

headdress, n. coiffure.
heading, n. title, caption.
headland, n. cape, foreland.
heading off. interception.
headlong, adv. headforemost;
precipitately, rashly; helter-
skelter, confusedly.
head off. intercept.
headsman, n. executioner.
headstrong, a. willful, perverse,
stubborn, froward.
heal, v. cure, repair.
healing, a. curative, sanative,
remedial, sanatory, lenitive,
medicinal, hygienist, sanitary.
healthful, a. healthy; wholesome.
healthy, a. hale, well, hearty;
salubrious, salutary. *Antonyms:*
unhealthy, ill, silky, delicate,
diseased.
heap, n. pile, mass, accumulation, lot, stack.
heap, v. amass, accumulate, pile,
stack.
hearer, n. auditor.
hearing, n. audition, listening;
audience; earshot, sound,
hearing distance.
hearsay, n. rumor, report, gossip,
bruit.
heart, n. cardia; conscience,
character; essence, core, pith,
kernel, marrow.
heart-broken, a. disconsolate,
inconsolable.
heartburn, n. cardialgia, water-
brash.
heartburning, . discontent,
resentment, envy.
heartless, a. acardiac; cruel,
pitiless.
heart-shaped, a. cordate.
hearty, a. cordial, heartfelt,
sincere; healthy, robust;
nourishing.
heat, n. warmth, caloric; cauma.
heat, n. vehemence, fire, ardor,
impetuosity, fervor, zeal,
intensity.

heat, v. warm, calefy.
heathen, a. pagan, heathenish,
paganic, gentile; irreligious.
heathen, n. pagan, idolater.
heathenism, n. idolatry, pagan-
ism, gentilism; irreligion,
godlessness.
heaven, n. Paradise, Eden,
Olympus, Nirvana.
heavenly, a. celestial, supernal;
divine, ravishing, sublime.
heaviness, n. weight,
ponderosity, gravity.
heavy, a. weighty, massive;
burdensome, oppressive,
onerous; unraided, soggy,
unleavened.
heavy hand. severity, oppression, tyranny, extortion.
hector, v. torment, tease, plague,
bully.
heed, v. mind, regard, consider,
notice.
heed, n. regard, attention, notice.
heedful, a. attentive, circumspect, cautious, vigilant.
Antonyms: inattentive, unmindful, careless, heedless.
height, n. altitude, loftiness;
elevation; stature, eminence;
sumit, apex, culmination.
heinous, a. atrocious, flagrant,
monstrous.
heir, n. inheritor; scion; coheir.
hell, n. inferno, infernal regions,
limbo, Hades, the grave.
hellish, a. infernal, malignant,
fiendish, atrocious.
helm, n. rudder, tiller, wheel;
steersman, pilot; command,
control.
helmet, n. casque, morion, sallet.
help, v. abet, assist, befriend,
aid, cooperate, second,
subsidize.
help, n. aid, assistance, succor,
support, facilitation, subsidy,
cooperation.
helper, n. assistant, ally, supporter, helpmeet, coadjutor,

G
H

confederate, deputy, aider.

helpful, a. assistant, conducive, useful, salutary.

helping, a. assisting, auxiliary.

helter-skelter, adv. irregularly, disorderly, headlong.

hen, n. partlet; pullet.

herald, n. messenger, precursor.

herald, v. proclaim, announce, foretell.

herd, n. drove; rabble, mob.

herdsman, n. ranchman, cowboy.

hereditary, a. ancestral, patrimonial, inheritable.

heritage, n. inheritance, patrimony; possession.

hermit, n. recluse, anchoret, eremite.

heroic, a. valiant, bold, daring, brave; desperate.

heroism, n. courage, valor, prowess, hesitancy, -n. indecision, vacillation, irresolution.

hesitate, v. doubt, falter, waver, scruple, demur, deliberate.

hesitation, n. indecision, doubt, reluctance, wavering.

hidden, a. covert, latent; recondite, abstruse.

hide, v. veil, cloak, conceal, dissemble, secrete, mask; lurk.

hideous, a. horrible, grim, grisly, repulsive, ugly, ghastly.

hiding, n. concealment, secretion.

high, a. lofty, tall, elevated.

high and dry. aground, beached.

high and mighty. arrogant, overbearing, lordly.

higher, a. supernal.

highest, a. loftiest, superlative, meridian, supreme.

highest point. meridian, culmination.

highfaluting, a. bombastic, pretentious, grandiose.

highflying, a. aspiring, presump-

tuous.

highgo, n. spree, revel.

highhanded, a. overbearing, arbitrary, despotic.

high jinks. revelry, carousal, wild sport.

highland, n. plateau.

high liver. gormand, epicure, gourmet, voluptuary.

high living, gormandism, sybaritism, epicurism. *Antonyms:* asceticism, moderation.

highminded, a. magnanimous, honorable, noble. *Antonyms:* mean, base, low, servile, abject.

highmindedness, n. magnanimity.

hightoned, a. shrill, acute; honorable; fashionable.

highwayman, n. bandit, desperado, outlaw, footpad.

hill, n. mound, eminence, knoll; monadnock; monticle; copple.

hilly, a. undulating, uneven.

hind, n. rustic, boor, peasant.

hinder, n. buttocks, rump, seat.

hinder, v. retard, obstruct, hamper, impede, forfend, thwart.

hindrance, n. retardation, hindering; obstacle, obstruction, restraint, encumbrance, check.

hint, v. intimate, suggest, imply, refer.

hint, n. allusion, suggestion, intimation, inkling.

hip, n. haunch, huckle; innominate, ischium, pubis.

hire, n. salary, wages, pay, stipend, compensation. -v. engage; let, lease.

hireling, a. mercenary, venal. -m. mercenary.

hiss, no. sibilation, hissing. -v. sibilate, whiz.

hissing, a. sibilant, sibilatory.

history, n. annals, chronicle,

record, account; autobiography.

hit, v. smite, buffet, strike.

hitch, n. catch, impediment, obstacle, contretemps. -v. hook, yoke, unite.

hoard, v. garner, amass, save.

hoard, n. store, supply, stock.

hoarse, a. harsh, discordant, husky, raucous.

hobgoblin, n. sprite, goblin.

hobo, n. tramp, vagrant.

hodgepodge, n. medley, farrago, potpourri.

hog, n. swine, porker; boar; sow.

hoggish, a. swinish, gluttonous.

hoitytoity, a. flighty, giddy.

hold, v. sustain, restrain, retain, withhold, arrest; contain; clutch, grasp.

hold back. check, restrain, impede.

holdback, n. check, hindrance, restraint.

holder, n. tenant, occupier.

hold in. restrain, curb, check, repress, retain.

holding, n. restraint, retention, checking, detention; tenure, incumbency. *Antonyms:* incontinence, release.

hole, n. cavity, excavation, pit, perforation, rent, opening. *Antonyms:* imperforation, closure.

holiday, n. festival.

holiness, n. sanctity, piety, godliness.

hollow, a. excavated, cavernous, vacant, void, empty; concave. *Antonyms:* convex, protuberant.

hollow, v. scoop, excavate, concave.

holy, a. sacred, consecrated, hallowed, saintly, godly, pious.

Holy Ghost. Paraclete, Holy Spirit, the Comforter, the Sanctifier.

holy water. asperges, aspergill, aspersoir, stoup, benitier, cruet.

homage, n. deference, obeisance, reverence, honor; fidelity; adoration.

home, n. domicile, residence, dwelling-place, abode, hearth; habitat, seat; asylum.

homeborn, a. native, indigenous.

homely, a. plain, uncomely; inelegant, rude.

homesickness, n. nostalgia.

homing instinct. orientation.

hone, n. oilstone.

honest, a. honorable, reputable; upright, sincere, ingenuous.

honesty, n. uprightness, probity, integrity, candor, sincerity.

honey combed, a. alveolate, cellular, faviform.

honey-dew, n. meligo, nectar.

honeysuckle, n. woodbine, caprifole.

honey-tongued, a. persuasive, seductive.

honor, n. respect, esteem, veneration, reverence, homage; probity. *Antonyms:* dishonor, disesteem, improbity, disrepute.

honor, v. esteem, respect, revere, venerate; dignify, exalt.

honorable, a. upright, honest, reputable, magnanimous.

honors, n.pl. titles, dignities, privileges.

hood, n. cowl, fascinator, capote, camail, chaperon, capuchin.

hooded, a. cowled, capistrate.

hoodlum, n. rowdy, larrikin.

hoodwink, v. deceive, impose upon, delude, dupe, overreach.

hook, n. hasp, clasp, catch; crook.

hook, v. fasten, catch, secure; entrap, ensnare.

hoot, v. shout, deride, denounce.

hop, v. spring, jump, skip, bound, leap, caper, gambol, dance.

hope, n. optimism, anticipation. *Antonyms:* despair, despera-

G
H

tion, pessimism.

hopeful, a. expectant, promising.

hopeless, a. despairing, desperate, unpromising.

hops, n. pl. humulin, lupuline.

horde, n. troop, gang, throng, multitude.

horn, n. antler; epithema; antenna.

horn, n. trumpet, bugle, cornet, trombone; cornucopia; shophar.

horning, n. charivari.

hornless, a. polled, mulley.

horns of a dilemma. alternatives.

horny, a. ceratose, cornified, callous.

horrible, a. dreadful, terrible, shocking, grim, ghastly, revolting, appalling.

horrid, a. offensive, detestable.

horror, n. abhorrence, dread, detestation.

horror-stricken, a. horror-struck, horrified, appalled.

horse, n. stallion, stud, sire; mare; colt, foal, filly; pony.

horse doctor. veterinarian, veterinary, surgeon, horse.

horse-fly, n. breese-fly, bot-fly.

horse-laugh, n. guffaw, cachinnation.

horseman, n. jockey; equestrian; cavalier.

horse-trader, n. jockey.

hose, n. hosiery; tubing.

hospital, n. infirmary, asylum, retreat.

host, n. entertainer; landlord; multitude, horde; army, legion.

hostile, a. antagonistic, inimical, repugnant.

hostility, n. enmity, animosity, opposition, warfare.

hostler, n. groom.

hot, a. torrid, sultry, fiery, scorching, grilling, tropical; vehement, passionate.

hot-blooded, a. ardent, irritable, excitable.

hotel, n. hostelry, inn, tavern.

hotel-keeper, . hosteler, host, landlord, inn-keeper.

hot springs. thermae.

hound, v. importune, harass.

house, n. dwelling, residence, abode; mansion, palace; tenement; chateau.

house, v. shelter, protect, harbor; abide, dwell.

household, n. family, menage.

housewarming, n. infare.

hovel, n. hut, shanty, shack, cabin, den, dugout.

howl, v. yowl, roar, ululate, yawl. -n. yowling, ululation, howling, wail.

hub, n. nave; protuberance.

hubbub, n. tumult, uproar, din, clamor, racket, commotion.

huckleberry, n. whortleberry.

huckster, n. peddler, hawker, chapman, cadger.

huff, n. petulance, tiff, pet.

huffy, a. petulant, touchy.

hug, n. embrace. -v. embrace, clasp.

huge, a. mammoth, colossal, vast.

hullabaloo, n. uproar, vociferation, din, clamor, tumult.

hum, n. drone, murmur, buzz; croon.

humble, a. lowly, meek, modest, unpretentious.

humble, v. humiliate, debase, abase.

humbug, n. imposition, hoax, deception, imposture, quackery; imposter, deceiver, cheat.

humbug, v. deceive, impose on.

humdrum, a. monotonous, tedious, prosy, tiresome. -n. monotony, tedium.

humiliate, v. humble, mortify, abash, disgrace.

humiliation, n. abasement, mortification, degradation;humbleness, meekness.

humility, n. meekness, lowliness, diffidence, modesty.

humor, n. disposition, temper, mood; jocularity, pleasantry, wit, satire; pl. caprices, whims, fancies.

humor, v. indulge, please, gratify. *Antonyms:* discipline, deny, curb, mortify.

humorist, n. wag, droll, wit.

humorous, a. facetious, droll, comical, waggish.

hump, n. protuberance, hunch.

humpbacked, a. hunchbacked, deformed.

humpy, a. protuberant, humped.

hunch, n. hump, protuberance; chunk, lump.

hundredfold, a. centuple.

hundred years. century, centennial.

Hungarian, n. Magyar.

hungry, a. voracious, ravenous, eager; starved, infertile, barren.

hunky, a. even, square, all-right.

hunt, v. chase, pursue, follow; search, seek, rummage, ferret; poach.

hunt, n. chase, pursuit, search, hunting.

hunter, n. huntsman, sportsman, Nimrod; seeker, persuer, chase.

hurly-burly, n. tumult, bustle, turmoil, commotion.

hurrah, n. cheer, huzza.

hurricane, n. cyclone, tornado.

hurried, a. cursory, hasty.

hurry, n. haste, speed, dispatch, expedition.

hurry, v. hasten, impel, expedite, accelerate, speed.

hurt, v. damage, wound, impair, harm, injure, offend.

hurt, n. injury, wound, detriment, harm.

husband, n. spouse, benedict. *Antonyms:* bachelor, celibate.

hush, v. silence, still, repress; appease.

husk, n. glume, hull, rind, shell.

husky, a. dry, raucous, harsh, guttural, hoarse.

hussy, n. jade, quean; jilt, flirt.

hustle, v. jostle.

hut, n. hovel, shack, shed.

hybrid, n. mongrel, crossbreed, cross. -a. mongrel, crossbred.

hypocrisy, n. dissimulation, Pharisaism.

hypocrite, n. dissembler, pharisee, formalist.

hypocritical, a. pharisaical, canting, dissembling, sanctimonious. *Antonyms:* sincere, unfeigned, ingenuous.

I

ice, n. igloo, iceberg, glacier, icicle, avalanche, skate, ski, skating.

icy, a. glacial, glacious.

idea, n. conception, notion, opinion, fancy, impression; intention.

ideal, a. faultless, consummate.

idiocy, n. imbecility, foolishness, fatuity, senselessness.

idiot, n. imbecile.

idle, a. leisure, vain, futile; indolent, inactive, lazy.

idleness, n. indolence, sloth, laziness; vanity.

idler, n. sluggard, drone, loafer.

idol, n. image, effigy.

idolize, v. deify, worship, adore.

ignis fatuus. Will-o'-the-wisp, Jack-with-a-lantern, decoy.

ignoble, a. humble, untitled; base.

ignominious, a. dishonorable, shameful, disreputable.

ignominy, n. disgrace, dishonor, reproach, shame, humiliation.

ignoramus, n. dunce, illiterate, wiseacre, dullard.

ignorance, n. illiteracy,

unenlightenment, nascence; quackery.

ignorant, a. illiterate, in erudite, unlearned, unlettered, nascent; quackish. *Antonyms:* educated, instructed, schooled, trained, learned.

ignorantly, adv. unknowingly, inadvertently, unwittingly.

ignorant person. ignoramus, illiterate.

ignore, v. disregard, slight, connive.

ill, a. ailing, sick, unwell; evil, adverse, bad.

ill at ease. uneasy, uncomfortable.

illegal, a. illicit, contraband, illegitimate.

illegality, n. unlawfulness, illegitimacy.

illegitimate, a. bastard, adulterant; illegal, illicit.

illegitimate, a. bastard; illegal, illicit; spurious.

illegitimate, v. illegitimatize, bastardize.

illiberal, a. ungenerous, stingy; narrow-minded, bigoted.

illiberality, n. parsimony, stinginess; narrow-mindedness, intolerance.

illicit, a. prohibited, unlawful.

illness, n. malady, sickness.

illogical, a. fallacious, sophistic.

illusion, n. mockery, hallucination, phantasm, delusion.

illusive, a. delusive, illusory, mocking.

illustrate, v. elucidate, picture, demonstrate.

illustration, n. elucidation; comparison, example, simile.

ill-will, n. malice, resentment, grudge, rancor, antipathy, hatred.

image, n. statue; effigy, figure; idol.

image breaker. iconoclast, vandal.

image breaking. iconoclasm, vandalism.

image worship. iconolatry, iconoduly.

imaginary, a. fancied, visionary, chimerical, illusive.

imagination, n. fancy, conception, notion, conceit, figment.

imagine, v. conceive, fancy; think, suppose, opine.

imbecile, n. idiot, whittling, fool.

imbecility, n. idiocy, fatuity, foolishness.

imbedded, a. enfonced.

imitate, v. copy, ape, counterfeit; personate, mimic, simulate; parody, caricature.

imitation, n. copy, counterfeit; mimicry, impersonation; parody, travesty, burlesque.

imitative, a. apish, copying, mimicking, mimetic.

imitator, n. copyist, follower, mimic, mime, ape, echo.

immanence, n. inherence, indwelling.

immanent, a. inherent, indwelling.

immature, a. undeveloped, embryonic, crude, unripe, premature.

immediately, adv.instantly, forthwith, directly, straightway, at once, now, instant. *Antonyms:* hereafter, by and by, after a while.

immense, a. vast, infinite, illimitable.

immerse, v. submerge, plunge into, dip, immerge, douse.

immersion, n. submersion, immersing; engrossment.

immoderate, a. excessive, exorbitant, inordinate, intemperate.

immodest, a. indecorous, indelicate, shameless; lewd, unchaste.

immoral, a. licentious, dissolute, vicious, profligate, loose, illicit.

immorality, n. vice, depravity, profligacy.

immortality, n. deathlessness, athanasia.

immovable, a. fast, permanent, impassive, firm.

impact, n. collision, forcible contact.

impart, v. communicate.

impartial, a. equitable, fair, disinterested, unbiased.

impartiality, n. fairness, equity, justice.

impassable, a. impenetrable, pathless.

impatient, a. restless, restive, fretful, eager.

impede, v. retard.

impediment, n. obstacle, barrier, stumbling block.

impending, a. imminent, threatening.

impenetrable, a. impervious, imperforable.

impenitence, n. in contrition, obduracy.

impenitent, a. in contrite, unrepentant, obdurate, recusant.

imperative, a. binding, compulsory, obligatory, imperious.

imperfect, a. defective, faulty, deficient, abortive, fallible, frail.

imperfection, n. defect, blemish, shortcoming, infirmity, deformity, vice, frailty, fallibility.

imperious, a. despotic, magisterial, domineering, tyrannical, imperative.

imperishable, a. permanent, enduring.

impersonate, v. personate; personify.

impersonation, n. personation, impersonating; impersonification.

impersonator, n. mimic, personator, mime, actor.

impertinent, a. irrelevant, inapplicable, impudent.

impervious, a. impermeable, imperviable.

impetus, n. momentum, force, impulse.

impish, a. malignant.

implacable, a. unappeasable, vindictive, pitiless.

implant, v. instill, inculcate, ingraft.

implied, a. tacit, inferential.

implore, v. beseech, supplicate, entreat, obsecrate.

imploring, n. supplication, obsecration.

impolite, a. discourteous, inurbane, rude, uncivil, disrespectful, saucy, insolent, impertinent.

impoliteness, n. discourtesy, inurbanity, incivility, insolence.

importance, n. moment, materiality, consequence; self-importance.

important, a. momentous, material, essential; pompous.

impose upon. delude, dupe, deceive.

imposing, a. impressive, stately, august.

impossibility, n. impracticability.

impossible, a. impracticable, unfeasible.

impostor, n. pretender, cheat, mountebank, quack.

imposture, n. fraud, imposition, deception.

impracticability, n. unfeasibility.

impracticable, a. impossible.

impregnate, v. fecundate.

impregnation, n. fecundation.

imprison, v. incarcerate, immure.

imprisonment, n. incarceration, durance, duress, confinement, commitment.

impromptu, a. improvised, offhand, extempre.

improper, a. indecorous, unseemly, indecent, priate, wrong.

impropriety, n. unsuitableness,

I
K

unfitness, indecorum, solecism.

improve, v. amend, ameliorate, rectify, better, mend; utilize, use; gain, get better.

improvement, n. betterment, amelioration; utilization.

impudence, n. insolence, impertinence, rudeness.

impudent, a. insolent, impertinent, flippant, pert, brazen, saucy.

impulse, n. motive, incentive; impulsion, impetus.

impulsive, a. passionate, capricious, hasty; impellent, propulsive.

impure, a. tainted, defiled, contaminated, polluted, vitiated, infected; adulterated, alloyed.

impurity, n. defilement, contamination, taint, pollution; adulteration, alloy, sophistication.

inability, n. incompetence, impotence, incapability, incompetency, inefficiency, disability.

in a body. altogether, en masse.

inaccuracy, n. inexactness, incorrectness, impropriety.

inaccurate, a. incorrect, inexact, erroneous, faulty, wrong.

inaction, n. inactivity, inertness, stagnation, idleness.

inactive, a. inert, motionless, quiescent, dormant, inoperative, sluggish, stagnant, dilatory.

inactivity, n. inaction, passivity, inertia, lethargy, dormancy, stagnation, torpor.

inadequate, a. insufficient, deficient; defective, incomplete, imperfect.

inappropriate, a. unsuitable, unbecoming, inapplicable.

inapt, a. irrelevant, unsuitable, inept, inapplicable.

inattention, n. inadvertence, abstraction, heedlessness, disregard, neglect, remissness.

inattentive, a. heedless, absent-minded, inadvertent, unmindful, careless.

inborn, a. congenital, inherent, innate, instinctive, ingenerate.

incapable, a. incompetent, disqualified, unfit, insusceptible.

incarnation, n. incarnification, avatar; personification.

incautious, a. unwary, inconsiderate, indiscreet, thoughtless.

incense, n. thurible, censer, thurification, thurify, frankincense, cense, thurifer.

incentive, n. motive, spur, incitement, stimulus, inducement, provocation.

incivility, n. discourtesy, rudeness, incomity, inurbanity, disrespect.

inclination, n. leaning, slant; tendency, propensity, proneness, penchant, prediliction.

incline, n. slant, slope, ascent, descent, grade. -v. lean, tend, dispose.

inclose, v. surround, encircle, circumscribe, encompass, enclose.

inclosure, n. surrounding, closure, barrier, fence, corral, stockade.

include, v. comprise, comprehend, inclose.

inclusion, n. comprisal.

income, n. revenue, proceeds; tontine, annuity.

incomparable, a. peerless, matchless, transcendent, inimitable, unrivalled, unapproachable.

incompetent, a. inefficient, unqualified, incapable; inadequate; unfit, unsuited.

incomplete, a. unfinished, defective, imperfect, deficient, partial, inchoate.

incomprehensible, a. inconceivable, abstruse, unfathomable.

inconsiderate, a. thoughtless, heedless, inattentive, careless.

inconsistency, n. discordance, incoherence, contrariety, incompatibility.

inconsistent, a. disagreeing, incoherent, contradictory, discrepant, incompatible.

inconstancy, n. fickleness, matuability, variableness, instability.

inconstant, a. fickle, changeable, volatile, fighty, mercurial, variable.

inconvenient, a. unhandy, incomodious, inopportune, untoward.

incorrect, a. inaccurate, erroneous, inexact, wrong; ungrammatical, solecistic.

incorrectness, n. inaccuracy, inexactness, error; impropriety.

increase, v. augment, advance, enlarge; multiply, be prolific; was; aggravate.

increase, n. augmentation, accretion, increment, accession, amplification, addition.

incremate, v. cremate, incinerate.

incremation, n. cremation.

incumbent, a. obligatory, imposed, binding.

incumbrance, n. hindrance, impediment, incubus; mortgage, claim, lien.

incurable, a. insanable, irremediable, immedicable; irremedicable, irreparable.

indebtedness, n. obligation; debts, liabilities.

indecency, n. immodesty, indelicacy, shamelessness, obscenity, rebaldry, lewdness.

indecent, a. immodest, obscene, indelicate, shameless, ribald, lewd, unchaste.

indecision, n. vacillation, indetermination, irresolution, wavering, inconstancy.

indecisive, a. inconclusive, vacillating, hesitating, irresolute, wavering.

indefatigable, a. untiring, persistent, unremitting sedulous, unflagging.

indefinite, a. vague, indeterminate, equivocal, ambiguous, inexplicit, inexact.

indelicacy, n. unrefinement, rudeness, indecorum, imodesty.

indelicate, a. unrefined, indecorous, immodest, unchaste, rude, vulgar.

indemnity, n. security, insurance; restitution, reimbursement, indemnification.

indentation, n. bruise, notch, depression, indenture, serrature, jag, engrailment, crenellation.

independence, n. freedom, self-government, liberty, autonomy; opulence, affluence.

independent, a. self-governing, autonomous; self-reliant; exclusive, irrespective; affluent.

indicate, v. designate, betoken, signify.

indication, n. designation, signifying; symptom, evidence, sign, token, manifestation.

indicator, n. [as in a hotel] annunciator.

indictment, n. accusation, charge, arraignment, crimination.

indifference, n. apathy, coolness, negligence, unconcern, nonchalance, insouciance; mediocrity..

indifferent, a. disinterested, unconcerned, nonchalant, perfunctory, apathetic, neutral, impartial..

indirect, a. roundabout, circuitous, tortuous.

indescreet, a. unwise, imprudent.

indiscretion, n. unwisdom, folly, imprudence; misstep, lapse.

indisposed, a. averse, disinclined, unwilling, loath, reluctant; sick, ill, unwell.

indisposition, n. disinclination, averseness, reluctance, unwillingness.indisputable, a. undeniable, incontestable, indubitable, incontrovertible.

indissolvable, a. indissoluble.

indocile, a. intractable, refractory, unruly.

indolence, n. idleness, laziness, indiligence, sloth, inactivity, faineance.

indolent, a. lazy, slothful, supine, dronish, listless.

inducement, n. incentive, incitement, motive, stimulus.

indulge, v. satisfy, gratify, luxuriate; humor, pamper, cocker; grant. *Antonyms:* mortify, deny, suppress, restrain.

indulgence, n. humoring, pampering, gratification; kindness, favor. *Antonyms:* morification, denial, restraint.

indulgent, a. forbearing, kind, lenient, lax, merciful.

industrial science. technology, polytechnics.

industrious, a. assiduous, diligent, sedulous, persistent, hard-working. *Antonyms:* idle, indolent, inactive, lazy.

industry, n. assiduity, diligence, activity; labor, work, exertion, efforts.

indwelling, n. immanence, inherence. -a. immanent, inherent.

ineffective, a. ineffectual, unavailing, inefficacious.

inefficient, a. ineffective, inefficacious; slack, remiss, incompetent.

inelastic, a. inductile, inextensible, rigid.

inelasticity, n. inductility, inextensibility, rigidity.

inelibible, a. disqualified.

inequality, n. disparity, disproportion, unevenness, irregularity; unfairness, injustice; inequation.

inexcusable, a. unpardonable, indefensible, unjustifiable, unwarrantable.

inexhaustible, a. exhaustless.

inexorable, a. unyielding, relentless, implacable, unmovable, unrelenting.

inexperienced, a. untrained, unpractised, undisciplined, raw, unskilled.

inexpert, a. maladroit, unskillful, bungling.

inexpressible, a. ineffable, unspeakable, unutterable.

infailibility, n. inerrability.

infallible, a. inerrable, unerring, sure, certain, undeniable.

infamous, a. disreputable, ignominious, scandalous, oprobrious, odious, heinous.

infamy, n. disgrace, ignominy, odium, obloquy, opprobrium.

infancy, n. babyhood; minority, nonage, pupilage.

infant, n. baby; minor.

infantile paralysis, poliomyelitis.

infatuate, v. enamor, charm. *Antonyms:* repel, disgust, disillusionize.

infection, n. contagion, contamination, vitiation, pollution.

infectious, a. contagious, pestiferous, epidemic, vitiating.

infer, v. deduce, imply, gather.

inference, n. deduction, conclusion, illation, corollary.

inferior, a. poorer, lower, subordinate, menial, minor, mediocre, subaltern.

inferior, n. subordinate. *Antonyms:* peer, equal, superior.

inferiority, n. subordinacy, mediocrity, deficiency.

infidel, n. free-thinker, atheist, unbeliever, skeptic.

infirmity, n. See weakness.

inflammable, a. combustible, accendible; irascible, irritable, excitable.

inflammation, n. phlogosis; phlegmasia.

inflammatory, a. phlogistic; seditious, incendiary.

inflate, v. expand, enlarge, distend.

inflated, a. distended, blown up; bombastic, pompous, grandiloquent, declamatory.

inflation, n. distention, expansion.

inflection, n. modulation, accent.

inflexibility, n. rigidty, stiffness; firmness, pertinacity, obstinacy, steadfastness.

inflexible, a. unyielding, rigid, impliable; immovable, resolute, steadfast.

influence, n. sway, control; persuasion, restaint; authority, ascendency, presitige.

influence, v. move, persuade, induce, sway, control, prevail upon, actuate, impel.

informal, a. inceremonious, inconventional, easy, natural, inconstrained.

informality, n. inceremoniousness.

information, n. knowledge, intelligence, instruction; complaint, accusation.

infringe, v. violate, transgress; encroach, trespass, intrench.

infringement, n. transgression, violation, breach, encroachment, trespass, intrenchment.

in full. unabridged, at length.

ingenious, a. inventive, resourceful.

ingratitude, n. unthankfulness.

ingredient, n. constituent, element, component, part.

inhabitant, n. dweller, denizen, residentiary, resident, citizen. *Antonyms:* sojourner, pilgrim, visitor.

inherent, a. innate, adhering, inexistent, inborn, inalienable.

inheritable, a. hereditable.

inheritance, n. heritage, patrimony, legacy.

inhuman, a. savage, barbarous, fiendish, brutal, cruel.

inhumanity, n. cruelty, brutality, barbarity, mercilessness.

injection, n. immission, injecting; enema, clyster, lavement.

injure, v. damage, harm, hurt, impair, disfigure, maim, mar, wound.

injurious, a. hurtful, harmful, detrimental, pernicious, deleterious, baneful, maleficent.

injury, n. damage, detriment, harm, hurt, wound, impairment, mutilation.

injustice, n. inequity, infairness; grievance.

inkling, n. hint, intimation, allusion.

inkstand, n. standish.

inky, a. atramentous, atramental.

inland, a. interior, internal.

inlet, n. entrance, ingress; bay, recess, bight, estuary, cove, frith, bayou.

inmate, n. occupant.

inn, n. lodging house, tavern, hotel; cabaret, caravensary.

innate, a. inborn, inherent, native.

inner, a. internal, interior; obscure.

innermost parts. recesses.

innocence, n. blamelessness, guilelessness, guiltlessness, impeccability.

innocent, a. blameless, guileless, guiltless, impeccable, inoffensive, sinless, artless.

inquiring, a. curious, inquisitive.

inquiry, n. question, query,

I
K

interrogation; research, investigation.

inquisitive, a. inquiring, mousing, curious, intrusive, prying, meddlesome. *Antonyms:* indifferent, unconcerned, uninterested.

insane, a. demented, crazy, mad, deranged, delirious, dementate; paranoiac. *Antonyms:* sane, rational.

insane asylum. bedlam, bethlehem, madhouse, retreat.

insanity, n. dementia, madness, lunacy, craziness, derangement. *Antonyms:* sanity, rationality, lucidity.

insatiable, a. unappeasable; voracious, rapacious, omnivorous.

inscrutable, a. incomprehensible, inexplicable, unsearchable.

insect- eaters, n.pl. Insectivora, Entomophaga.

insect-eating, a. insectivorous, entomophagous.

insect powder. insecticide, pyrethrum.

insecure, a. risky, unsafe, precarious, rickety, unstable, dangerous.

insecurity, n. unsafety, risk, instability, precariousness.

insensibility, n. unconsciousness, torpor, coma, narcosis, lethargy, narcoma.

insensible, a. unfeeling, numb, insensate, torpid, unimpressible, unsusceptible, unconscious.

inseparable, a. indivisible, indissoluble.

insert, v. interpolate, intercalate, interject, ingraft, inosculate.

insertion, n. interjection, interpolation, intercalation.

inside, a. internal, inner, interior.

insides, n.pl. entrails; recesses.

insight, n. discernment.

insignificance, n. unimportance, pettiness, immateriality, triviality, inanity.

insignificant, n. meaningless; unimportant, immaterial, petty, trivial, paltry.

insincere, a. disingenuous, dissembling, false, hypocritical, affected, deceitful.

insincerity, n. duplicity, disingenuousness, hypocrisy.

insinuation, n. innuendo, intimation; ingratiation.

insist, v. persist, press, urge, contend.

insistence, n. persistence, pertinacity, importunity, contention, instance.

insistent, a. persistent, importunate, insisting.

insnare, v. ensnare, entrap, seduce, inveigle, allure.

insolation, n. sunstroke, siriasis; sun bath.

insolence, n. impudence, contumely, impertinence, offrontery, disrespect.

insolent, a. impudent, contrumelious, overbearing, disrespectful.

insoluble, a. indissoluble; unesplainable, insolvable, inexplicable.

inspect, v. examine.

inspiration, n. inhalation; divine afflatus, theopneusty.

inspiring, a. inspiriting, elevating, promethean.

in spite of. notwithstanding, despite, nevertheless.

install, v. instate, induct.

installation, n. induction.

instance, n. persistency, request, solicitation, urgency; example, cse, illustration.

instantly, adv. immediately, forthwith, at onec, instanter, urgently, persistently.

instep, n. metatarsus, acrotarsium.

instruct, v. teach, indoctrinate, edify, enlighten, coach.

instruction, n. nurture, tuition, teaching, information, indoctrination, education, admonition.

instrutive, a. edifying, didactic, preceptive, mentorial; propaedeutic.

instructor, n. teacher, preceptor, tutor, master, coach, mentor, counselor, monitor, trainer.

instrument, n. tool, utensil, implement; agent, means, medium.

insufferable, a. intolerable, unendurable; detestable, offensive.

insufficiency, n. deficiency, inadequacy.

insufficient, a. inadequate, deficient, incommensurate, lacking.

insult, n. indignity, affront.

insult, v. offend, affront, flout.

insulting, a. offensive, contemtuous, scurrilous.

insurance, n. assurance, indemnity.

insure, v. assure, indemnify; underwrite.

insurgency, n. revolt, rebellion, mutiny.

insurgent, a. rebellious, mutinous, insurrectionary.

insurgent, n. rebel, revolter, mutineer, insurrectionist.

intaglio, n. diaglyph. *Antonyms:* cameo.

intelligence, n. knowledge, discernment, insight, acumen.

intelligent, a. clever, discerning, astute, bright, knowing, apt, sensible.

intemperance, n. excess, immoderation, debauchery.

intemperate, a. immoderate, excessive, unrestrained.

intend, v. design, purpose, propose, contemplate, plan.

intended, n. fiance [male],

fiancee [female].

intense, a. extreme, excruciating.

intensify, v. aggravate, exacerbate, heighten.

intention, n. design, plan, purpose, aim.

intentional, a. deliberate, premeditated. *Antonyms:* unintentional, inadvertent, accidental.

intercede, v. mediate, interpose, propitiate.

intercessor, n. mediator, interceder, propitiator, makepeace.

interchange, n. reciprocation, reciprocity, permutation; alternation.

interest, n. concern; share, portion, part, participation. *Antonyms:* boredom, ennui, indifference, unconcern.

interested, a. concerned; prejudiced, partial. *Antonyms:* disinterested, unconcerned, bored.

interfere, v. clash, conflict; intermeddle, interpose, intervene.

interference, n. clashing, collision; intermeddling, interposition, intervention.

interlining, n. interlineation.

interloper, n. intruder, interferer.

intermediate, a. intervening, interjacent; interlocutory.

intermittent, a. remittent, periodical, recurrent.

internal, a. inward, interior, inside, inner; esoteric; inherent.

interpret, v. construe, translate, render.

interpretation, n. rendering, rendition, translation; exegesis, hermeneutics, isagogics, dittology.

interrogation point, eroteme.

interval, n. interstice [space between]; interim, meantime.

intervening a. intermediate, interjacent.

intervention, n. interference, interposition; mediation, intercession.

intestines, n.pl. entrails, bowels, inwards, guts.

intolerable, a. insufferable, unendurable.

intolerance, n. bigotry, dogmatism.

intolerant, a. bigoted, unforbearing, illiberal.

intrenchment, n. earthwork, fortification; encroachment, infringement, invasion, inroad.

intricacy, n. complication, entanglement, eomplexity.

intricate, a. complicated, entangled, involved, labyrinthian, mazy.

intrigue, n. conspiracy, machination, cabal, plot; amour, liaison.

intrigue, v. plot, scheme, machinate, cabal.

intriguer, n. machinator, plotter, schemer.

intriguing, a. scheming, wily.

intrinsic, a. inherent, innate, real, genuine. *Antonyms:* extrinsic.

introduction, n. preface, proem, exordium, prelude, prolegomenon, prologue, foreword.

introductory, a. preliminary, premial, prefatory.

intrude, v. infringe, invade, encroach, obtrude, interlope.

intrusion, n. encroachment, obtrusion, infringement, interloping.

intrusive, a. obtrusive. *Antonyms:* unintrusive, unobtrusive, retiring.

intrust, v. commit, confide.

invade, v. infringe, encroach, trespass, intrench, trench.

invalid, a. null, void, of no efficacy; baseless, unfounded.

invalid, a. valetudinary.

invalid, n. valetudinarian.

invalidate, v. annul, abrogate, cancel, quash, nullify.

invalidation, n. nullification, abrogation, annulment.

invalidism, n. valetudinarianism.

invasion, n. irruption, foray, raid, aggression; violation, infringement, encroachment, intrenchment.

inveigle, v. wheedle, seduce.

inveiglement, n. wheedling, seduction.

investigate, v. probe, sift, examine.

investigation, n. examination, inquiry, research.

invidious, a. objectionable, offensive.

invincible, a. indomitable, unconquerable.

invisible, a. inperceptible, microscopic.

invitation, n. bidding, call, summons.

invite, v. bid, ask, summon; allure, induce, entice.

invocation, n. prayer, supplication.

involuntary, a. uncontrollable, instinctive, automaticy, compulsory, forced.

inwards, n.pl. entrails intenstines, bowels, guts; viscera; giblets, inmeats.

iota, n. scintila, tittle, atom, mite, jot, whit, bit, particle.

Ireland, n. Erin, Emerald Isle.

iridescent, a. prismatic, nacreous.

iris, n. flower-de-luce, flag.

Irish, a. Hibernian.

Irishman, n. Hibernian, Milesian, Teague, Pat, Paddy.

iron, v. smooth; mangle.

irons, n.pl. fetters, chains, handcuffs, shackles, manacles, hampers, gyves.

ironworker's pneumonia.

siderosis.

irrecoverable, a. irretrievable.

irregular, a. inconformable, abnormal, anomalous, exceptional, unusual, rose, baroque, aberrant.

irregularity, n. inconformableness, abnormality, asymmetry, anomaly, aberration, intermittency.

irreligious, a. ungodly, impious, godless, sacrilegious, blasphemous, profane.

irresolute, a. wavering, vacillating, inconstant, fickle, doubleminded.

irresolution, n. indecision, vacillation, inconstancy, fickleness.

irresponsible, a. unaccountable, unanswerable, unreliable.

irritable, a. irascible, fretful, spleeny, choleric, petulant, fiery, captious.

irritate, v. intensify, stimulate; provoke, vex, annoy, offend, chafe.

isinglass, n. fishglue, ichrhyocol; mica; carlock.

island, n. isle, eyot, holm, islet; atol.

isolate, v. insulate, segregate, dissociate, detach, separate.

isolated, a. insulated, separate, solitary, segragated.

isolation, n. insulation, segragation; lonliness, solitude.

issue, v. gush, disembogue; sally forth, debouch; proceed, emanate, ensue, follow, result.

Italian laborers. padrone.

itch, n. psora, scabies; prurigo; sycosis; sczema; pruriency.

itching, a. tingling, prurient.

ivory, n. eburnean, eburnine, eburin.

ivy, n. hederaceous, hederal, hederic, hederose.

J

jab, n. thrust, punch, dig.

jabber, n. gibberish, chatter, gabble, babble.

jackass, n. donkey; dolt, simpleton, witling, ignoramus, fool.

jacket, n. coat, jerkin, blouse, spencer, bolero, pea-jacket.

jade, n. nephrite, jadeite; nag, plug.

jag, n. notch, cleft, barb, protuberance. v. notch.

jagged, a. cleft, jaggy, notched, serrated, erose, sharp.

jail, n. prison, lockup, calaboose, workhouse, limbo.

jail bird. prisoner.

jailer, n. warden, turnkey, sheriff.

jail fever. typhus fever.

jam, n. preserve, conserve; crowd, throng, crush.

jam, v. squeeze, crowd, press, wedge in, bruise.

jamboree, n. carousal, revelry, carouse, spree.

jangle, n. clashing, clang, discord, dissonance; wrangling, quarrel, dispute.

jangle, v. clash, clang; quarrel, wrangle, dispute, altercate.

jangling, a. discordant, dissonant, clashing, inharmonious.

janitor, n. doorkeeper, porter, *concierge*.

Japan, n. Nippon, Flowery Kingdom.

japan, n. lacquer, varnish, enamel.

jar, n. crock; gurglet; shock, jolt, vibration. v. jolt, jounce, shock, discompose, unsettle; grate.

jargon, n. gibberish, drivel, babble, gabble, twaddle, bosh. slang.

jaundice, n. icterus. v. prejudice.

jaundiced, a. prejudiced, biased, warped.

jaunty, a. airy, showy, finical,

I
K

affected, fine.

jaw, n. jawbone, jowl; maxilla.

jealous, a. suspicious, distrustful.

jealousy, n. suspicion, distrust.

jeer, v. mock, deride, ridicule, taunt, jibe.

jeering, n. mockery, derision, ridicule, scoffing, sneer, taunt.

jellylike, a. gelatinous, colloid.

jeopard, v. imperil, risk, expose, endanger, hazard.

jeopardize, v. jeopard.

jeopardy, n. danger, peril, hazard, exposure.

jerky, a. abrupt, unconnected.

jest, n. joke, witticism, quip.

jester, n. joker, wag; buffoon, merry-andrew, clown, harlequin, zany.

jesting, n. joking, jest, raillery, banter, persiflage, facetiousness.

jesting, a. waggish, jocular, facetious, sportive.

jet, v. spurt, spout, gush; protrude, project. n. spouting, spurt, gush.

Jew, n. Hebrew, Israelite, Judahite, Judean, Semite, Yid; Rabbi.

jewel, n. gem, brilliant.

jewelry, n. jewels; bijoutry.

Jewish, a. Hebrew, Judaic, Israelitish, Hebraic, Semitic.

Jezebel, n. virago, she-devil, fury, Gorgon, termagant.

jibe, v. agree, harmonize, fit.

jiffy, n. moment, instant, second, trice.

jill, n. coquette, flirt; sweetheart, gill.

jilt, n. coquette, flirt.

jingle, n. tinkling, jingling, tintinnabulation; rhyme. v. tinkle.

job, n. task; situation, position.

jog, n. shake, jolt, shove; hitch, break.

jog, n. push, shake, jostle; suggest to, notify, remind.

join, v. connect, couple, unite, combine, associate, add, append.

Antonyms: disjoin, disconnect.

joiner, n. link, coupling, bond; woodworker, carpenter.

joint, n. gimbal joint, dove-tail joint, joggle joint, mortise joint, mitre, dowel.

joint, n. articulation; suture, commissure, knuckle.

joint, a. combined, joined, united.

jointed, a. articulated, hinged; knotted, gnarled.

joke, n. jest, witticism, jocosity, sally, *jeu d'esprit*, quip, quirk.

joke, v. rally, banter, jest.

joking, n. jesting, rallying, banter.

jokingly, adv. sportively, jestingly, waggishly, jocularly.

jolly, a. jovial, vivacious, congenial, convivial, mirthful, sportive, gay.

jolly, v. make good-natured, joke, jest, cheer, encourage.

jolt, n. jar, shock, jounce, jolting. v. shake, jar, jounce.

jot, n. iota, point, tittle, bit, mite, atom, scintilla.

jotting, n. memorandum, note, entry.

jounce, n. jolt, shake, jolting. v. jolt, shake, jar.

journal, n. day-book, daily register, record; diary; periodical, publication, magazine, gazette.

journey, n. trip, tour, pilgrimage, excursion, travel, jaunt.

journeyman, n. handicraftsman, artisan. *Antonyms*: apprentice, amateur.

joust, v. tilt.

jovial, a. jolly, mirthful, gay, merry, sportive, hilarious, gleeful.

joviality, n. gayety, jollity, sportiveness, liveliness.

joy, n. gladness, exultation, jubilation, mirth, festivity, glee, elation.

joyful, a. joyous, glad, elated, jubilant, exhilarating, happy.

joyous, a. joyful.

jubilant, a. joyful, exultant, triumphant.

jubilation, n. rejoicing, exultation, triumph.

Judas, n. betrayer, traitor.

Judas, a. traitorous, treacherous, disloyal, perfidious.

judge, v. adjudge, adjudicate, try; discern, distinguish, discriminate.

judge, n. justice, judger; arbitrator, arbiter, umpire, referee; connoisseur, critic.

judgment, n. decision, adjudication, arbitrament, arbitration, adjudgment; sentence, decree.

judgment-seat, n. court, tribunal, bar, judicatory.

judicial, a. judicative, judicatory, juridical, judiciary.

judicious, a. prudent, discreet, well-advised.

jug, n. pitcher, ewer, demijohn, flagon; bellarmine, long-beard.

juggler, n. prestidigitator, magician, conjurer; cheat, impostor; jongleur.

juice, n. sap, lush; must.

juicy, a. succulent, sappy, lush, luscious. *Antonyms*: juiceless, sapless, dry.

jumble, v. confuse, disarrange, entangle, mix.

jumble, n. disorder, confusion, disarray, mixture, entanglement, chaos.

jump, v. spring, bound, leap, hop, caper, vault; bounce, jolt.

junction, n. union, coalition; juncture.

juncture, n. joint, seam; crisis, conjuncture, point, exigency.

jungle, n. thicket, brake, boscage, brush.

juryman, n. juror.

just, a. upright, honest, conscientious, honorable, straightforward; condign, merited. *Antonyms*: dishonest, inequitable, undeserved.

just, adv. precisely, exactly; closely, nearly, almost; barely, scarcely, only.

justice, n. justness, equity, impartiality; judge. *Antonyms*: inequity, injustice.

justifiable, a. warrantable, defensible, vindicable.

justification, n. vindication, exculpation, exoneration, defense.

justifier, n. justificator, vindicator, defender.

justify, v. vindicate, warrant, excuse, exonerate, exculpate, absolve, defend.

justle, v. clash, bump, jostle, collide.

justly, adv. honestly, fairly, equitably, impartially.

justness, n. justice, fairness, equity, impartiality, condignness.

jut, v. jut out, project, protrude. n. projection, jutty.

juvenile, a. youthful, young, immature.

juvenility, n. youthfulness, immaturity.

K

keel over. overturn, capsize, tip over.

keen, a. sharp, acute, trenchant; penetrating, shrewd, astute, discerning.

keep, n. custody, charge; maintenance, support; stronghold, donjon; condition, case.

keep, v. detain, restrain, hold, retain, repress, withhold; preserve.

keep back. reserve, withhold; restrain, repress, check.

keep company with. associate with, accompany, go with.

keep down. hold in subjection, restrain, hinder, subdue.

keeper, n. warden; superintendent, curator, custodian, guardian, attendant.

keep from. abstain from, refrain from.

keeping, n. holding, restraint, custody, guard, guardianship, protection.

keeping back. reservation, reserving, withholding; restraint, repression, checking.

keep on. proceed, continue, persist.

keepsake, n. memento, souvenir.

keep to. adhere to.

keep under. hold in subjection, subdue, mortify.

keep up. maintain, continue.

kernel, n. seed, grain; nucleus; gist, core, pith, substance, essence, marrow.

kerosene, n. coal oil, petroleum.

kettle, n. caldron.

key, n. pitch, tone.

key, n. clew, solution, guide, explanation, elucidation, clavis.

keyboard, n. clavier.

kick, v. spurn, calcitrate, recalcitrate, winch; resist; oppose; recoil.

kick, n. kicking, opposition.

kicking, n. spurning, recalcitration, calcitration, winch, opposition, resistance.

kicking, a. recalcitrant, calcitrant, resistant.

kidnap, n. abduct.

kidnapper, n. abductor, man-stealer.

kidnapping, n. abduction.

kidney-shaped, a. reniform.

kidney stone. nephrite, jade.

kill, v. slay, slaughter, murder, assassinate, butcher, despatch, execute, lynch.

killer, n. slayer, murderer, butcher, assassin, assassinator, executor, destroyer.

killing, n. slaying, slaughter, butchering, butchery, assassination, massacre.

killing, a. fatal, mortal, deadly, destructive; captivating, charming, fascinating.

kilt, n. filibeg.

kin, n. relationship, relatives, relations, kindred, kinsfolk, kinsmen.

kin, a. kindred.

kind, a. indulgent, compassionate, merciful, lenient, clement, benignant, gracious.

kind, n. variety, genus, species, strain, breed, nature, genre, sort.

kind-hearted, a. compassionate, lenient, clement, kind.

kindle, v. enkindle, fire, ignite, incite, inflame, rouse.

kindling, n. enkindling, incitement, accension.

kindly, a. kind.

kindness, n. compassion, benignity, benevolence, kindliness, graciousness, clemency, compassionateness.

kindred, n. relationship; relatives, relations, kinsfolk, kin, kinsmen.

kindred, a. related, congenial, allied, similar.

king, n. monarch, sovereign, potentate, regulus.

kingdom, n. empire, dominion, sovereignty, monarchy, realm.

kingly, a. royal, regal, monarchical; sovereign, august, majestic, grand. *Antonyms*: servile, mean, abject, slavish, unkingly.

kink, v. snarl, become entangled.

kink, n. snarl, knot, entanglement, twist; crotchet, whim, caprice.

kinky, a. snarled, tangled, knotted; crotchety, eccentric, capricious.

kinsman, n. relative.
kiss, n. osculate.
kiss, n. osculation, buss, smack; pax.
kissing, n. osculation. a. osculant, osculatory.
kitchen, n. cookroom, cuisine, scullery.
knack, n. gimcrack, trinket, toy, plaything, knickknack.
knarled, a. knotted, gnarled, knurly, gnarly, knotty, knurled.
knave, n. villain, rascal, scamp.
knavery, n. villainy, rascality, scoundrelism, chicanery, knavishness, roguery.
knees, n. pl. marrowbones.
knickknack, n. gimcrack, gewgaw, bauble, trinket, knack, curio, bric-a-brac.
knife, n. dagger, stiletto, dirk, poniard, bowie-knife.
knight, n. man-at-arms; champion, partisan, lover, gallant.
knighthood, n. chivalry.
knightly, a. chivalrous, gallant.
knob, n. excrescence, boss, lump, tubercle, knop, stud, hard.
knock, v. rap; clash, bump; strike, beat. n. blow, stroke, rap.
knock about. wander about, saunter, stroll.
knock down. fell, floor, prostrate.
knoll, n. hillock, mound.
knot, n. entanglement, snarl, intricacy, complication; cluster, group.
knot, v. entangle, tie, snarl. *Antonyms*: disentangle, unravel, untie.
knotted, a. knurled, knaggy, gnarled, gnarly; snarled, entangled, interwoven.
knotty, a. knotted, gnarled, crossgrained; intricate, difficult, complicated.
knowable, a. ascertainable, cognizable, cognoscible,
intelligible, recognizable. *Antonyms*: unknowable, unascertainable, incognoscible, unrecognizable.
knowing, a. intelligent, sagacious, wise, clever; expressive, significant; artful, sharp, cunning.
knowingly, adv. consciously, intelligently, wittingly, designedly.
knowledge, n. learning, lore, erudition, culture, enlightenment, attainments, information. *Antonyms*: sciolism, ignorance, inerudition.
knuckle to. submit to, yield, cringe, obey.
kodak, n. camera [portable], *an invented term, the trademark of the Eastman Company.*

L

labor, n. toil, work, drudgery, task, industry, travail.
labored, a. studied, elaborate, overwrought, stiff, unnatural.
laborer, n. toiler, workman, stevedore, roustabout, drudge, hack.
laborious, a. toilsome, arduous, onerous; diligent, industrious, sedulous.
labyrinth, n. maze, intricacy, complexity.
lace, n. string, cord, thong, aglet.
lacerate, v. tear, rend, mangle, laniate, harrow, wound.
laceration, n. tearing, rending, laniation, harrowing, wound.
lack, v. need, want, be in need of, require.
lack, n. want, need, deficiency, dearth, paucity, scarcity.
lackadaisical, a. pensive, dreamy, languishing, die-away.
lacking, a. deficient, insufficient, unsupplied, shy, wanting,

L
M

devoid.

lag, v. fall behind, loiter, linger, delay, saunter.

lake, n. pond; lagoon.

lamb, n. eanling, yeanling, lambkin, cosset.

lame, v. disable, maim, cripple, hamstring.

lame, a. crippled, hobbling, limping, halt, deformed.

lament, v. bemoan, weep, wail, deplore, grieve, bewail, mourn.

lamentable, a. deplorable, grievous, pitiable, distressing, sorrowful.

lamented, a. mourned for, deplored.

lampoon, v. libel, defame, satirize.

lance, n. spear, javelin, harpoon.

land, n. terra firma; country; freehold; ground, soil, earth; realty, real estate.

land, v. disembark, debark; capture.

landing, n. disembarkation, debarkation; wharf, dock, quay; capture.

landlord, n. host, hotel-keeper, inn-keeper, Boniface; owner, proprietor.

Land of promise. Canaan.

landscape, n. scene, scenery, view, prospect.

language, n. speech, tongue, vernacular; dialect; idiom, phraseology, diction.

lanky, a, gangling, overgrown.

lapse, n. slip, misstep, indiscretion; backsliding; devolution.

lard, n. grease; leaflard, flare; axunge. v. interlard.

large, a. big, extensive, huge, unwieldy, vast, massive, immense.

lariat, n. lasso, reata.

lark, n. frolic.

larva, n. caterpillar, grub, maggot; pl. larvae.

lascivious, a. lewd, libidinous, salacious.

lash, n. scourge, thong, whip.

lash, v. scourge, castigate, flagellate; satirize, scold, rate.

lashing, n. scourging, castigation, flagellation; satire, scolding, rating.

lasso, n. lariat, cabestro, reata.

last, a. final, hindmost, farthest, latest, ultimate.

last, v. continue, endure, remain.

lasting, a. enduring, durable, permanent, imperishable, abiding. *Antonyms*: ephemeral, transitory, fleeting, transient, fugitive, impermanent.

lastly, adv. finally.

late, a. tardy, delayed; recent.

lately, adv. recently.

latent, a. concealed, dormant, undeveloped, hidden.

later, a. subsequent, posterior.

latitude, n. breadth, width; room, range, scope, extent, freedom; laxity.

lattice, n. trellis, lattice-work; cancelli; grille.

laud, v. extol, praise.

laudable, a. praiseworthy, commendable. *Antonyms*: illaudable, unpraiseworthy, indign.

laugh, v. cachinnate, roar, giggle, snicker, titter, chuckle.

laughable, a. risible, comic, ludicrous, droll, facetious, farcical, amusing.

laughing, a. merry, gleeful, mirthful, smiling.

laughing gas. protoxide of nitrogen, nitrous oxide, hyponitrous oxide.

laughter, n. mirth, laugh, cachinnation, giggle, snicker, roar.

launch, v. set afloat; set going, start; throw, hurl; expatiate, descant.

lavish, a. profuse, prodigal, free, unstinted; superabundant.

lavish, v. spend lavishly, bestow with profusion.

law, n. statute, ordinance, edict, enactment, decree, canon, usage.

law-breaker, n. criminal, malefactor, culprit, felon, delinquent, offender, sinner.

law-breaking, n. crime, misdemeanor, transgression, violation.

lawful, n. legal, legitimate, licit, legalized.

lawfulness, n. legality, legitimacy. *Antonyms*: unlawfulness, illegality.

lawing, n. litigation, lawsuit.

lawless, a. anarchical, riotous, mobocratic, licentious.

lawlessness, n. anarchy, unrestraint, abandon, mobocracy, license, riot.

lawmaker, n. legislator, lawgiver, Solon.

lawsuit, n. litigation, case, suit, action.

lawyer, n. attorney, counselor, barrister, counsel, advocate, attorney-at-law.

lax, a. loose, slack, flabby, relaxed; loose; vague.

laxative, a. aperient.

lay, v. deposit, place; impose, assess; impute, charge, ascribe, attribute.

layer, n. stratum, course, tier.

lay open. uncover, reveal, expose, disclose, exhibit, show.

lay over. overlay, cover, apply; defer, postpone, prorogue.

lay siege to. besiege, beset, bombard, obsess.

lay to heart. take to heart, be grieved at, feel keenly, consider seriously.

lay up. store, treasure, save, hoard, garner; confine, disable.

lay wait for. lie in ambush for.

laziness, n. indolence, sloth.

lazy, a. indolent, slothful, sluggard, dronish. *Antonyms*: diligent, industrious, sedulous, hardworking.

lazy person. sluggard, drone, idler.

lead, v. guide, conduct, escort, direct; precede; induce, entice, influence.

lead astray. mislead, seduce.

leader, n. guide, commander, coryphaeus, pilot, bellwether, protagonist, chief.

leaf, n. blade, spire; folio; lithophyll [fossil leaf].

league, n. alliance, confederation, coalition, confederacy, union, federation, association.

lean, v. incline, slope, recline, tend; rely, depend; careen.

lean, a. thin, lank, spare, meager, poor, skinny, gaunt.

lean-to, n. penthouse, addition, shed.

leap, v. spring, jump, vault, bound, caper, gambol, prance.

learn, v. master, acquire knowledge.

learned, a. educated, erudite, lettered, scholarly.

learning, n. education, erudition, lore, scholarship knowledge.

lease, v. let, demise, rent.

least, n. minimum.

leave, v. depart from, vacate, retire from; abandon, forsake, desert; abstain from.

lecture, n. discourse, address, dissertation, prelection; reproof, scolding.

leg, n. limb, shank, skin.

legacy, n. bequest, devise.

legal, a. lawful, legitimate. *Antonym*: illegal.

legality, n. lawfulness, legitimacy. *Antonym*: illegality.

legalize, v. legitimize. *Antonyms*: illegalize, illegitimize.

legend, n. fable, myth; posy, inscription, motto.

legendary, a. mythical, tradi-

L
M

tional.

legible, a. readable, decipherable. *Antonym:* illegible.

legion, n. host, horde, army.

legitimate, a. lawful. *Antonym:* illegitimate.

lend, v. loan.

lengthen, v. extend, elongate, stretch, prolong, protract; expatiate, amplify.

lengthwise, adv. longitudinally.

lengthy, a. long, prolix, protracted, verbose.

lenient, a. compassionate.

lenity, n. clemency, mercy, lenience.

Lent, n. Quadragesima.

lessen, v. reduce, diminish, minify, depreciate, minimize, decrease.

lessening, n. reduction, diminution, decrease, decrement, depreciation, mitigation, shrinkage.

lesson, n. task, exercise.

let, v. allow, permit, suffer; lease, rent.

lethargy, n. drowsiness, stupor, unconsciousness.

letter, n. initial [first letter].

letter-carrier, n. postman, mail-carrier, courier, mail-man, postboy, post.

letters, n. pl. correspondence.

letters, n. pl. learning, literature, erudition, humanities.

let-up, n. abatement, assuagement, respite, subsidence.

level, a. even, flat, plain, smooth, flush, plump; horizontal; steady. *Antonyms:* undulating, uneven, concave, convex, warped.

levity, n. lightness, buoyancy; gayety, frivolity.

lewd, a. unchaste, lustful, licentious; libidinous, lecherous, incontinent. *Antonyms:* chaste, modest, pure.

lewdness, n. unchastity, incontinence, lust, lechery, ribaldry, salacity. *Antonyms:* chastity, modesty, purity.

liability, n. exposure, accountability, responsibility, amenability. *Antonyms:* immunity, exemption.

liabilities, n. pl. debts, obligations, indebtedness.

liable, a. exposed, subject, accountable, answerable, amenable, found. *Antonyms:* exempt, immune.

libel, n. defamation, lampoon, roorback.

libellous, a. defamatory, slanderous, calumnious.

liberal, a. generous, open-handed, bounteous, munificent, unstinted, princely. *Antonyms:* illiberal, ungenerous, stingy, limited, narrow, bigoted.

liberty, n. freedom, independence; privilege, permission. *Antonyms:* captivity, bondage, servitude, subjection, constraint, serfdom, slavery.

license, v. legalize, permit.

licentious, a. immoral, dissolute, profligate, lewd, libertine, rakish, lascivious

lick, v. lap; flog, thrash, chastise, castigate, trounce, drub.

licking, n. flogging, chastisement, castigation, punishment, thrashing, whipping.

lid, n. cover.

lie, n. untruth, falsehood, fib; fiction, fabrication; subterfuge.

lie close. cuddle, nestle, snuggle.

lien, n. incumbrance.

life, n. existence, being, animation, vitality; vivacity, spiritedness, energy.

lifeless, a. dead, inanimate, spiritless, devitalized.

lift, v. raise, elevate.

lift, n. lifting, raising, elevation;

help, assistance, aid; elevator, dumb waiter.

light, a. buoyant; easy, inoppressive; active, nimble, deft, fleet, swift, spry.

light, v. ignite, illumine, illuminate.

light-fingered, a. thievish, pilfering.

like, a. similar, alike, cognate, analogous, homogeneous.

like, v. fancy, approve of; prefer, choose, wish.

likelihood, n. probability, verisimilitude. *Antonyms*: unlikelihood, improbability.

liken, v. compare.

likeness, n. similitude, resemblance, similarity, appearance, guise, analogy; portrait.

liking, n. fondness, partiality, affection, approval, preference, predilection. *Antonyms*: distaste, aversion, inappetency, hatred, antipathy, disapproval.

limb, n. branch, bough.

limber, a. flexible, pliant, limp, pliable, supple, lithe, lithesome.

limit, n. bound, boundary, confine, extent; restriction, check, restraint, limitation.

limp, a. flaccid, flabby, limber, soft, flexible.

linen, n. napery; lingerie; damask.

linger, v. loiter, saunter, tarry, lag.

link, v. join, unite, connect, couple, concatenate.

liquid, n. fluid.

list, n. catalogue, roster, schedule, register; selvage, selvedge, listing.

listen, v. hearken; eavesdrop; auscultate. *Antonyms*: disregard, ignore, scorn.

listless, a. inattentive, indifferent, supine, heedless, unconcerned.

litigation, n. lawsuit.

litter, n. stretcher; mulch;

disorder, untidiness; farrow.

little, a. small, diminutive, minute, tiny, wee, puny, dwarfish.

little by little. piecemeal, gradually.

live, v. exist; dwell, reside, abide.

liveliness, n. animation, vivacity, sprightliness, briskness, activity, lilt.

live longer than. survive, outlive.

lively, a. animated, spirited, vivacious, vigorous, active, brisk. *Antonyms*: slow, sluggish, inactive, quiet.

livid, a. ecchymosed, bruised, black and blue.

living, n. life, existence, being; livelihood, sustenance, subsistence.

living again. redivivus, resurrected, revived, resurgent.

living in seclusion. eremitism, anchoretism, reclusion, seclusion, retirement.

living together. cohabitation.

living upon others. parasitic. n. parasitism.

load, v. encumber, lade, burden, freight.

loaf, v. lounge about, loiter.

loathe, v. abhor, hate, detest, abominate, despise, execrate, recoil from.

location, n. situation, locality, place.

lock-jaw, n. tetanus.

logical, a. consistent, sound. *Antonym*: illogical.

loiter, v. saunter, linger.

lone, a. alone, lonely, isolated, desolate; unfrequented, solitary.

long, v. yearn for, hanker for, crave.

long life. longevity.

longshoreman, n. stevedore.

long-suffering, a. forbearing, uncomplaining, patient. n. forbearance, patience,

L
M

longanimity.

look, v. glance, gaze, stare, see, con, gloat, glare.

look, n. glance, glimpse, inspection, scrutiny, gaze; expression.

looking for. anticipation, expectation; search.

looking forward. anticipation, expectation, prospect, foresight.

looking-glass, n. mirror; cheval glass.

look into. inspect, examine, probe, investigate.

look on. see, witness; regard, consider, deem, view.

lookout, n. observatory; watch-tower, conning tower, responsibility.

look over. examine, scrutinize, reconnoiter.

look upon. regard, esteem, consider.

look up to. honor, respect, defer to, venerate, reverence.

loop, n. staple, noose, bight.

loophole, n. excuse, plea, pretext.

loose, v. release, disengage, free, disentangle, liberate, absolve.

looseness, n. laxity, slackness, relaxation.

loot, n. spoil, booty, plunder, prize; plundering, pillage.

lopsided, a. unbalanced, disproportioned.

lord, n. nobleman, peer, magnate, grandee; liege, suzerain.

Lord, have mercy upon us. Kyrie eleison.

lordly, a. overbearing, domineering, despotic, arrogant, imperious, uppish.

Lord's Prayer. Pater noster.

Lord's Supper. communion, Eucharist.

lose, v. miss, forfeit.

lose ground. retire, recede, retreat, decline.

loss, n. forfeiture.

lost, a. forfeited, missing; derelict, adrift; misspent, misemployed.

lot, n. destiny, doom, fortune, fate; portion, parcel, part, allotment; much, many.

loth, a. disinclined, unwilling, reluctant, averse, loath, indisposed.

loud, a. deafening, stentorian, resonant, clarion; clamorous, vociferous, boisterous.

lounge, v. recline, loll.

lousiness, n. phthiriasis, pediculosis, pediculation.

lout, n. booby, boor, bumpkin, lubber, gawky.

loutish, a. boorish, lubberly, gawky, ungentlemanly.

lovable, a. amiable, winsome, lovely, winning.

lovableness, n. amability, winsomeness, amiability.

love, n. affection, devotion, infatuation, passion; amorousness.

lovely, a. charming, delightful, delectable, amiable, pleasing.

lover, n. amoroso, inamorato, swain, suitor, admirer, philander.

loving, a. affectionate; enamored; amative, amorous, erotic.

loving-kindness, n. tenderness, mercy, compassion.

low, a. depressed; base, mean, vulgar, raffish, ignominious, undignified.

lower, v. drop; depress, reduce; decrease, diminish, fall, humble.

lower, a. nether, under.

lowest, a. nethermost.

low life. obscurity.

lowliness, n. humility, meekness, self-abasement.

low-lived, a. mean, dishonorable, ignominious, base.

lowly, a. humble, meek, unassuming.

low-minded, a. groveling, abject, sordid, base-minded.

loyal, a. true, constant, faithful, devoted, stanch, unwavering.

loyalty, n. fidelity, constancy, faithfulness, devotion, fealty, allegiance.

lozenge, n. tablet, troche, pastille.

luck, n. fortune, chance, fortuity, haphazard, chance, hap, hazard.

lucky, a. fortunate; favorable, auspicious, propitious.

lug, v. drag, pull, tug, haul.

luggage, n. baggage, traps.

lukewarm, a. tepid; indifferent, cool, unconcerned.

lull, v. hush, still, quiet, tranquilize; subside, abate.

lumbering, a. unwieldly, ponderous, cumbersome, ungraceful.

lump, n. mass, aggregation, aggregate. —v. mass, amass.

lumpish, a. inert, heavy; stupid, dull, stolid.

lunatic, n. madman, maniac, bedlamite.

lunch, n. luncheon, refection.

luncheon, n. collation, refreshment, nuncheon, tiffin.

lunge, v. allonge, longe, thrust.

lurch, v. sway, stagger, roll; dodge, shift, evade, bilk.

lure, n. decoy, enticement, bait.

lure, v. entice, tempt, seduce, allure, decoy.

lurking-place, n. ambush, retreat, cover.

luscious, a. delicious, delectable; cloying, fulsome, unctuous.

lush, a. juicy, succulent.

lust, n. venereal appetite, concupiscence, salacity, sexual desire. *Antonym*: anaphrodisia.

luster, n. brightness, gloss, glitter, sheen, brilliancy.

lusterless, a. dull, lackluster.

lustful, a. lascivious, concupiscent, lecherous, licentious, libidinous.

lustre, n. brilliancy, glitter, radiance, resplendence.

lusty, a. robust, sturdy, stalwart, strapping, muscular.

luxuriance, n. exuberance, rampancy, richness.

luxurious, a. voluptuous, epicurean, sybaritic.

luxury, n. voluptuousness, epicurism, sybaritism, luxuriousness.

lying, a. untruthful, false, mendacious, deceitful.

lying, n. falsehood, lie, untruth, mendacity, fabrication, fiction.

lying down. reclining, recumbent, accumbent.

lying in wait. ambush, ambuscade.

M

machine, n. automation.

mad, a. crazy, insane, demented, maniacal, raving; indignant.

madden, v. incense, anger, enrage, infuriate, provoke.

made up. devised, fabricated, artificial, sham, false, counterfeit.

madhouse, n. bedlam, insane asylum.

madman, n. maniac, lunatic, bedlamite; monomaniac.

madness, n. dementia, insanity, craziness, mania, lunacy.

magazine, n. storehouse, depot, repository; periodical, publication.

magic, n. enchantment, conjuration, wizardry.

magic, a. magical, necromantic, talismanic.

magician, n. conjurer, prestidigitator, sorcerer, wizard.

magnet, n. loadstone.

L
M

magnificence, n. grandeur, sublimity, splendor, majesty.

magnificent, a. splendid, superb, sublime, majestic, stately, grand.

magnify, v. augment, amplify, enlarge; overstate, exaggerate.

maiden, a. virgin; chaste, undefiled, pure; unused, fresh, new.

maidenhead, n. maidenhood; hymen [virginal membrane].

maidenhood, n. maidhood, girlhood, virginity.

mail, v. post.

mail-carrier, n. postman, letter-carrier, courier.

main, a. principal, leading, chief, capital, cardinal, paramount.

main, n. ocean, high sea; gross, bulk, majority; strength, power.

mainland, n. continent.

mainly, adv. principally, chiefly, largely.

maintain, v. support, sustain; affirm, assert, contend, claim; conduct.

majestic, a. august, imperial, regal, splendid, magnificent, imposing.

majesty, n. grandeur, magnificence, augustness, splendor.

major, a. greater, larger. *Antonym*: minor.

majority, n. seniority, manhood; plurality. *Antonyms*: minority, youth.

make, v. force, compel, coerce, constrain, require, necessitate.

make, n. construction, shape, form, structure, conformation.

make believe, a. feigned, mock, sham, counterfeit, spurious, supposititious, simulated.

make believe, n. pretense, simulation, affectation, feint.

make good. fulfill, vindicate, justify, establish; indemnify, reimburse.

make headway. advance,

progress, thrive, prosper.

make known. declare, announce, publish, report, proclaim.

make little of. belittle, decry, disparage.

make love to. court, woo, spark.

make out. decipher.

make over. transfer, alienate, convey; remodel, rebuild.

make peace between. mediate, intercede, reconcile, propitiate, pacify, conciliate.

maker, n. manufacturer, constructor, producer.

makeshift, n. expedient, substitute.

make sport of. deride, ridicule, jeer.

make up. reconcile, adjust, compose, settle; collect, amass.

making, n. construction, fabrication, workmanship, invention.

malady, n. disorder, distemper, ailment, complaint, disease.

malaria, n. miasma, miasm; fever and ague.

male, n. masculine; staminate [Bot.].

malice, n. hatred, rancor, malevolence, animosity.

malicious, a. hateful, malevolent, rancorous, malignant.

malpractice, n. evil practice, misdoing, misbehavior.

man, v. mortal, person, individual, adult, someone; mankind.

manacle, n. handcuff, fetter, shackle.

manage, v. conduct, administer, supervise, manipulate, superintend.

management, n. administration, conduct, guidance, regulation, superintendence.

mandate, n. command, edict, order, injunction, precept.

mandatory, a. directory,

commandatory, preceptive.

man-eater, n. cannibal, anthropophagite.

maneuver, n. management, ruse, stratagem, artifice, trick, finesse.

manful, a. manly, resolute, brave.

mangle, v. mutilate, maim, dismember, hack; smooth, calender.

mangy, a. scabby, scurvy.

manhood, n. maturity, majority, man's estate, manliness.

mania, n. madness, insanity, craziness.

maniac, n. madman, bedlamite.

manifest, v. show, exhibit, reveal, disclose.

manipulate, v. handle, operate, manage.

manipulation, n. handling, management.

manly, a. manlike, resolute, brave, strong, dignified.

manner, n. mode, method, style, fashion, way; bearing, demeanor.

mannish, a. masculine, vigorous, bold. *Antonyms*: effeminate, feminine.

mansion, n. palace; manor-house, hall.

man-stealer, n. kidnapper, abductor.

mantle, n. cape, cloak; pallium; mantel-piece, mantel shelf.

manual, n. handbook.

manufacture, n. making, fabrication, construction.

manufacturing, a. industrial.

manure, n. fertilizer, dung, compost, guano.

manuscript, n. copy.

many, a. various, numerous, sundry, divers, manifold.

many-times, adv. frequently, oftentimes, often, repeatedly.

many-ways, adv. variously, multifariously, diversely.

map, n. chart.

map, v. sketch, plan, delineate, picture.

mar, n. defacement, disfigurement, blemish, injury, defect.

margin, n. confine, border, edge, limit, skirt, brink, rim.

marine, a. maritime, naval, nautical, oceanic.

marionette, n. puppet.

maritime, a. marine, naval, nautical.

mark, v. note, notice, remark, observe, see; indicate, betoken.

marked, a. designated, noticeable, conspicuous, notable, salient.

market, n. mart, emporium, exchange, market-place.

marriage, n. matrimony, wedlock; wedding, nuptials, espousals, nuptial rites. *Antonyms*: celibacy, divorce, bachelorhood, maidenhood.

marry, v. wed, espouse.

marsh, n. swamp, morass, fen, slough, bog, quagmire.

mart, n. market, emporium.

martial, a. military.

marvel, n. wonder, prodigy; amazement.

marvel, v. wonder.

marvelous, a. wonderful, amazing, stupendous, astonishing.

masculine, a. male; manly, virile, manful. *Antonym*: feminine.

mask, n. disguise, pretext, subterfuge, screen, cloak, veil, ruse.

mask, v. disguise, masquerade, veil.

mass, n. aggregate, aggregation, totality, lump, heap, assemblage.

massacre, n. carnage, butchery [of human beings], slaughter, havoc.

Mass Book. missal.

L
M

massive, a. ponderous, bulky, immense, huge, cumbersome, massy.

master, n. director, lord, commander, ruler, manager, governor.

masterful, a. domineering, imperious, arbitrary.

masterly, a. skillful, proficient, adroit, dexterous, finished.

masturbation, n. onanism, self-abuse, self-pollution.

mat, n. rug; matting; petate.

match, v. rival, equal, cope with; contend, pit, oppose; tally.

matchless, a. peerless, incomparable, inimitable, unequalled.

mate, n. companion, associate, friend, chum, crony, compeer, intimate, partner.

mate, v. oppose, cope with, vie with, compete with; match, marry.

material, n. substance, matter, fabric, stuff, cloth, staple; plasma.

matrimonial, a. connubial, nuptial, hymeneal, conjugal.

matrimony, n. marriage, wedlock.

matron, n. dame.

matronly, a. elderly, dignified, matronal.

matted, a. tangled, snarled, entangled.

matter, n. substance, material, body; essence, pith, embodiment.

matter, v. import, signify, be of importance, maturate, suppurate.

matter-of-fact, a. practical, pragmatical, unimaginative, commonplace, prosaic.

mature, a. full-grown, ripe, developed, perfect; prepared, finished.

maturity, n. development, ripeness, perfection, completion. *Antonym*: immaturity.

maul, v. pound, pommel, beat, club, cudgel.

maybe, adv. perhaps, possibly, peradventure, haply.

maze, v. perplex, bewilder, confuse, puzzle.

meadow, n. mead, lea.

meager, a. poor, emaciated, gaunt; barren, sterile, unproductive, arid.

mean, a. contemptible, despicable, low-minded, base, abject, groveling, dishonorable.

meander, v. wind, turn.

meandering, a. winding, tortuous, crooked, serpentine, meandrous.

meaning, n. signification, significance, import, acceptation, intent.

meaningly, adv. significantly.

means, n. property, possessions, wealth, resources, riches, estate.

meantime, n. interval, interim, meanwhile.

measles, n. rubeola.

measure, n. gauge, rule; dimensions, capacity, size, extent.

measure, v. gauge, mete; appraise, estimate, compute, adjust.

measurement, n. mensuration; dimensions, size, extent, area, capacity, bulk.

meat, n. flesh [of animals].

meat pie. mince pie; pasty.

mechanic, n. mechanician, artisan, artificer, handicraftsman, craftsman.

mechanical, a. automatic, involuntary.

medal, n. medallion.

meddle, v. interfere, interpose, intermeddle, obtrude.

meddlesome, a. officious, intrusive, obtrusive, pragmatical, intermeddling.

mediation, n. intercession.

medical, a. medicinal, therapeutical, therapeutic, curative.

medicine, n. materia medica, medicament, remedy, restorative, corrective, specific, physic.

mediocre, a. middling, ordinary, medium, commonplace.

mediocrity, n. commonplaceness, indifference, middle state.

meditate, v. contemplate, muse, ponder, cogitate, reflect, think.

medium, a. intermediate, middling, mean, average, mediocre.

medley, n. mixture, jumble, hodgepodge, potpourri, olio, melange, farrago.

meek, a. humble, unassuming, modest, retiring, docile, lowly.

meet, v. encounter, confront, collide, converge, engage; intercept. *Antonyms*: avoid, elude, escape, disperse, scatter.

meet, a. suitable, proper, befitting, seemly, appropriate.

meeting, n. assembly, assemblage, congregation, convention, convocation, conference.

melancholy, n. despondency, hypochondria, dejection, disconsolation, melancholia.

melodious, a. tuneful, harmonious, dulcet, musical, sweet, euphonious.

melody, n. music; descant, tune, song, air, theme. *Antonyms*: discord, dissonance.

melt, v. dissolve, liquefy, thaw, fuse, soften, blend, swale, colliquate.

meltable, a. dissolvable, soluble, liquefiable, fusible.

melted, a. molten.

melting, a. dissolving, thawing; affecting, touching.

member, n. part, organ, limb; constituent, component, part.

memento, n. souvenir, keepsake, memorial.

memoir, n. biography, autobiography.

memorandum, n. record, minute, note.

memorial, a. commemorative.

memory, n. remembrance, recollection, reminiscence; retrospection. *Antonyms*: oblivion, forgetfulness, Lethe, amnesia, ecmnesia.

menace, n. threat, threatening.

mend, v. repair, patch; improve.

mendacious, a. lying, untruthful, false, deceitful.

mending, n. repairing, patching, restoration; improvement.

menial, a. serving; low, servile.

mental, a. intellectual.

mentor, n. monitor, counselor, guide.

mercantile, a. trading, commercial.

mercenary, a. hired, hireling, purchased; greedy, sordid, avaricious, grasping.

merchandise, n. wares, goods, commodities.

merchant, n. trader, dealer, trafficker, shopkeeper, tradesman.

merciful, a. pitiful, lenient, clement, compassionate, benignant, indulgent, kind.

merciless, a. unmerciful, remorseless, cruel, pitiless, ruthless, inexorable, implacable.

mercy, n. clemency, pity, lenity, leniency, lenience, compassion.

merely, a. purely, absolutely; simply, barely, only.

merge, v. swallow up, absorb, immerse, take in; be swallowed up, be absorbed.

merger, n. absorption.

merit, n. desert, worth, meed,

L
M

worthiness; worth, excellence.
Antonym: demerit.

merit, v. deserve, earn.

meritorious, a. worthy, commendable, meedful, deserving.

merriment, n. mirth, gayety, glee, levity, laughter, sportiveness.

merry, a. mirthful, gay, jolly, gleeful, jovial, sportive.

mesh, n. net, network.

mess, n. rations, food; mixture, medley, farrago, litter.

message, n. communication, notice, word; telegram, despatch, cablegram.

messenger, n. courier, herald, forerunner, precursor, harbinger, mercury, emissary.

metaphor, n. simile.

meteor, n. fireball, shooting star; bolis, bolide.

meticulous, a. timid, fearful, diffident.

mettle, n. spirit, disposition; pluck, nerve, hardihood, stamina, spirit.

midday, n. noon, meridian, noontide.

middle, a. mean, medial; intermediate, intervening.

middle, n. center, midst.

middle class. *bourgeoisie.*

middleman, n. factor, go-between, agent, broker, commissioner.

midwife, n. accoucheuse, obstetrician [female].

midwifery, n. obstetrics, tocology.

might, n. strength, power, force, puissance, potency.

mighty, a. strong, powerful, potent, invincible.

mild, a. gentle, indulgent, tender, merciful, clement, lenient.
Antonyms: severe, drastic, rigorous, violent, harsh.

mildew, n. mould, mustiness, must, blight.

military, a. martial.

military command. strategy, generalship, tactics, logistics.

milkman, n. dairyman.

mimic, n. mime, mimicker, imitator, personator.

mimic, v. personate, ape, imitate, mock.

mince, v. hash.

mind, v. obey, regard; consider, heed, mark, note. *Antonyms*: disobey, disregard, ignore.

mind, n. intellect, faculties; opinion, judgment; temperament, humor, disposition.

mindful, a. heedful, regardful, observant.

mindless, a. irrational; unmindful, heedless, inattentive.

mingle, v. blend, mix, intermix, amalgamate, intermingle, incorporate.

minister, n. ambassador, envoy, plenipotentiary, delegate, ecclesiastic, parson.

minister, v. administer, serve; officiate.

ministry, n. ministration; cabinet, administration.

minor, a. subordinate, secondary, less, smaller.

minority, n. nonage, pupilage.

mint, v. coin.

minute, a. little, tiny, microscopic, diminutive; critical, precise.

minute, n. moment; memorandum, record, item, note.

miraculous, a. supernatural, hyperphysical, incredible.

mirror, n. reflector, looking-glass, speculum; cheval glass.

mirror, v. reflect.

mirth, n. merriment, jollity, glee, gayety, fun.

misapply, v. misemploy, pervert, misuse.

miscarriage, n. frustration, failure; abortion.

miscellaneous, a. mixed, diversified, promiscuous, heterogeneous, diverse, multifarious.

misdeed, n. offense, misdemeanor.

misdemeanor, n. offense,
transgression.

miserable, a. wretched; abject;
deplorable, grievous, pitiable,
calamitous.

misfortune, n. disaster, calamity,
frustration, mischance, reverse,
affliction.

misgiving, n. doubt, suspicion,
evil premonition.

misinterpret, v. misconstrue.

misleading, a. delusive, deceitful, fallacious, illusive.

misrepresent, v. falsify, distort.

miss, n. failure, miscarriage;
omission, oversight, default,
mistake, error.

miss, v. fail, miscarry, skip, omit,
overlook.

missile, n. projectile, dejectile.

missing, a. absent, wanting.

mission, n. commission, delega-
tion; errand, trust.

missionary, n. evangelist,
missioner, revivalist, propagan-
dist.

misspelling, n. cacography.

misstate, v. falsify, distort,
misrepresent.

mist, n. mizzle, misle, drizzle;
fog, haze, brume.

mistake, n. misunderstanding,
misapprehension, misconcep-
tion; error, blunder, oversight.

mistranslate, v. misrender,
misconstrue, misinterpret.

mistreat, v. misuse, abuse,
maltreat.

mistress, n. matron, superior;
sweetheart, flame, Dulcinea,
ladylove.

mistrust, v. doubt, question,
suspect, distrust, apprehend.

misty, a. obscure, hazy, foggy,
brumous.

misunderstand, v. misconceive,
miscomprehend, misappre-

hend.

misuse, v. misapply, prostitute,
pervert, profane; maltreat,
abuse.

mitigate, v. meliorate, alleviate,
assuage, temper.

mix, v. mingle, blend, combine,
concoct, incorporate, amalgamate.

mixture, n. blending, mingling,
amalgamation, incorporation,
conglomeration, infusion.

mob, n. rabble, rabblerout;
populace, canaille, riffraff.

mock, a. sham, spurious,
counterfeit, imitational.

mock, v. mimic, flout, taunt,
imitate, gibe, ridicule, jeer.

mocker, n. scorner, scoffer,
jeerer; mimic.

mockery, n. mimicry, ridicule,
derision, jeering, scouting;
counterfeit, sham.

mode, n. manner, method,
fashion, vogue, style.

model, n. pattern, prototype,
exemplar, gauge, criterion,
standard.

model, v. fashion, mould, shape.

moderate, v. temper, appease,
diminish, mitigate, reduce.

moderate, a. sparing, temperate,
frugal; reasonable, calm,
deliberate.

moderation, n. mitigation,
diminution; temperance,
restraint; calmness.

modest, a. unassuming, shy,
unpretentious, unpretending,
unobtrusive, retiring.

modesty, n. unobtrusiveness,
humility; delicacy, chastity,
purity, decency, pudicity.
Antonyms: immodesty, boldness, indelicacy.

modify, v. limit, qualify, adjust.

modulate, v. inflect; harmonize,
attune, adjust, adapt.

moist, a. damp, humid, dank.

moisten, v. dampen, damp, wet.

L
M

moisture, n. dampness, humidity; humor.

molasses, n. treacle.

molecule, n. atom, monad.

molest, v. disturb, trouble, annoy.

molestation, n. disturbance.

moment, n. instant, minute, jiffy, trice; force, momentum.

momentary, a. instantaneous, transient.

momentum, n. impetus, force, moment.

monarch, n. sovereign.

monastery, n. abbey, priory, cloister, convent; hospice.

monetary, a. pecuniary.

money, n. currency, coin, capital, funds, finances, change, legal tender.

monitor, n. mentor, adviser, counselor.

monk, n. religious, monastic, cenobite, anchoret, friar, *abbe*, fakir.

monogram, n. cipher.

monopolize, v. engross, forestall.

monotonous, a. unvaried, uniform, uninteresting, hum-drum,tedious.

monster, n. prodigy, enormity, abnormality, monstrosity.

monstrosity, n. abnormality, monster, *lusus naturae*.

monstrous, a. abnormal; enormous, colossal; atrocious.

monthly, a. mensal, menstrual.

monument, n. tombstone, memorial; cenotaph; dolmen, cromlech.

mood, n. humor.

moon, n. satellite; Luna, Cynthia.

moonshine, n. balderdash, flummery, fustian, nonsense.

moot, a. undecided, unsettled, debatable.

mop, n. malkin, swab; merkin.

mopish, a. dejected, glum, dumpish, listless, dull, spiritless.

moral, a. ethical; virtuous, good; accountable, responsible; probable. *Antonyms*: immoral, licentious.

morality, n. virtue, rectitude, probity, goodness. *Antonym*: immorality.

morning, n. forenoon; dawn, daybreak, aurora, cock-crowing, sunrise.

morsel, n. bite, mouthful; fragment, crumb, scrap.

mortally, adv. fatally.

mortification, n. gangrene; chagrin, humiliation, abasement, embarrassment; repression, subjection.

mosaic, a. tessellated, inlaid, variegated.

most, n. majority.

mother, n. materfamilias, matron, matriarch; generatrix; dam.

motherhood, n. maternity.

motherly, a. maternal.

mother-of-pearl, n. nacre.

motion, n. movement, activity; gesture, signal, gesticulation. *Antonyms*: inertia, rest, stagnation, immobility, quiescence, repose.

motionless, a. stationary, inert, stagnant, quiescent.

motive, n. incentive, inducement, incitement.

mould, n. matrix, matrice; pattern, model; mouldiness, mildew, blight.

mould, v. form, shape, model, cast; knead.

mount, v. ascent; bestride.

mourn, v. deplore, lament, regret, grieve, repine, sorrow, bemoan, bewail.

mournful, a. sorrowful, lugubrious, doleful, woful.

mourning, n. sorrow, grief, bereavement; weeds.

mouse, n. murine, rodent; pl. mice, vermin.

mouthpiece, n. embouchure;

spokesman.

movable, a. portable, mobile. *Antonyms*: immovable, fast, immobile.

move, v. transfer; migrate, immigrate, emigrate, remove; impel, propel.

movement, n. motion, locomotion, transference, removal.

moving, a. motive.

mow, v. reap.

mucus, n. phlegm.

mud, n. mire, ooze, muck; silt.

mud bath. illutation.

muddiness, n. turbidness, feculence, obscurity, miriness.

muddle, v. confuse, fuddle, bewilder.

muddled, a. confused, addled.

muddy, a. feculent, turbid, roily; opaque, intransparent, confused, involved, incoherent.

muffle, v. wrap, envelop; deaden, subdue.

muffler, n. scarf, tippet.

mull, v. ruminate, ponder, cogitate.

multitude, n. crowd, throng, host.

mum, a. silent, speechless, dumb, mute.

mumble, v. mutter, maunder, mump.

mumbling, a. muttering, inarticulate, indistinct, incoherent.

mumps, n. parotitis; sullenness, the sulks.

munch, v. craunch.

murder, n. homicide.

murderer, n. homicide.

murderous, a. sanguinary, homicidal, fell.

muriatic acid. hydrochloric acid.

murky, a. lowering, dark.

murmur, v. grumble, complain, repine.

murmur, n. plaint, complaint; purl, babble; undertone.

murmuring, a. complaining, querulous, repining.

muscle, n. brawn, thew; sinew, tendon.

muscular, a. brawny, thewy, sinewy, stalwart.

muse, v. contemplate, ruminate, brood, ponder, mull, reflect.

mushroom, a. ephemeral, transitory.

music, n. melody, symphony, harmony; melodics, harmonics.

musical, a. melodious, harmonious, tuneful, symphonious.

muskmelon, n. cantaloupe.

muster, v. assemble, marshal.

musty, a. mildewed, fusty, mouldy, frowzy, rank, stale.

mute, a. dumb, obmutescent; silent, speechless.

mutilation, n. maim, dismemberment, mangling.

mutinous, a. rebellious, insubordinate, seditious, insurgent, insurrectionary.

mutiny, n. insurrection, rebellion, insubordination, revolt.

mutter, v. maunder.

muttering, a. inarticulate, indistinct, maundering.

mutual, a. reciprocal.

mutuality, n. correlation, reciprocation, interchange.

muzzle, v. restrain, repress.

mysterious, a. inscrutable, cryptic, obscure, unexplainable, enigmatical, unfathomed.

mystery, n. secret, enigma, riddle, intricacy, arcanum.

mystic, a. occult, esoteric, cabalistic, mystical.

mystification, n. bewilderment, perplexity, obfuscation.

mystify, v. bewilder, perplex, obfuscate, befog, nonplus.

mystifying, a. perplexing, confusing, bewildering, mysterious.

myth, n. legend, tradition, fable.

mythical, a. fabulous, legendary, traditional.

L
M

N

nab, v., grab, snatch, seize.

nag, v., plague, tease, twit, hector, torment, scold.

naive, a, artless, innocent, ingenuous, frank.

naked, v. nude, undressed, bare; unexaggerated, uncolored, exact, literal.

nakedness, n. nudity, bareness; exactness, literalness, accuracy.

name, n. appellation, designation, denomination; epithet, title, cognomen.

name, v. entitle, denominate, style, call, christen, dub.

nameless, a. unnamed; undistinguished, inglorious, unknown, obscure; anonymous.

narcotic, n. stupefacient, sedative, anaesthetic, opiate, anodyne.

narrate, v. recount, recite, tell about, relate.

narration, n. narrative, relation, recital, story.

narrative, n. narration, account, portrayal, story, tale.

narrow, a. limited, circumscribed, incapacious, contracted, straitened, cramped.

narrow, v. contract, reduce, constrict, restrict, limit, cramp, confine.

narrowing, n. contraction, reduction, constriction, limitation, circumscription.

narrow-minded, a. illiberal, bigoted, intolerant, narrow, uncatholic.

narrow-mindedness, n. illiberality, bigotry, bias, intolerance, insularity, uncatholicity.

narrowness, n. contractedness, incapaciousness, circumscription.

narrows, n. strait, sound.

nastiness, n. squalor, filthiness, pollution, filth, corruption, dirtiness.

nasty, a. filthy, squalid, foul, polluted, dirty; indecent.

native, a. natal; indigenous, natural, aboriginal, autochthonal, vernacular.

natives, n. pl. aborigines.

natural, a. native, inborn, congenital, innate, characteristic; original.

naturalization, n. denization.

naturalize, v. familiarize, accustom, habituate, acclimatize, adapt, acclimate.

nature, n. creation, universe, cosmos, world; kind, sort.

naughty, a. disobedient, mischievous, perverse, froward, refractory.

nausea, n. seasickness; qualm, squeamishness, queasiness, qualmishness.

nauseate, v. sicken, disgust, revolt; recoil from; abhor, abominate.

nauseous, a. disgusting, nauseating, offensive, sickening, fulsome, distasteful.

nautical, a. naval, marine, maritime, oceanic.

naval, a. nautical, marine, maritime.

navigate, v. sail, cruise; guide, steer, direct; circumnavigate.

near, a. nigh, close, adjacent, neighboring, contiguous, proximate. *Antonyms*: distant, remote, far.

nearness, n. closeness, proximity, propinquity, contiguity, adjacency, imminence.

near-sighted, a. myopic, short-sighted, purblind.

near-sighted person. myope.

neat, a. tidy, orderly, trim, clean, cleanly; tasteful. *Antonyms*: dowdy, slovenly, slatternly, untidy, tawdry, gaudy.

necessary, a. requisite, essential, needed, needful, indispensable; inevitable, unavoidable. *Antonyms*: nonessential, unnecessary, optional, discretional, casual, needless.

necessary, n. requisite, requirement, essential.

necessity, n. requisite, necessary, requirement, essential; exigency, urgency. *Antonyms*: choice, option, contingency, doubtfulness, possibility.

necktie, n. cravat, neckcloth, scarf, tie.

need, n. want, necessity, extremity, strait, exigency, urgency.

need, v. require, lack, want.

needful, a. requisite, necessary, essential, indispensable, required.

needless, a. unnecessary, groundless, unfounded.

needy, a. destitute, indigent, penniless, impecunious.

negation, n. denial, disavowal.

negative, n. denial, refusal. *Antonym*: affirmative.

neglect, n. disregard, omission, negligence, default, dereliction, remissness, oversight.

neglect, v. disregard, slight, overlook, ignore, omit.

negligence, n. neglect, remissness, oversight, heedlessness, laches [Law].

negligent, a. neglectful, heedless, indifferent, slack, remiss, regardless. *Antonyms*: careful, attentive, heedful.

negotiable, a. transferable.

neighborhood, n. vicinity, vicinage, locality, neighbors, venue [Law].

neighboring, a. adjacent, contiguous, neighbor, near.

nerve, n. boldness, audacity, presumption, effrontery,

courage, assurance.

nerve, v. brace, strengthen, fortify, invigorate, energize

nervous, a. excitable, sensitive, timorous.

nestle, v. cuddle, snuggle.

network, n. mesh, interlacement, reticulation; plexus, rete, ganglion.

neutrality, n. indifference.

neutralize, v. counteract, counterbalance, invalidate.

nevertheless, adv. or conj. yet, however, notwithstanding.

new, a. recent, fresh, modern, novel, newfangled, neoteric.

newly, adv. lately, recently, freshly; anew, afresh, again.

news, n. tidings, word, report.

New York. Gotham.

nice, a. fastidious, exacting, particular, punctilious, queasy, finical.

nicety, n. niceness, precision; punctilio, subtlety, fine point.

niche, n. recess, cavity, nook, tabernacle.

nick, n. notch, indentation, dent, score, dint.

nick, v. notch, mar, deface, indent.

nickname, n. sobriquet.

night, n. darkness.

nightly, a. nocturnal.

nightmare, n. incubus, cacodemon, succubus.

nimble, a. agile, sprightly, deft, lively, swift, brisk. *Antonyms*: slow, sluggish, clumsy, dilatory, unready, dull, heavy.

nip, v. pinch; clip, cut off; blast, kill; chill, deaden.

nitrogen, n. azote.

no, n. refusal, denial, negative.

nobility, n. nobleness, high-mindedness, magnanimity, excellence, superiority, dignity.

noble, a. eminent, exalted, magnanimous, superior;

N O

stately, magnificent.

noble, n. nobleman, peer, grandee. *Antonyms*: commoner, proletary, plebeian.

nobody, n. nonentity, jackstraw.

nod, n. bow.

nodding, n. bowing, nutation. — a. annuent, bowing, nutant.

noise, n. sound; racket, clamor, din, outcry, clatter, uproar.

noiseless, a. still, silent, quiet, inaudible.

noisy, a. clamorous, boisterous, vociferous, turbulent, riotous.

nonchalant, a. indifferent, cool, unconcerned, *insouciant*.

nonconformist, n. dissenter, recusant.

nonconformity, n. recusancy, dissent.

nondescript, a. undescribed, unclassifiable.

nonessential, a. unimportant, incidental, adventitious.

nonsense, n. absurdity, twaddle, bosh, fudge, silliness.

nook, n. retreat, corner, recess.

noon, n. meridian, noonday, noontide, midday.

normal, a. natural, regular. *Antonyms*: abnormal, unnatural.

northern, a. boreal, north, arctic, northerly, septentrion.

north star. polestar, lodestar, Cynosure, Polaris.

north wind. Boreas.

nose, n. snout, nozzle, spout, proboscis, muzzle.

nosebleeding, n. epistaxis.

nostalgia, n. homesickness.

notable, a. noticeable, conspicuous, plain, evident; signal, remarkable, famous.

notch, v. nick, score, indent, crenellate.

notched, a. serrated, crenated, incised, emarginated.

note, n. billet; memorandum, minute, record; remark,

comment.

note-book, n. memorandum-book, commonplace book, adversaria, journal, diary.

noted, a. celebrated, renowned, eminent, distinguished, famous.

noteworthy, a. memorable, remarkable.

nothing, n. non-existence, nonentity; begatelle; naught, cipher, zero, null.

nothingness, n. nihility, non-existence, nullity.

notice, n. observation, cognizance, note, heed, attention, regard.

notice, v. see, observe, note, heed, recognize, perceive. *Antonyms*: ignore, connive, skip, neglect, slight, overlook, disregard.

noticeable, a. observable, appreciable, conspicuous, salient, prominent. *Antonyms*: unobservable, inappreciable, inconspicuous.

notify, v. inform, acquaint, tell, apprise, give notice to.

notion, n. conception, idea, concept; opinion, judgment, belief.

notoriety, n. repute [unfavorable], publicity.

notorious, a. talked of, evident, obvious, noted, famous [usually unfavorable].

notwithstanding, conj. despite, nevertheless, however.

noun, n. substantive.

nourish, v. feed, nurture; support; encourage, foster, cherish.

nourishing, a. nutritious.

nourishment, n. nutrition; food, nutriment.

novel, a. new, recent, fresh, unusual, rare, unique, innovative.

novel, n. fiction, romance, story, tale.

novelty, n. newness; change, curiosity, innovation.

novice, n. tyro; probationer, proselyte, convert, novitiate.

now, adv. instantly, immediately, at once, instanter.

now and then. occasionally, at intervals, infrequently, intermittently, sometimes, periodically, once in a while.

noxious, a. injurious, baneful, unwholesome, noisome.

nucleus, n. kernel, core, heart, center.

nudge, v. poke [with the elbow].

nuisance, n. plague, pest, bane, infliction, bore, offense.

null, a. invalid, nugatory.

nullify, v. invalidate, abrogate, cancel, repeal, countermand.

numb, a. deadened, unfeeling, insensible, benumbed.

numb, v. benumb, deaden.

number, v. enumerate, figure up, count, numerate.

number, n. numeral, figure, digit, integer; collection, multitude.

numerous, a. many, plentiful, multitudmous.

numskull, n. dolt, dullard, dunce, lackwit, simpleton.

nunnery, n. convent, cloister, mynchery [ruins].

nuptial, a hymeneal, bridal.

nuptials, n. pl. wedding, marriage, espousal.

nurse, v. suckle; nourish, cherish, foster, succor, foment, encourage.

nurture, n. care, training; food, nourishment.

nurture, v. feed, nourish, nurse; educate, train, school.

nutriment, n. nourishment, food, aliment.

nutrition, n. nourishment, feeding; nutriment, food.

nutritious, a. nourishing,

nutritive. *Antonym*: innutritious.

O

oar, n. paddle, scull, spoon oar.

oath, n. adjuration, pledge, sworn promise; curse, profanity, swearing.

oath-breaking, n. perjury.

obedience, n. compliance, submission, subservience; dutifulness. *Antonyms*: disobedience, incompliance, defiance, revolt, insubordination.

obedient, a. submissive, tractable, deferential, subservient, compliant. *Antonyms*: unsubmissive, intractable, disobedient.

obey, v. comply, submit to, heed, regard, be ruled by.

object, v. disapprove, oppose, demur, contravene, gainsay, except, cavil.

object, n. thing, article; goal, purpose, aim, motive, intent.

objection, n. exception, scruple, demurrer, cavil. *Antonyms*: approval, acquiescence.

objectionable, a. exceptionable, offensive, obnoxious, undesirable, displeasing.

obligation, n. accountableness, responsibility, incumbency, duty, indebtedness; agreement.

obligatory, a. binding, incumbent, imperative, coercive. *Antonyms*: optional, discretional.

oblige, v. constrain, obligate; please, gratify, accommodate; coerce, compel.

obliging, a. complaisant, gracious, accommodating, affable, debonair, deferential, yielding.

obliterate, v. efface, erase, blot out, remove, destroy, expunge.

oblivious, a. unmindful, uncon-

N O

scious, forgetful, heedless, disregardful.

obnoxious, a. subject, liable; offensive, odious, hateful, displeasing.

obscene, a. smutty, lewd, gross, indecent, immodest, indelicate.

obscenity, n. lewdness, smut, ribaldry, indecency, bawdiness, immodesty.

obscure, a. abstruse, vague, recondite, indefinite, ambiguous; humble.

obscure, v. darken, obfuscate, bedim, eclipse; involve, dissemble.

obscurity, n. ambiguity, vagueness; privacy, seclusion, retirement; darkness.

obsolete, a. disused, archaic, antiquated, unfashionable, old-fashioned.

obstacle, n. obstruction, barrier, impediment, hindrance, stumbling-block.

obstetrician, n. midwife, accoucheur.

obstinate, a. incompliant, intractable, mulish, perverse, dogged, contumacious, stubborn. *Antonyms*: amenable, yielding, tractable, submissive, compliant, obedient.

obstruct, v. impede, oppose, retard, barricade, blockade, clog.

obtain, v. gain, get, procure, acquire, win, attain, secure.

obtainable, a. procurable, attainable, accessible. *Antonyms*: unobtainable, unprocurable, unattainable, inaccessible.

obtrusive, a. officious, meddlesome, intrusive, forward. *Antonyms*: inobtrusive, retiring.

obvious, a. plain, evident, palpable, manifest, patent, self-evident.

occult, a. mystic, mystical, abstruse, recondite, secret, unrevealed.

occupant, n. occupier, tenant, holder, incumbent, possessor, lessee.

occupation, n. occupancy, tenure, incumbency; vocation, employment.

occupational, a. vocational.

occupy, v. hold, keep, possess, fill; engage, absorb.

odd, a. unmatched, single, uneven; singular, peculiar, unusual, unique.

oddity, n. oddness, singularity; curiosity, nondescript, marvel, wonder.

odds and ends. remnants, fragments, orts, culls, scraps.

odious, a. detestable, abominable, execrable, offensive, repulsive, hateful, loathsome.

odor, n. smell, aroma, fragrance, scent, redolence, perfume, savor; stink.

odorless, a. inodorous, savorless, scentless.

odorous, a. odoriferous, fragrant, savory, aromatic, balmy, scented.

offend, v. displease, affront, provoke, mortify, exasperate.

offender, n. delinquent, wrong-doer, trespasser, male-factor, culprit, criminal.

offense, n. crime, wrong, sin, outrage, indignity; displeasure.

offensive, a. obnoxious, displeasing, noisome, distasteful, insolent, abusive.

offer, v. tender, proffer, propose, propound, volunteer, bid.

offer, n. tender, proposition, bid, overture, proffer.

offering, n. overture, proposition, bid; sacrifice, oblation; offertory; corban.

offhand, a. extemporaneous, impromptu, improvised,

unstudied.

office, n. duty, function, service, work, charge, trust, business.

officer, n. office-holder, magistrate, dignitary; incumbent.

officially, adv. ex-officio.

offset, n. set-off, counterbalance, equivalent. —v. counterbalance, counterpoise.

offshoot, n. scion, branch.

offspring, n. children, issue, progeny, posterity, descendants.

often, adv. frequently, repeatedly, oftentimes, ofttimes. *Antonyms*: seldom, infrequently.

oil, v. lubricate.

oily, a. unctuous, oleaginous, emulsive, lubricous; glib, fluent, plausible.

ointment, n. unguent, embrocation, salve.

old, a. aged, elderly, senescent, decrepit, venerable, patriarchal.

old age. senility, dotage, superannuation, decrepitude.

old-fashioned, a. antiquated, archaic, *passe*, antique, obsolete.

old maid. spinster.

old man. veteran, patriarch, Nestor, elder, oldster.

old-time. a. late, former, quondam.

old woman. beldame, crone, gammer; witch, hag, harridan.

omen, n. foretoken, sign, augury, portent, presage, prognostic, auspice.

ominous, a. portentous, monitory, premonitory, threatening.

omission, n. default, oversight, neglect, pretermission, omittance, nonperformance.

omit, v. leave out, skip, pretermit, disregard, neglect, overlook, ignore, delete.

omittance, n. omission, forbearance, default, neglect, over-

sight.

one, n. unit.

oneness, n. unity, singleness, individuality, unanimity.

onerous, a. laborious, difficult, arduous.

one-sided, a. unilateral; partial, unfair, inequitable, *ex parte*.

onion, n. scallion, eschallot, shallot.

onlooker, n. looker-on, bystander, spectator, beholder, witness, eye-witness.

on the sly. sly, covertly, furtively, clandestinely, surreptitiously, secretly.

ooze, v. filter, exude, percolate, transude, seep.

opaque, a. intransparent; obscure, unintelligible.

open, a. accessible, clear, unobstructed, unrestricted; ajar, unlocked.

open, v. spread, expand, unfold, evolve; reveal, disclose.

opening, a. beginning, introductory, initiatory, preliminary.

openly, adv. publicly, unreservedly, candidly.

open-mouthed, a. gaping, yawning; greedy, clamorous, ravenous, rapacious, eager.

opinion, n. belief, judgment, impression; decision, ruling, verdict, sentence.

opponent, n. adversary, antagonist, rival, competitor.

opportune, a. timely, seasonable, apropos, felicitous, appropriate.

oppose, v. combat, resist, confront, withstand, oppugn, impugn. *Antonyms*: yield, acquiesce, concur, agree.

opposer, n. opponent, antagonist.

opposing, a. conflicting, antagonistic, contending, opposite, adverse.

opposite, a. contrary, adverse,

N O

diametrical, antagonistic,
inverse, reverse.

opposition, n. resistance,
counteraction, hostility, repulse,
rebuff, recalcitration.

oppress, v. burden, overwhelm,
aggrieve, tyrannize, persecute,
overpower.

oppression, n. tyranny, persecu-
tion, extortion, hardship,
severity.

oppressive, a. rigorous, tyrannical, extortionate, burdensome.

oppressor, n. tyrant, persecutor,
extortioner.

option, n. choice, preference,
election, discretion, alternative.
antonyms: constraint, coercion,
compulsion.

optional, a. discretional, elective.
Antonyms: compulsory,
coercive, obligatory.

oral, a. spoken, verbal, parole,
vocal, nuncupative.

oration, n. declamation, rhetoric.

ordeal, n. crucible.

order, n. mandate, command,
precept, direction, decree,
decretal.

order, v. methodize, systematize,
regulate; bid, command,
dictate, enjoin.

ordering, n. distribution, disposition, regulation.

orderly, a. systematic, methodical, well-regulated, regular;
peaceable.

ordinary, a. common, regular,
conventional, commonplace,
mediocre, average, usual.

organic, a. constitutional, vital,
fundamental, essential,
inherent, instrumental.

organization, n. organism;
formation, construction,
making.

organize, v. arrange, systematize, form.

origin, n. source, beginning,
derivation, rise, origination.

original, a. first, primeval,
aboriginal, primitive, arche-
typal, primordial. *Antonyms*:
derivative, copied.

original, n. origin, archetype,
prototype, model, pattern.

ornament, n. decoration,
embellishment, adornment,
garniture, ornamentation.

ornament, v. decorate, embellish, garnish, bedeck, grace,
beautify.

ornamentation, n. adornment,
garniture, embellishment.

ornate, a. ornamented, decorated, embellished, florid,
adorned.

orthodox, a. *Antonym*: heterodox.

oscillate, v. fluctuate, vacillate.

ostentatious, a. showy, pompous, spectacular, gaudy,
pretentious.

oust, v. eject, evict, dispossess,
dislodge, remove, displace,
expel, depose.

out, adv. away, absent, abroad;
outright, aloud, audibly.

out and out. wholly, completely,
openly. —a. absolute, unqualified, undisguised.

outbreak, n. eruption, outburst,
uprising.

outburst, n. eruption, outbreak,
paroxysm, access, ebullition.

outcast, n. pariah, castaway,
reprobate.

outcome, n. consequence,
outgrowth, result, issue,
upshot, eventuation.

outdo, v. excel, surpass, outvie,
outstrip, exceed.

outer, a. external, exterior.

outermost, a. extreme, uttermost, utmost.

outfit, n. equipment.

outflow, n. effusion, outpouring.

outlandish, a. grotesque,
bizarre, barbarous, unconventional, freakish.

outlast, v. outwear, survive.

outlaw, n. bandit, desperado. — v. proscribe.

outlay, n. expenditure, disbursement.

outlet, n. egress, vent, exit.

outline, n. contour, circumference, periphery, profile, sketch, draught, scenario.

outlive, n. survive.

outlook, n. prospect, view, vista; watch-tower; foresight.

outlying, a. remote, detached, distant, frontier.

out of joint. unhinged, dislocated.

out of order. disordered, disarranged, jumbled, chaotic, disorganized.

out of place. misplaced; improper, unbecoming.

out of reach. inaccessible, unattainable.

outrage, n. indignity, affront, insult, assault.

outrageous, a. atrocious, nefarious, wanton, flagrant, unwarrantable, furious, monstrous, villainous.

outright, adv. unconditionally, utterly.

outside, n. exterior.

outside, a. external.

outskirt, n. edge, border, purlieu, suburb, frontier.

outspoken, a. unreserved, frank, explicit, blunt, ingenuous.

outward, a. external, exterior, outer, superficial, surface, extrinsic.

outweigh, v. overweigh, overbalance, preponderate.

outweighing, n. preponderance, preponderation. —a. preponderant.

outwit, v. circumvent, outgeneral, defeat.

oval, a. elliptical.

over, adv. across, crosswise, athwart, transversely.

overbearing, a. haughty, arrogant, dictatorial, magisterial, lordly, dogmatical.

overcharge, n. extortion.

overcoat, n. great coat, topcoat, ulster, raglan, inverness, surtout, paletot.

overcome, v. surmount, conquer, subdue, master, vanquish, overpower, subjugate.

overcoming, a. conquering, overmastering, overwhelming, irresistible.

overconfident, a. rash, presumptuous, incautious.

overdo, v. overwork, overtask, overtax, exhaust; exaggerate.

overeat, v. gorge, glut, satiate.

overfeed, v. surfeit, stuff, satiate, gorge, pamper.

overfill, v. surcharge.

overflow, n. deluge, flood, inundation; exuberance, superabundance, profusion.

overflow, v. inundate, deluge, engulf.

overflowing, n. overflow, inundation; exuberance, copiousness, superabundance.

overhang, n. projection.

overhead, adv. aloft, above.

overlapping, a. obvolute, obvoluted, imbricate, imbricated. —n. imbrication.

overlook,— v. supervise, oversee; inspect, overhaul, examine, neglect, disregard.

overpower, v. vanquish, subdue, conquer, overcome, defeat, crush, overwhelm.

overpowering, a. overwhelming, conquering, irresistible, overmastering.

overpowering, n. vanquishment, conquering, defeat, subjugation, overthrow.

override, v. trample upon, supersede, annul, abrogate.

overrule, v. annul, rescind, abrogate, revoke, supersede,

N
O

set aside.

overruling, a. predominant, prevailing, controlling.

overruling, n. abrogation, cancellation, rescission.

overrun, v. infringe, invade.

oversee, v. superintend, supervise.

overseer, n. superintendent, supervisor, inspector, taskmaster, foreman, monitor.

oversight, n. superintendence, supervision, care, inspection, surveillance, control.

overstate, v. exaggerate.

overstep, v. exceed, trespass, infringe, intrench, encroach.

oversupply, n. excess, superabundance, surfeit, glut, repletion.

overt, a. public, apparent, unconcealed, patent.

overthrow, v. upset, overturn; demolish, prostrate, subvert, defeat.

overthrow, n. overthrowing, demolition, subversion, undoing, reversal, prostration.

overvalue, v. overrate, overestimate, overprize.

overweight, n. preponderance.

overwhelm, v. overflow, submerge, ingulf, drown, overpower, crush.

overwhelming, a. irresistible, overpowering.

owing, n. indebtedness.

owing, a. due, payable, unpaid; ascribable, traceable, imputable.

own, v. admit, acknowledge, confess, allow, concede, grant; possess. *Antonyms*: disown, deny.

owner, n. proprietor.

ownership, n. proprietorship, claim, title.

P

pacifiable, a. placable, appeasable, conciliable.

pacify, v. appease, quiet, calm, mollify, propitiate, transquilize.

pack, n. bundle, bale, parcel, package; multitude, number.

pack, v. compress, stow, truss; load, encumber.

package, n. bundle, packet, bale, parcel, pack, budget.

pact, n. compact, covenant, concordat.

pad, n. cushion, bolster; saddle-cloth, housing.

page, n. footboy, buttons; folio.

page number. folio.

pail, n. bucket; piggin.

pain, v. hurt, torture, rack; distress, grieve, afflict, aggrieve.

pain, n. punishment, penalty; suffering, ache, smart. *Antonyms*: ease, comfort, relief, solace.

painful, a. distressing, agonizing, excruciating, dolorous, racking.

painstaking, a. diligent, particular, precise, scrupulous. *Antonyms*: slovenly, negligent.

paint, n. pigment; cosmetic, rouge.

paint, v. delineate, portray, lim, depict, picture, sketch.

pair, n. two, brace, couple, span, team, yoke.

pal, n. partner, mate, confederate, associate, accomplice.

palace, n. mansion, castle, pretorium.

pale, a. pallid, wan, colorless, ghastly, blanched, cadaverous. *Antonyms*: ruddy, buxom, flushed, blowzed.

paleness, n. pallidness, pallor, wanness, colorlessness, etiolation.

palliate, v. excuse, apologize for,

gloss over, extenuate; moderate.

palliation, n. extenuation, glossing over, excuse, apology; moderation.

pamper, v. overfeed, feed luxuriously; indulge, gratify, spoil.

pamphlet, n. brochure, booklet, tract.

pan, n. basin, chafer.

pancake, n. griddlecake, flapjack, fritter.

pander, n. bawd, pimp, procurer, whoremonger.

panic, n. consternation, terror, alarm.

panic-stricken, a. panic-struck, alarmed, dismayed, terrified, appalled.

pant, n. gasp, gasping.

pant, v. gasp; long, hunger, yearn, thirst.

panther, n. puma, cougar, jaguar.

panting, n. anhelation, gasping; longing, hunger, desire, thirst.

paper, n. document; essay, dissertation, article; journal, newspaper.

par, n. equality, equivalence.

parade, n. pomp, display, ostentation, show; procession, pageant. —v. display, flaunt, show off.

paradise, n. garden of Eden; Elysium; Heaven.

parallel, a. like, similar, equal, analogous.

paralysis, n. palsy.

paralyze, v. benumb, deaden, stun, unnerve.

paraphernalia, n. equipments, accouterments, ornaments.

parasite, n. hanger-on, toady, sycophant, fawner.

parcel, n. bundle, package; collection, lot; tract, plot, piece.

pardon, n. absolution, remission, amnesty, forgiveness, condonation. *Antonyms*: retribution, vengeance, retaliation, implacability, penalty.

pardon, v. absolve, remit, forgive, condone.

pardonable, a. venial, excusable. *Antonyms*: unpardonable, inexcusable.

pare, v. peel.

parentage, n. extraction, descent, pedigree, ancestry, family, birth, lineage.

parsonage, n. rectory; manse; living, benefice.

part, n. portion, fraction, division, piece, constituent, installment.

part, v. divide, sever, disunite, dissever, sunder, dissociate.

partake, v. share, participate in.

partaking, n. participation.

parted, a. separated, divided, severed, disunited, isolated, detached.

partial, a. warped, biased, prejudiced; imperfect, incomplete.

partiality, n. bias, favoritism; predilection, inclination, fondness.

particular, a. special, especial, specific; minute, precise, detailed. *Antonyms*: indiscriminate, slatternly, promiscuous, general.

particular, n. detail.

parting, a. farewell, valedictory.

parting, n. division, disunion, severance, separation; leave-taking, farewell.

partition, n. division, distribution, apportionment, allotment.

partner, n. copartner, coadjustor; colleague, associate, confederate.

parts, n. pl. talents, gifts, faculties, endowments; regions.

party, n. clique, faction, set, circle, ring, cabal.

pass, v. elapse, lapse; transmit, deliver, hand; go, move.

P
R

pass, n. passageway, defile, passage; thrust, passado, lunge.

passable, a. navigable, traversable, penetrable; tolerable, mediocre. *Antonyms*: impassable, impervious, impenetrable.

passage, n. transit; fare; clause, sentence, paragraph; enactment.

passing, a. exceeding, surpassing; transient, momentary, transitory.

passion, n. suffering, pain, agony; emotion, ardor, feeling.

passionate, a. irascible, quick-tempered, choleric, excitable.

passionless, a. impassive, phlegmatic, stoical, unemotional, dispassionate, apathetic.

passive, a. inactive, quiet, inert, receptive, quiescent; patient.

passport, n. pass, safe-conduct; sea letter.

password, n. countersign; watchword, sesame.

past, a. bygone, elapsed; preterite, preterit.

pastime, n. amusement, sport, diversion, recreation, divertisement, entertainment.

patch, n. clout; tract, plot, parcel. —v. mend, repair, vamp, revamp.

patent, a. evident, obvious, manifest, apparent.

path, n. footway, runway, course, passage, route, avenue.

pathetic, a. plaintive, pitiable, piteous, mournful, sad.

patience, n. long-suffering, fortitude, resignation, submission, sufferance; indulgence. *Antonyms*: impatience, restiveness, resistance.

patient, a. uncomplaining, submissive, resigned, passive, long-suffering, indulgent; diligent.

patron, n. supporter, promoter, defender, guardian, benefactor; customer.

pattern, n. model, exemplar, original, prototype, archetype; specimen.

pause, n. intermission, suspension, break; hesitation; break.

pause, v. stop, hesitate, desist, waver, intermit.

pawn, v. pledge, impawn.

pay, v. compensate, remunerate, recompense, requite, indemnify, reward. *Antonyms*: repudiate, protest, bilk, defraud.

payable, a. due, unpaid, outstanding; remunerable.

pay back. reimburse, refund, restore, repay, requite.

paying, a. profitable, lucrative, gainful, remunerative.

payment, n. paying, compensation, remuneration, liquidation, discharge, reparation. *Antonyms*: nonpayment, protest, repudiation, default.

peace, n. concord, amity, harmony; tranquility, quietness.

peaceable, a. amicable, inoffensive; tranquil, serene, undisturbed. *Antonyms*: bellicose, belligerent, contentious, rebellious, pugnacious.

peaceably, adv. amicably.

peaceful, a. amicable, tranquil, peaceable, halcyon.

peacemaker, n. mediator, intercessor, pacificator, make-peace, arbitrator, intermediary.

peacemaking, a. pacificatory, conciliatory, intercessory, propitiatory, mediatorial.

peace-offering, n. atonement, reparation, amends.

peak, n. apex, pinnacle, summit, crest, spire, point.

peaked, a. pointed; sickly, thin,

pale, emaciated.

peculation, n. embezzlement.

peculiar, a. individual, personal, particular; singular, eccentric, erratic.

peculiarity, n. characteristic, trait, attribute, idiosyncrasy, eccentricity, oddness.

peddle, v. hawk, vend.

pedigree, n. lineage, ancestry, descent, extraction, genealogy.

peek, v. peep.

peel, n. rind, skin. —v. pare, decorticate. *Antonym:* pulp.

peep, v. chirp, cheep, pule; peer, peek, pry.

peevish, a. petulant, querulous, captious, spleeny, fretful, impatient, cross.

penalty, n. punishment, retribution; forfeiture, fine.

pending, a. undecided, unsettled. —prep. during.

penetrable, a. permeable, pervious. *Antonym:* impenetrable.

penetrate, v. pierce, perforate; comprehend, understand; explore;interpenetrate.

penetration, n. piercing, perforation; acuteness, discernment, sharpness; interpenetration.

penitence, n. contrition, repentance, remorse, compunction. *Antonym:* impenitence.

penitentiary, n. prison.

penmanship, n. writing, calligraphy, pencraft, chirography.

penniless, a. impecunious, indigent, destitute.

pensive, a. meditative, dreamy, lackadaisical, introspective, thoughtful, sad, grave.

people, n. folks; inhabitants, population; citizens; populace, commonalty.

people, v. populate, colonize.

peppery, a. pungent; irascible, hot-tempered, choleric.

perceive, v. see, discern,

observe; apprehend, comprehend, understand.

perception, n. cognizance, discernment; sensation, feeling. *Antonym:* imperception.

perchance, adv. perhaps, peradventure, possibly, maybe.

percolate, v. ooze, strain, filter, transude.

perfect, a. consummate, faultless, flawless, exquisite, inviolate, impeccable.

perfect, v. consummate, elaborate, retouch, develop.

perforate, v. bore through, pierce, penetrate, drill.

perform, v. accomplish, execute, do.

performance, n. execution, achievement, accomplishment; trick, feat, exploit.

perfume, n. fragrance, aroma, redolence, sachet, incense.

perhaps, adv. perchance, peradventure, possibly, haply.

perilous, a. dangerous, hazardous, imperiled, unsafe.

period, n. interval.

perishable, a. destructible, impermanent, mortal. *Antonyms:* imperishable, permanent.

perjury, n. oath-breaking.

permanent, a. stable, immutable, durable, imperishable, unchangeable. *Antonyms:* impermanent, evanescent, ephemeral, transient.

permeable, a. penetrable, pervious, pervadible. *Antonym:* impermeable.

permission, n. consent, allowance, license, leave, permit, authorization. *Antonyms:* refusal, denial, embargo, injunction, veto.

permit, v. allow, consent to, suffer, tolerate, let, authorize. *Antonyms:* refuse, disallow,

P
R

prohibit, resist.

permit, n. warrant, license, leave, permission.

perpendicular, a. upright, vertical. *Antonyms*: horizontal, oblique.

perplex, v. bewilder, puzzle, pose, confuse, mystify, distract.

perplexity, n. bewilderment, distraction, confusion, disconcertion, doubt, uncertainty.

persecute, v. harass, oppress, tyrannize, torment.

perseverance, n. persistence, diligence, constancy.

persevere, v. persist, continue.

persevering, a. persistent, steadfast, untiring, indefatigable,pertinacious, unremitting; indomitable. *Antonyms*: inconstant, fickle, unsteadfast.

persist, v. persevere.

persistency, n. perseverance, doggedness, pertinacity, obstinacy, contumacy, insistence.

persistent, a. contumacious, persevering, insistent, pertinacious, tenacious.

personality, n. individuality; reflection, stricture, animadversion, criticism.

personally, adv. individually.

personate, v. impersonate.

perspire, v. sweat.

persuade, v. induce.

persuasion, n. inducement, suasion, incitement; creed, belief. *Antonyms*: dissuasion, coercion, constraint.

pertain, v. appertain.

pertinence, n. relevancy, applicability, propriety. *Antonyms*: impertinence, irrelevance.

pertinent, a. relevant, apposite, applicable, proper. *Antonyms*: impertinent, irrelevant.

perturb, v. disquiet, excite, disturb, agitate, discompose, distress.

perturbed, a. excited, distressed, worried, discomposed, agitated.

perusal, n. reading.

perverse, a. perverted, misdirected, erring, depraved, vitiated; intractable.

perversion, n. debasement, vitiation, corruption, falsification.

pervert, v. lead astray, corrupt, debase, vitiate; misuse.

pessimistic, a. gloomy, foreboding, hopeless.

pest, n. pestilence, plague, scourge; curse, nuisance, annoyance.

pester, v. plague, badger, harass, harry, tease, torment.

pestilence, n. plague, scourge, fatal epidemic.

pet, n. fondling, darling, favorite.

pet, v. humor, coddle, fondle, cosset, caress, indulge.

petition, n. entreaty, supplication, prayer.

petitioner, n. suppliant, applicant, solicitor.

petrify, v. lapidify, fossilize.

petty, a. small, insignificant, trivial, trifling.

phantom, n. spectre, apparition, ghost.

pharmacist, n. apothecary, druggist, pharmaceutist.

phase, n. aspect, appearance.

phase, v. disconcert, disturb, discompose, affect.

phlegmatic, a. unemotional, cold, dull, sluggish.

photograph, n. heliograph.

photography, n. heliography.

phrase, n. idiom, diction, phraseology.

physic, n. medicine; cathartic, purge, purgative.

physic, v. purge.

physical, a. material, bodily.
physical structure. physique.
piano, n. pianoforte.
pick, v. pluck; pick out, select, choose, cull, glean.
picket, n. stake, pale, paling; sentry, guard, watchman, sentinel.
pickle, n. brine; dilemma, predicament, plight; marinade.
picture, v. delineate, sketch, draw, represent, depict.
picture, n. drawing, painting, engraving, half-tone photograph, print.
piddling, a. trifling, inconsiderable, insignificant, piffling, inconsequential.
piece, n. scrap, swatch, clout, chunk, slice, clipping.
pier, n. wharf, dock, jetty, buttress.
pierce, v. transfix, stab, impale, gore; penetrate.
piercing, a. penetrating, keen, sharp, thrilling, poignant.
piety, n. sanctity, godliness, holiness.
pigheaded, a. stubborn, perverse.
pig pen, n. sty, pigsty, piggery.
pile, n. heap, stack, accumulation.
pilfer, v. filch, purloin.
pilgrim, n. wayfarer, traveler, sojourner, crusader.
pilgrimage, n. journey, expedition, sojourn, crusade.
pillage, n. devastation, plundering, rapine, spoliation; spoil.
pillar, n. column, pier, shaft, post.
pillow, n. cushion, bolster.
pilot, n. steersman, helmsman; director, guide, conductor.
pimple, n. eruption, papule, pustule.
pinch, v. squeeze, compress, twinge, tweak, gripe, nip.
pinch, v. arrest.
pine, v. droop, languish, waste; yearn, long. —n. deal.
pious, a. religious, devout, saintly, righteous, reverent. *Antonym*: impious.
pipe, n. tube, conduit, aqueduct.
piquancy, n. pungency, sharpness, spiciness; raciness, liveliness.
pit, n. hollow, hole, excavation, cavity; abyss.
pitch, n. slope, declivity, slant.
pitch, v. cast, hurl, toss, throw, fling, heave, chuck.
pitfall, n. snare, trap, pit.
pitiful, a. tender-hearted, compassionate, merciful, lenient, ruthful, clement.
pittance, n. dole.
pity, n. compassion, mercy, ruth, commiseration, condolence, sympathy.
pity, v. have pity for, condole with, commiserate.
place, n. position, site, situation, locality; rendezvous.
place, v. deposit, locate, dispose, put, set, station.
place between. interpose.
plague, n. pestilence.
plague, v. hector, tantalize, tease, badger, pester.
plain, a. evident, manifest, explicit, obvious, unmistakable, apparent. *Antonyms*: ambiguous, equivocal, indistinct, indecipherable, elaborate, luxurious.
plain, adv. plainly, distinctly, bluntly, candidly, explicitly.
plain-spoken, a. frank, candid, unreserved, outspoken.
plaintiff, n. complainant.
plan, v. scheme, project, intend, devise, contrive, design, purpose.
plant, v. sow; settle; establish.
plastic, a. formative, creative; impressible, fictile.
platform, n. rostrum, stage, dais.
plausible, a. specious; glib,

P
R

fluent, oily, smooth-tongued.
Antonym: implausible.

play, v. frolic, sport, gambol,
disport, frisk, skip.

play, n. game, pastime, amusement, recreation, diversion,
sport.

playful, a. sportive, frolicsome,
prankish, jocular, sprightly.

plaything, n. bauble, gimcrack,
toy.

play-writer, n. playwright,
dramatist.

plead, v. reason, argue; apologize, defend, advocate,
intercede.

pleader, n. intercessor, defender,
advocate.

pleasant, a. agreeable, genial,
congenial, affable, amiable,
enjoyable. *Antonyms*: unpleasant, disagreeable, uncongenial,
repellent.

pleasantry, n. badinage, banter,
raillery, witticism, joke, jest.

please, v. rejoice, gladden,
delight, gratify, cheer; elate.

pleasing, a. pleasant, delightful,
gratifying, delectable, gracious,
winning.

pleasure, n. gratification,
enjoyment, happiness, delectation, delight; amusement.
Antonym: displeasure.

pledge, n. gage, security,
hostage, guarantee.

pledge, v. pawn, impawn,
hypothecate, plight.

plentiful, a. abundant, bounteous, ample, galore, copious,
full. *Antonyms*: scarce,
deficient, inadequate, insufficient, scant.

plenty, n. abundance, sufficiency,
plenitude.

pliability, n. flexibility, suppleness, pliancy, limberness,
ductility, malleability. *Antonyms*:
inflexibility, rigidity.

pliable, a. flexible, pliant, supple,

limber, lithesome, lithe.
Antonyms: impliable, inflexible.

plight, n. condition, state,
dilemma, predicament,
situation, scrape.

plight, v. pawn, pledge; promise,
betroth.

plot, v. conspire, intrigue, cabal,
complot, machinate, scheme.

pluck, v. pull, draw; pick, gather.

plug, n. stopper, stopple, bung,
tampoon, spile.

plump, a. fleshy, bouncing,
chubby, fat, portly, stout.

plunder, n. booty, spoil, loot,
pillage, robbery.

plunge, v. souse, immerse,
submerge, dip, douse; dive,
pitch.

pocket-book, n. purse, wallet.

poem, n. sonnet, ballad, verse,
distich, lyric.

poetry, n. verse, rhyme, poems,
poesy, orthometry. *Antonym*:
prose.

poignant, a. pricking, piercing,
pungent.

point, v. aim, level, direct; show,
indicate, designate.

pointed, a. sharp, picked,
peaked, tapering, conical.
Antonyms: pointless, dull.

pointer, n. indicator, index.

poise, n. equipoise, balance,
equilibrium.

poise, v. balance, librate.

poison, n. venom, virus, toxine,
toxicant, irritant, taint.

poisonous, a. toxic, toxical,
venomous, noxious, baneful.
Antonyms: nonpoisonous,
antidotal.

poke, v. stir up, excite; punch,
thrust; gore, hook; grope.

poke fun at. ridicule, deride.

poky, a. slow, dull, tiresome,
tedious, prosaic.

polish, n. gloss, luster, sheen,
glaze, glazing.

polite, a. courtly, civil, courteous,

suave, urbane, deferential.

politeness, n. courtliness, courtesy, civility, suavity, urbanity.

politic, a. political; judicious, discreet, shrewd, astute; diplomatic.

politician, n. statesman, statist; demagogue.

pollute, v. defile, contaminate, corrupt, infect, debase, vitiate.

pompous, a. stately; imposing, august; pretentious, grandiose.

pond, n. lake [small]; lagoon.

ponder, v. meditate, reflect, ruminate, think, muse.

ponderous, a. massive, heavy, cumbersome; dull, spiritless; momentous, important.

poor, a. indigent, impecunious, needy, poverty-stricken, straitened, necessitous.

poorhouse, n. almshouse, infirmary.

pope, n. bishop of Rome, pontiff.

populace, n. commonalty, proletariat, rabble.

popular, a. approved.

popularity, n. favor, esteem, approbation, celebrity.

population, n. inhabitants.

porch, n. piazza, stoop, veranda.

porous, a. permeable, penetrable, pervious, percolable. *Antonyms*: imporous, compact.

port, n. harbor, haven; port-hole, embrasure; larboard.

portion, n. part, section, piece; allotment, quota, share.

portly, a. dignified, imposing, stately, commanding; fleshy, obese.

portray, v. delineate, depict, picture, draw, sketch, paint, describe.

position, n. situation, post; attitude, posture; situation, place.

positive, a. definite, precise, unequivocal, explicit, categori-

cal, unmistakable.

posse, n. crowd, throng, multitude.

possess, v. own; have, hold, occupy, seize, take, appropriate.

possession, n. ownership, occupancy, tenure, fruition, retention, occupation.

possessor, n. owner, proprietor; occupant, tenant, holder.

possibility, n. potentiality, contingency. *Antonym*: impossibility.

possible, a. potential, *in posse,* contingent, practicable. *Antonym*: impossible.

possibly, adv. maybe, perhaps, perchance, peradventure, haply.

post, n. column, pillar, pilaster; position, seat, station.

post, v. placard, announce; mail.

posted, a. informed.

poster, n. placard, bulletin, bill.

posterior, a. later, subsequent, ensuing, succeeding; hinder, rear.

post-mortem, n. autopsy, necropsy.

postpone, v. defer, delay, put off, procrastinate, adjourn, prorogue.

postponement, n. deferring, delay, procrastination.

posture, n. attitude.

potent, a. powerful, forcible, cogent, effective, strong.

pound, v. beat; comminute, pulverize, bray, triturate.

pour, v. decant.

poverty, n. penury, indigence, need, destitution, privation, neediness.

powder, n. dust, pulverulence; cosmetic, rouge.

power, n. potency, might, cogency, efficacy, force.

powerful, a. mighty, potent, drastic, efficacious, intense,

P
R

strong.
powerless, a. impotent.
practicability, n. feasibility.
practical, a. pragmatical.
Antonyms: impractical,
Utopian, chimerical.
practice, n. custom, usage,
habit; exercise, application,
drill, rehearsal.
practice, v. exercise, apply, do,
train, drill, rehearse.
praise, n. commendation,
laudation, approbation,
encomium. *Antonyms*: condemnation, dispraise, disapprobation, disparagement.
praise, v. laud, extol, commend,
eulogize, panegyrize, applaud.
Antonyms: condemn, de-
nounce, disparage, deprecate,
criticize.
praiseworthy, a. laudable,
commendable. *Antonyms*:
illaudable, unpraiseworthy,
indign.
prance, v. cavort.
prank, n. trick, antic, frolic, caper.
prankish, a. playful, frolicsome,
sportive, mischievous, gamesome.
pray, v. invoke, supplicate,
entreat, implore, beg, petition,
intercede.
prayer, n. invocation, orison,
collect, suffrage, supplication.
preach, v. exhort.
preacher, n. homilist, exhorter,
predicant, pulpiteer; missionary, evangelist, revivalist.
preaching, n. sermon, homily,
exhortation.
precarious, a. uncertain,
insecure, unassured, doubtful.
preceding, a. foregoing.
precept, n. commandment,
maxim, rule, adage, behest,
injunction.
precious, a. costly, expensive;
valuable; dear, beloved,
adored, idolized.

precise, a. exact; formal,
punctilious, particular, prim,
prudish.
precision, n. exactness, accuracy; formalness, prudery.
predatory, a. predacious,
plundering.
predestination, n. foreordina-
tion, foreordainment.
predict, v. prophesy, foretell,
prognosticate, forebode,
portend.
prediction, n. prophecy, soothsaying, divination, augury,
prognostication.
predominant, a. dominant,
overruling, ascendant, supreme.
preface, n. prologue, prelude.
prejudice, n. prejudgment, bias;
harm, mischief, detriment.
preposterous, a. absurd,
ridiculous, irrational,
inconsistent,foolish.
present, n. gift, donation,
largess, gratuity, douceur.
preserve, v. conserve. —n.
compote.
press, n. pressure, urgency.
press, v. squeeze, crowd,
compress; urge, crowd;
express.
pressing, a. urgent, importunate,
exigent.
pretend, v. claim; simulate, feign,
affect.
pretense, n. assumption, claim,
pretension; simulation, affectation; pretext.
pretty, a. comely, fair; personable, considerable. *Antonyms*:
plain, homely, uncomely, ugly.
prevent, v. thwart, hinder,
obstruct, preclude, obviate,
forestall.
prevention, n. obstruction,
thwarting, interruption, hindrance, preclusion.
preventive, a. deterrent, prophy-
lactic, obviating. —n. prophy-

lactic.

previous, a. former, foregoing, antecedent, prior, anterior.

prey, n. spoil, loot, plunder, booty; victim, quarry.

prick, v. puncture, pierce, perforate; goad, spur, incite; sting.

pride, n. self-esteem, self-respect; haughtiness, arrogance, hauteur, superciliousness. *antonyms*: humility, shame, self-abasement, modesty, lowliness.

priestly, a. sacerdotal.

prim, a. formal, precise, demure, prudish.

primitive, a. pristine, primordial, primeval, primal; antique.

principal, a. leading, chief, cardinal, paramount, main, foremost.

printing, n. typography; [for the blind] Braille.

prior, a. previous, former, antedecent, anterior.

priority, n. antecedence, anteriority, precedence.

prison, n. penitentiary, bridewell, jail, house of correction, clink, bastille. —v. imprison, incarcerate.

privacy, n. retirement, seclusion; retreat, solitude, concealment.

private, a. personal, individual; secret, secluded, covert, sequestered.

privation, n. deprivation, degradation; destitution, poverty, need; absence.

privilege, n. liberty, right, franchise, prerogative, immunity, advantage.

prize, v. value, esteem.

prize-fighter, n. pugilist.

probability, n. likelihood, verisimilitude, credibleness.

probable, a. likely, credible, reasonable.

probe, v. investigate, examine.

procession, n. parade, cavalcade, cortege, train, retinue, file.

procure, v. get, obtain, acquire.

prodigal, a. wasteful, extravagant, lavish, profuse.

profane, v. violate, desecrate; debase, prostitute, defile.

profane, a. unconsecrated, secular; unsanctified, unholy; blasphemous.

profess, v. acknowledge, avow, admit; claim, pretend.

profession, n. acknowledgement, avowal; vocation, businesscalling.

proficient, a. expert, adept, skilled.

profit, n. gain, emolument, dividend.

profitable, a. remunerative, lucrative, gainful, beneficial.

profound, a. abysmal, deep; abstruse, recondite. *Antonym*: shallow.

progress, n. progression, advancement, improvement.

prominent, a. protuberant; conspicuous, salient; eminent, distinguished.

promiscuous, a. indiscriminate.

promise, n. pledge, word, parole, plight, betrothal, troth.

promise, v. pledge, covenant, assure, plight.

promote, v. advance, forward; exalt, elevate, raise.

promotion, n. preferment, exaltation, advancement, furtherance.

prompt, a. quick, expeditious, ready; punctual, timely.

pronunciation, n. orthoepy; utterance, articulation, enunciation.

proof, n. verification, corroboration, attestation, certification, confirmation. *Antonyms*: disproof, refutation.

proper, a. appropriate, meet,

P
R

suitable, seemly, condign, appertinent. *Antonyms*: improper, inappropriate, unsuitable.

property, n. attribute, trait; estate, wealth, chattels, goods.

prophecy, n. prediction, foretelling, divination, soothsaying, prognostication.

prophet, n. prognosticator, vaticinator, soothsayer, diviner, oracle, seer.

prosperity, n. weal, success, well-being. *Antonyms*: adversity, reverses, disaster.

prostitute, n. harlot, whore, strumpet, courtesan.

prostitution, n. harlotry, social evil, whoredom; perversion, misuse, profanation.

protect, v. shield, defend, guard, fortify, screen, shelter, befriend.

protection, n. defense, shield, shelter, tutelage, refuge.

protector, n. defender, guardian, patron.

proud, a. arrogant, vain, haughty, overbearing, supercilious.

provable, a. demonstrable.

prove, n. verify, corroborate, substantiate, demonstrate. *Antonyms*: disprove, refute.

provide, v. supply, furnish; stipulate, covenant, agree.

provider, n. furnisher, caterer, purveyor, provisor.

provoke, n. incite, stimulate, instigate, rouse; exasperate, displease.

prudence, n. discretion, caution.

prudent, a. discreet, cautious, circumspect, provident. *Antonyms*: imprudent, incautious.

publish, v. promulgate, proclaim, circulate, blazon, announce. *Antonyms*: suppress, withhold.

puddle, n. pool, plashet, plash.

puke, v. vomit.

pull, v. draw, tug, haul, tow, drag.

pulverize, v. triturate, comminute, levigate, bray.

pump, v. interrogate, question, quiz.

punch, v. push, poke; pierce, bore, perforate, puncture.

puncture, v. prick, perforate, pierce.

pungent, a. pricking, stinging; poignant, sharp, excruciating, severe.

punish, v. chastise, castigate, chasten, discipline.

punishment, n. chastisement, castigation, scourging, discipline, penalty. *Antonyms*: immunity, impunity, acquittal, exoneration.

puny, a. undeveloped, small, undersized, diminutive, stunted.

pup, n. puppy, whelp.

pupil, n. scholar; learner, disciple, catechumen.

purchase, v. buy.

pure, a. chaste, virtuous, innocent, undefiled, unpolluted, inviolated.

purge, n. physic, purgative, cathartic.

purification, n. depuration, expurgation, defecation, refinement, cleansing.

purify, v. cleanse, refine, expurgate, sublime, clarify.

purity, n. chastity.

purport, n. meaning, signification, import. —v. mean, intend, signify, import.

purpose, n. aim, object, design, intent, goal, view, drift.

purpose, v. intend, design, contemplate.

push, v. shove, impel.

push, n. energy, spiritedness, enterprise, aggressiveness; crowd, gang, posse.

pushing, a. enterprising, energetic, intrusive, forward, officious, obtrusive, aggressive.

put back. replace, restore, reinstate; retard, impede, delay, hinder.

put between. interpose.

put down. deposit; crush, quell, suppress, repress, vanquish.

put in. insert, inject, interpolate, interpose, thrust in.

put-off, n. shift, evasion, subterfuge, ruse, parry.

put off. discard, doff; delay, defer, postpone, procrastinate.

put out. eject, oust, remove, evict, dispossess, dislodge.

putting back. hindering, delay, retardation; replacement, restoration, reinstatement.

putting in practice. application.

putting off. delay, deferment, postponement, procrastination.

putting on. investing, investiture; assumption, arrogation; instigation, incitement.

puzzle, v. mystify, pose, nonplus, perplex, bewilder, confuse.

puzzle, n. enigma, conundrum, intricacy, maze, crux, riddle.

puzzling, a. enigmatical, perplexing, inexplicable, inscrutable, intricate, bewildering.

Q

quack, n. charlatan, empiric, pretender, mountebank.

quack, a. empirical, charlatanic, quackish.

quackery, n. empiricism, charlatanism, charlatanry, mountebankery.

quaint, a. fanciful, whimsical, odd, curious, grotesque, old-fashioned.

quake, v. quiver, tremble, shake, shudder, vibrate.

quake, n. agitation, trembling, shaking, vibration, quivering.

qualification, n. condition, restriction, modification, limitation; endowment.

qualified, a. modified, limited; competent, eligible, fitted, capable.

qualify, v. modify, limit, restrict, condition; fit, prepare.

qualify, n. nature, character, sort, strain, condition; characteristic.

qualm, n. nausea; compunction, regret, uneasiness.

qualmish, a. nauseated.

quandary, n. perplexity, predicament, dilemma, puzzle, difficulty, strait.

quantity, n. amount.

quarrel, n. altercation, disagreement, dispute, brawl, affray, fray.

quarrel, v. wrangle, altercate, dispute, contend, squabble, bicker.

quarrelsome, a. disputatious, contentious, irascible, choleric, litigious.

quarry, n. stone pit; game, prey.

quarters, n. pl. rooms, lodging; posts, stations, cantonment, barracks.

quash, v. crush, subdue, extinguish, quell, suppress; annul, overrule.

quaver, n. shaking, trembling, quiver. —v. shake, tremble, quiver.

queen, n. consort.

queer, a. odd, erratic, eccentric, peculiar, singular, unusual.

queer, v. ridicule, banter, rally; spoil, discourage.

quench, v. slake; extinguish, stifle, suppress.

query, n. question.

quest, n. search, seeking, pursuit; request, desire, solicitation, inquiry.

question, n. interrogation, inquiry, query, quizzing, quiz, examination.

questionable, a. suspicious, disputable, doubtful, debatable,

P
R

problematical.

questioner, n. inquirer, interrogator, inquisitor, querist, quizzer.

questioning, a. interrogatory, inquisitive, qiuzzical, inquisitorial, catechistic.

question mark. interrogation point, eroteme.

quibble, n. shift, evasion, cavil, sophism, subterfuge, subtlety.

quibbling, a. trifling, evasive, prevaricative, caviling, elusive, sophistical.

quick, a. hasty, swift, fast, speedy, fleet, hurried, rapid. *Antonyms*: slow, dilatory, sluggish.

quicken, v. revive, vivify, vitalize, resuscitate, animate, excite. *Antonyms*: impede, retard, hinder, obstruct, check.

quickness, n. fleetness, expedition, rapidity, celerity, alacrity, agility.

quiet, a. calm, still, pacific, motionless, unmoved, stagnant, placid. *Antonyms*: noisy, tumultuous, boisterous, hoidenish, rude, stormy.

quiet, v. still, hush, lull, appease, allay, compose. *Antonyms*: arouse, aggravate, exasperate, intensify, increase.

quietness, n. stillness, quiescence, quiet, repose, calmness, tranquillity.

quilt, n. coverlet, bedquilt, counterpane.

quirk, n. evasion, subterfuge, shift, quibble, prevarication, equivocation.

quit, v. cease, stop, desist, discontinue, forbear, break off. *Antonyms*: continue, persist, stay.

quiver, v. tremble, shake, shudder, quake.

quivering, a. trembling, tremulous, shuddering, shaking.

quiz, v. puzzle, banter, chaff; question.

quiz, n. puzzle, conundrum, poser; examination.

quota, n. portion, share, allotment, apportionment.

quotation, n. citation, excerpt.

quotation marks. guillemets.

quote, v. cite, repeat, paraphrase, excerpt.

R

rabbit, n. hare, coney, bunny, cottontail.

rabid, a. violent, raging, furious; intolerant, fanatical, uncompromising.

rabies, n. hydrophobia.

rack, n. pain, torture, agony.

rack, v. stretch, strain, torture, agonize; harass.

racy, a. fine-flavored, pungent, rich; spirited, piquant, fresh and lively. *Antonyms*: insipid, vapid, tasteless, flavorless, dull.

radiance, n. effulgence, refulgence, brilliancy, brightness.

radiate, v. shine, beam, gleam; diverge.

radiated, a. divergent.

radiation, n. irradiance, irradiation; divergence. *Antonym*: convergence.

radical, a. original, fundamental; extreme, thorough-going; primitive. *Antonyms*: conservative, moderate, slight, trifling, derivative.

radically, adv. fundamentally.

raffle, n. lottery.

raft, n. float, catamaran.

rag, n. tatter, flitter, shred, patch, frazzle, fragment.

ragamuffin, n. tatterdemalion, scarecrow.

rage, n. fury, wrath, passion; vogue, mode, fashion.

rage, v. storm, fume, rave.

rent, a. rent, torn, frazzled; rough, jagged.

raging, a. furious, raving, infuriated, wroth, frenzied.

raid, n. foray, incursion.

railroad, n. railway.

rain, n. drizzle, mizzle, mist, misle; shower. *Antonym:* drought.

rainbow, n. iris.

rainy, a. showery, wet, pluvious, pluvial.

raise, v. uplift, lift; hoist, heave; erect, build.

raising, n. uplifting, lifting, elevation, hoisting; erection, rearing.

rally, v. collect, reunite; recover, recuperate; assemble.

ram, n. buck.

ram, v. cram, stuff, compress.

ramble, v. rove, range, stroll, stray, straggle, roam, wander.

rambling, a. roving, wandering; discursive, digressive, incoherent.

rampage, n. debauchery, passion, excess, unrestraint.

rampant, a. exuberant, luxuriant, rank, wanton, excessive.

rampart, n. fortification, bulwark, security, vallum.

rancid, a. musty, tainted, rank, frowzy.

rancorous, a. malevolent, vindictive, malignant, hateful, virulent, bitter.

random, a. haphazard, chance, stray, aimless, hazarded.

range, v. arrange, rank, class, classify; rove, roam.

range, n. extent, reach, sweep, compass, scope, latitude.

rank, a. exuberant, luxuriant, rampant, vigorous; violent, extreme.

rank, n. row, line, range, order, tier, series.

ransack, v. rummage.

ransom, n. release, liberation, redemption, deliverance.

ransom, v. redeem, rescue, liberate, deliver.

rant, v. declaim, spout, rave, vociferate.

ranting, a. bombastic.

rap, v. knock. —n. knock, thump, thwack.

rapacious, a. predatory, predaceous, ravenous.

rape, n. constupration, defloration, ravishment, violation.

rape, v. ravish, constuprate, violate, deflower.

rapid, a. swift, fast, fleet, expeditious, cursory, quick.

rapidity, n. swiftness, celerity, velocity, haste, speed, fleetness.

rapidly, adv. swiftly, fast, post, haste.

rapture, n. ecstasy, transport, delight, bliss, beatitude.

rapturous, a. ecstatic, beatific, delightful, ravishing, transporting.

rare, a. uncommon, unusual, strange, infrequent, singular, curious.

rarely, adv. infrequently, seldom.

rascal, n. rogue, scoundrel, scamp, knave, villain.

rash, a. incautious, precipitate, overhasty, indiscreet, inconsiderate.

rash, n. exanthema, eruption, efflorescence.

rashness, n. temerity, precipitancy, indiscretion, incaution, recklessness.

rate, v. estimate, value, appraise; access; scold, censure.

ratification, n. confirmation, sanction, substantiation, corroboration.

ratify, v. confirm, sanction, substantiate, corroborate.

ration, n. allowance, portion, allotment.

rational, a. reasoning; intelligent,

P
R

sane, sound, judicious, wise.
Antonyms: irrational, insane,
injudicious, unwise, unreasonable.

rationale, n. explanation,
exposition, reason.

rattle, v. clatter; chatter, prate,
babble.

ravage, n. plunder, pillage,
devastation, spoliation, sack.

rave, v. rage, rant, storm.

ravel, v. unravel.

ravenous, a. voracious, rapacious, ravening, insatiable.

ravine, n. gorge, defile, clough,
lin, gully, gulch.

raving, a. irrational, delirious,
maniacal, wild, phrenetic.

ravish, v. transport, enrapture,
enchant; rape.

ravishing, a. rapturous, ecstatic,
transporting, beatific, delightful.

ravishment, n. ecstasy, transport, rapture; rape.

raw, a. uncooked; unprepared,
crude; immature, unripe.

ray, n. beam, gleam.

reach, v. attain.

reachable, a. attainable, accessible.

react, v. repeat; resist, oppose;
rebound, recoil.

read, v. peruse.

readable, a. legible. *Antonyms*:
unreadable, illegible.

readiness, n. promptness,
facility, alacrity. *Antonyms*:
unreadiness, reluctance.

reading, n. perusal; recitation,
prelection.

real, a. genuine, veritable, actual,
true. *Antonyms*:
fictitious,unreal, spurious,
ostensible, artificial.

reality, n. actuality, verity.
Antonyms: unreality, phantasm,
simulation, phantom.

realization, n. fulfillment,
effectuation.

realize, v. effectuate.

really, adv. actually, truly, indeed,
veritably, verily.

realm, n. kingdom, dominion;
domain, region, sphere,
department.

realty, n. real estate.

ream, n. twenty quires, 480 to
516 sheets.

rear, a. hindmost.

rear, v. raise, lift, elevate; erect,
build; bring up.

rearing, n. elevation, raising;
erection.

reason, n. motive, consideration,
design, purpose, rationality,
logic.

reason, v. ratiocinate, syllogize;
argue, remonstrate, expostulate.

reasonable, a. rational; logical,
just; conscionable, fair,
moderate, equitable.

reasoning, n. ratiocination,
argumentation, syllogism,
discursus.

rebate, n. deduction, discount,
allowance.

rebel, n. insurgent, revolter,
turncoat.

rebel, v. revolt, mutiny.

rebellion, n. insurrection,
insurgency, mutiny, sedition,
revolt, insubordination.

rebellious, a. insurgent, seditious, mutinous, insubordinate,
refractory. *Antonyms*: dutiful,
submissive, docile, compliant.

rebound, v. recoil, ricochet;
reverberate.

rebound, n. rebounding, resil-
ience, repercussion, recoil,
ricochet.

rebuff, n. repulse, resistance,
opposition, repellence.

rebuke, v. reprove, unbraid,
censure, reprehend, chide,
admonish.

rebuke, n. reproof, censure;
chastisement, punishment.

recall, v. revoke, annul, retract,

recant, rescind, repeal.

recalling, a. revocatory.

recant, v. retract, abjure.

recapitulate, v. summarize.

receipt, n. receiving, reception; formula, recipe, formulary; voucher.

receive, v. take, accept; admit, allow; welcome; hold, contain.

receiver, n. recipient, donee; beneficiary; fence [receiver of stolen goods].

recent, a. new, late.

receptacle, n. container, repository.

reception, n. receipt, receiving; levee, soiree, function.

recess, n. retreat, withdrawal, retirement; intermission; alcove, niche.

recipe, n. formula, receipt.

recipient, n. receiver, beneficiary, donee, conferree.

reciprocity, n. reciprocation, interchange.

recital, n. recitation, narration, narrative.

recite, v. relate, recount, repeat, deliver; cantillate.

reckless, a. heedless, inconsiderate, unmindful, thoughtless, temerarious, rash.

reckon, v. compute, calculate, count, enumerate; esteem, regard.

reckoning, n. computation, calculation, enumeration; settlement, adjustment.

reclaim, v. tame, domesticate; reform.

reclining, a. recumbent, leaning, lying. ?v. recumbence, reclination.

recluse, a. solitary, eremitic.

recluse, n. solitary, eremite, anchoret, hermit.

reclusion, n. seclusion, eremitism.

recoil, v. rebound, react; flinch, shrink, quail.

recollect, v. remember.

recollection, n. remembrance, memory, reminiscence.

recommend, v. commend, praise.

recommendation, n. commendation.

reconcile, v. conciliate, propitiate, pacify; harmonize, adjust, settle. *Antonyms*: estrange, disaffect, alienate.

reconciliation, n. conciliation, pacification, appeasement, reunion.

record, n. register, memoir, diary, chronicle, minute, memorandum.

records, n. pl. annals, archives.

recover, v. regain, reclaim, retrieve, repair, recoup.

recoverable, a. retrievable.

recovery, n. retrieval, recuperation, regaining, restoration, convalescence.

recreation, n. pastime, amusement, relaxation, diversion, sport, fun.

rectify, v. correct, amend.

rectitude, n. probity, integrity, uprightness, honesty, virtue.

rector, n. pastor, clergyman, priest.

rectory, n. parsonage.

red, n. carmine, crimson, scarlet, cerise, garnet, vermilion.

red, a. florid, blushing, flushed, ruby, ruddy.

redeem, v. repurchase; regain, recover; ransom, rescue, deliver.

redeemer, n. ransomer, deliverer, savior.

redemption, n. repurchase; ransom, salvation, deliverance, rescue.

redoubtable, a. formidable, terrible; valiant, courageous, brave.

red pepper. cayenne pepper.

redress, n. reparation, amends,

indemnification, relief.

reduce, v. diminish, lower, degrade, minimize, depress, debase.

reduction, n. diminution, abatement, minimization, decrement, debasement; subjugation.

redundance, n. superabundance, superfluity, excess.

redundant, a. superabundant, superfluous, excessive, plethoric.

reek, n. fume, vapor, exhalation, effuvium, steam.

reel, v. stagger.

refer, v. allude.

referable, a. attributable, ascribable, traceable, assignable.

referee, n. umpire, judge, arbitrator, arbiter.

refine, v. purify, defecate, clarify, sublimate, subtilize, sublime.

refined, a. exquisite, polished, fine, well-bred, courtly, cultured.

refinement, n. culture, elegance, polish, fastidiousness;purification. *Antonyms:* vulgarity, coarseness, crudity, barbarity.

reflect, v. mirror; rebound, revert; meditate, ruminate, consider, contemplate.

reflection, n. meditation, contemplation, rumination; stricture, animadversion.

reform, v. reclaim, regenerate, convert, amend.

reformable, a. corrigible. *Antonym:* irreformable.

reformation, n. reform, reclamation, betterment, improvement.

refraction, n. deflection.

refrain, v. restrain, curb, check; forbear, abstain, desist.

refresh, v. revive, enliven, reanimate; renovate, renew, restore.

refreshing, a. reviving, reanimating, cooling, reinvigorating, refective.

refreshment, n. collation, lunch, refection, regalement.

refuge, n. stronghold, asylum, retreat, covert; shelter.

refugee, n. fugitive, runaway.

refund, v. repay, return, restore.

refusal, n. dissent, denial, nonacceptance, negation; option, preemption.

refuse, v. deny, decline; reject, rebuff, repulse.

refutable, a. confutable. *Antonym:* irrefutable.

refutation, n. confutation, disproof.

refute, v. confute, disprove.

regain, v. recover, retrieve.

regal, a. kingly, royal.

regard, v. heed, observe, consider.

regard, n. respect, esteem, estimation, opinion; respect. *Antonyms:* disregard, heedlessness.

regardful, a. mindful, heedful, attentive, observant.

regardless, a. heedless, careless, unmindful, inattentive, indifferent.

regards, n. pl. compliments, respects.

region, n. district, quarter, locality, neighborhood, vicinity.

register, n. list, roll, schedule, roster; registrar, recorder.

register, v. record, enroll, matriculate.

registration, n. registry, enrollment, matriculation.

regret, n. sorrow, compunction, deprecation, rue.

regret, v. deplore, be sorry for, rue, deprecate.

regular, a. formal, normal, conventional; systematic; steady.

regularity, n. uniformity, symmetry, shapeliness, constancy, order. *Antonyms*: irregularity, inconstancy, unshapeliness, disorder.

reign, n. sovereignty, rule, dominion; regnancy.

reject, v. cast away, discard; refuse, decline, rebuff, repulse.

rejection, n. refusal, declination, rebuff, repulse, discarding.

rejoice, v. glory, exult; gladden, cheer, delight, please, exhilarate.

rejoicing, n. joy, gladness, exultation, delight, pleasure.

relate, v. recount, narrate, tell.

related, a. allied, cognate, german, agnate, akin, kindred.

relation, n. connection, bearing, relationship, reference, correlation, alliance. *Antonyms*: irrelation, alienage.

relationship, n. kindred, affinity, alliance, kinship, cognation.

relative, a. relating, referring, respecting, pertaining.

relative, n. relation, kinsman, kinswoman, connection.

relax, v. loosen, slacken; abate, diminish, mitigate.

relaxation, n. loosening, slackening; diversion, recreation, rest.

relay, n. reinforcement.

release, v. liberate, loose, discharge, free, acquit.

release, n. liberation, discharge, deliverance, acquittance.

relentless, a. ruthless, implacable, unrelenting, inexorable, unmerciful.

relevancy, n. pertinency, applicability, relevance.

relevant, a. pertinent, germane, apposite.

reliability, n. trustworthiness.

reliable, a. trustworthy, trusty, dependable.

reliance, n. dependence, confidence, trust.

reliant, a. confident, trusting.

relics, n. pl. leavings, remains, remnants.

relief, n. alleviation, mitigation, comfort, ease, succor.

relieve, v. assuage, alleviate, allay, lesson.

relieve, v. assuage, alleviate, allay, lesson, remedy.

relieving, a. mitigative, assuasive, palliative, remedial, emollient.

religious, a. pious, godly, devout, righteous, devotional; strict.

relinquish, v. surrender, waive, forego, renounce, cede, abandon, desert.

relinquishment, n. surrender, abandonment, renunciation.

reluctance, n. unwillingness, disinclination, aversion.

reluctant, a. disinclined, unwilling, averse, loath, indisposed.

rely, v. depend.

remainder, n. residue, remnant, balance, rest, surplus.

remaining, a. residual, remanent, remainder.

remains, n. pl. relics, debris, remnants; corpse.

remand, v. recommit, send back. —n. recommitment.

remark, v. notice, observe, heed, see, note.

remark, n. comment, observation.

remarkable, a. noteworthy, striking, extraordinary, wonderful, notable.

remedy, v. heal, cure, repair, relieve, redress, alleviate.

remedy, n. medicine, cure, antidote, corrective, specific.

remember, v. recollect, recall.

remembrance, n. recollection, memory, reminiscence; souvenir, keepsake. *Antonyms*: forgetfulness, amnesia, amnesty, oblivion.

reminder, n. remembrancer.

remiss, a. negligent, derelict, careless, slack, heedless, neglectful.

remission, n. surrender, relinquishment; discharge, acquittance; abatement.

remnant, n. remainder, residue, rest; fragment, piece.

remorse, n. self-reproach, sorrow, regret; penitence; pity, compassion, sympathy.

remorseless, a. implacable, ruthless, merciless, unmerciful.

remote, a. distant.

removal, n. displacement, dislodgement, transference, expulsion, elimination, dismissal.

remove, v. move, displace, transfer, dislodge; dismiss, discharge.

remunerative, a. profitable, lucrative.

rend, v. tear, rive, lacerate, cleave, sunder.

render, v. repay, restore; translate, interpret, construe.

rendering, n. repayment, restoration; contribution, surrender.

renegade, n. deserter, recreant, backslider, turncoat; rebel.

renew, v. renovate, rejuvenate, restore, rebuild, remodel, reconstruct.

renewal, n. renovation, repair, restoration, redintegration, reconstruction.

renounce, v. disclaim, disown, repudiate; reject.

renovation, n. restoration, renewal, rehabilitation, reconstruction.

renown, n. celebrity, repute, fame, notoriety, note.

renowned, a. famous, celebrated, eminent, far-famed, illustrious. *Antonyms:* unrenowned, obscure, inglorious, unknown.

rent, v. lease, let, hire.

renter, n. lessee, tenant.

renunciation, n. abjuration, denial, disownment, disclaimer.

repair, v. mend, restore, patch, tinker, revamp, darn.

repair, n. renovation, restoration, reconstruction, reparation, rehabilitation.

reparable, a. restorable, retrievable. *Antonyms:* irreparable, irretrievable.

reparation, n. restoration, rehabilitation, instauration, renovation; atonement, restitution.

repay, v. refund, restore, reimburse; recompense.

repeal, v. revoke, rescind, abrogate.

repeat, v. iterate, reiterate, verbigerate.

repeating, n. repetition, iteration, reiteration; verbigeration.

repel, v. repulse, rebuff, resist, oppose.

repellence, n. repulsion, rebuff, opposition.

repentance, n. penitence, contrition, compunction, remorse. *Antonym:* impenitence.

repetition, n. iteration, reiteration, recurrence.

replace, v. restore, refund, repay.

replacement, n. restoration, reinstatement.

reply, v. answer, respond, rejoin, retort.

report, n. rumor, hearsay, bruit; account, statement.

report, v. announce, communicate, describe. *Antonyms:* suppress, withhold, reserve.

repose, n. rest, inactivity, motionlessness; composure, tranquillity.

repository, n. depository, storehouse, depot, magazine.

represent, v. show, typify, symbolize; personate.

representative, n. deputy, delegate, vicar, proxy, agent, substitute.

repress, v. quell, subdue, suppress, overpower, restrain.

repression, n. suppression, restraint, quelling, check.

reproach, v. censure, upbraid, rebuke, reprimand, revile.

reproachful, a. upbraiding, opprobrious, abusive; shameful, disgraceful, scandalous.

reprobate, a. abandoned, depraved, profligate, incorrigible. —n. castaway, outcast, wretch.

reproduce, v. portray, duplicate, imitate; generate, beget, propagate.

reproduction, n. duplication, copy, imitation; generation, procreation, propagation.

reprovable, a. culpable, censurable, reprehensible, blamable, reproachable.

repudiate, v. reject, renounce, disavow, abjure, disclaim.

repugnance, n. aversion, reluctance, unwillingness, hostility, antipathy.

repugnant, a. hostile, contrary, refractory, adverse, offensive.

repulse, v. repel, reject.

repulsive, a. repellent, offensive, forbidding, revolting.

reputation, n. repute, name, credit, esteem, honor.

repute, n. reputation, esteem, credit.

request, n. asking, solicitation, demand, instance, prayer.

request, v. ask, supplicate, petition, beg, entreat.

require, v. demand, claim, exact, need, want, necessitate, enjoin.

requirement, n. demand, requisition, requisite; command, essential, need.

requisite, a. necessary, required, essential, indispensable.

requital, n. recompense, remuneration, retribution, retaliation, reprisal.

rescue, n. deliverance, liberation, salvation, ransom.

rescue, v. release, deliver, liberate, recapture, redeem, save.

resemblance, n. likeness, similitude, similarity, analogy.

resentment, n. dudgeon, umbrage, displeasure, grudge.

reserve, n. reticence, constraint, uncommunicativeness.

reserved, a. retained, withheld, excepted; uncommunicative.

residence, n. dwelling, domiciliation, abode, habitancy.

resident, n. denizen, inhabitant, dweller, residentiary.

residue, n. remainder, remnant, residuum, rest, balance.

resign, v. demit, abdicate, withdraw, surrender, relinquish, submit.

resignation, n. surrender, abdication, demit, forbearance.

resigned, a. surrendered; uncomplaining, submissive, patient.

resist, v. oppose, withstand, impugn, oppugn, defy.

resistance, n. opposition, renitence, recalcitration, oppugnation.

resistant, a. resisting, opposing, renitent.

resolute, a. determined, unwavering, unflinching, steadfast, firm, pertinacious.

resolution, n. firmness, determination, pertinacity, persistence, steadfastness.

resolve, v. determine; dissolve, liquefy.

resolve, n. resolution, determination, intention, purpose, design.

P
R

resound, n. echo, reverberation.

resounding, a. resonant.

resource, n. resort, expedient, device, shift.

resources, n. pl. assets, means.

respect, n. care, caution, regard; esteem, veneration.

respect, v. esteem, venerate, revere, honor, reverence.

respectable, a. reputable, honorable, estimable; moderate, fair, average.

respectful, a. deferential, courteous, polite, obeisant, reverent. *Antonyms*: disrespectful, discourteous, defiant, irreverent.

respective, a. relative; particular, own.

respects, n. pl. compliments, regards, devoirs.

response, n. reply, answer, rejoinder, retort.

responsibility, n. accountability, liability, duty, trust.

responsible, a. accountable, answerable, amenable. *Antonyms*: irresponsible, unaccountable, independent.

responsive, a. responding, antiphonal.

rest, n. quiet, quietness, inactivity, repose, east, tranquillity. *Antonyms*: activity, agitation, unrest, commotion.

rest, v. stop, halt, pause, desist; repose, recline.

restaurant, n. cafe, eating-house, chophouse, refectory, buffet.

resting, a. reclining, lying, incumbent.

restitution, n. repayment, restoration, return, indemnification; reparation.

restive, a. restless, impatient, fidgety, intractable, uneasy.

restless, a. restive, fidgety, agitated, unquiet, uneasy.

restlessness, n. restiveness, the fidgets, uneasiness, agitation, turbulence, dysphoria.

restoration, n. return, restitution; replacement, reinstatement, reparation.

restore, v. repair, renew, reconstruct, rehabilitate.

restrain, v. repress, suppress, check, bridle, curb, constrain.

restraint, n. repression, constraint, check, suppression, limitation, prevention.

restrict, v. restrain, limit, confine, repress, curb, circumscribe.

restriction, n. restraint, constraint, confinement, repression, circumscription, limitation.

result, v. terminate, end, eventuate, redound, issue, accrue, ensue.

result, n. consequence, effect, issue, event, outcome.

resume, n. recapitulation, summary, abstract.

resurrect, v. disentomb, disinter, unbury, exhume.

resurrection, n. resurgence, revivification.

retain, v. keep, hold, reserve.

retainment, v. retention.

retaliate, v. avenge, requite, repay.

retaliation, n. revenge, requital, retribution.

retard, v. impede.

retarding, n. retardation.

retentive, a. tenacious. *Antonyms*: unretentive, irretentive.

reticence, n. reserve, uncommunicativeness, taciturnity.

reticent, a. taciturn, reserved, uncommunicative.

retire, v. withdraw, retreat, recede, retrocede, leave, secede.

retired, a. secluded, sequestered, unfrequented, withdrawn.

retiring, a. diffident, shy, coy,

shrinking, reserved, modest.

retract, v. recant, rescind, recall, disavow.

retreat, n. retirement, withdrawal; refuge, asylum, seclusion.

retreat, v. retire, withdraw, recede.

retribution, n. retaliation, repayment, requital.

retrograde, v. retrocede, recede, decline, deteriorate.

return, v. restore, repay, refund, replace; recur, regress.

return, n. restoration, restitution, repayment, requital, retribution, redress.

returning, a. recurrent, recurring, intermittent.

reveal, v. disclose, unveil, expose, divulge, impart.

revel, n. carousal, festivity, saturnalia.

revel, v. carouse; luxuriate, wanton.

revelation, n. disclosure, divulgement, exposition, apocalypse.

revenge, v. avenge, retaliate, wreak, vengeance.

revenge, n. vengeance, retaliation.

revengeful, a. vindictive, implacable, resentful, rancorous.

revenue, n. income.

revere, v. venerate, reverence, honor, respect.

reverence, n. veneration.

reverence, v. revere, venerate.

reverent, a. reverential, humble.

reverse, v. invert; overthrow, subvert, overturn; revoke, annul.

reverse, n. opposite, contrary, counterpart, reversal; misfortune, failure.

review, v. reconsider, revise, reexamine, retrace.

review, n. reexamination, reconsideration, retrospect,

revision.

revisal, n. revision, emendation, recension.

revision, n. revisal, recension, emendation.

revival, n. revivification, reanimation, resuscitation, restoration.

revivalist, n. evangelist.

revive, v. resuscitate, reanimate, quicken, revivify, reinspirit, revitalize.

revocation, n. recall, repeal, reversal, abjuration, recantation.

revoke, v. repeal, reverse, recant, rescind, abrogate.

revolt, n. rebellion, sedition, uprising, mutiny, insurrection.

revolt, v. rebel, mutiny; disgust, nauseate, shock, offend.

revolter, n. insurgent, rebel, mutineer, renegade.

revolting, a. nauseating, repulsive, fulsome, abhorrent, disgusting.

revolution, n. rotation, gyration; rebellion, revolt.

revolve, v. rotate, spin, gyrate, turn; devolve; brood over.

revolver, n. pistol, repeater.

revolving, a. rotary, gyrating, gyratory, rotatory. —n. revolution, rotation.

reward, n. recompense, requital, guerdon, meed, remuneration.

reward, v. requite, recompense.

rhyme, n. jingle, poetry.

ribald, a. indelicate, gross, indecent, obscene, lewd.

rich, a. wealthy, opulent, affluent, well-to-do, moneyed; abundant. *Antonyms*: poor, infertile, indigent, plain.

richness, n. opulence, wealth, affluence; abundance, profusion. *Antonyms*: poverty, infertility.

rid, a. free, clear, disencumbered.

rid, v. free, disburden, relieve,

disencumber, dispose of,
dispatch.
riddle, n. enigma, puzzle,
problem.
ridicule, n. mockery, gibe, jeer,
burlesque.
ridicule, v. deride, satirize, scoff,
rally, banter.
ridiculous, a. preposterous,
absurd, farcical, burlesque,
ludicrous.
rifle, v. strip, fleece, despoil,
pillage, devastate.
right, a. just, true, equitable,
honest, rightful, lawful.
right, v. correct, rectify, emend;
make restitution, redress.
right, n. prerogative, privilege,
immunity, exemption.
right, n. uprightness, rectitude,
probity, integrity.
right away. immediately, straightway, right off, instantly,
instanter, at one.
righteous, a. pious, religious,
devout, godly; saintly.
righteousness, n. godliness,
holiness, sanctity. *Antonym*:
unrighteousness.
right-handed, a. dexterous.
rigid, a. inflexible, stiff, unyielding, unpliant; rigorous, severe.
rigidity, n. stiffness, inflexibility,
severity, rigor.
rigmarole, n. nonsense, flummery, balderdash, twaddle.
rigor, n. rigidity, inflexibility,
austerity, severity.
rigorous, a. severe, stringent,
strict, unyielding; inclement,
severe.
rile, v. roil; anger, vex, offend.
rim, n. brim, margin, edge, brink,
verge, border.
rind, n. skin, peel. *Antonym*:
pulp.
ring, v. sound, resound, reverberate; toll, knell, chime.
ring, n. circle, hoop; grommet.
ringing, n. sounding, resounding,

reverberation, tolling, clang,
chime.
ringlet, n. tress, curl, lock.
ringworm, n. circular herpes,
serpigo.
riot, n. tumult, uproar; revelry.
rioter, n. reveler, carouser,
roysterer.
riotous, a. wanton, luxuriant,
unrestrained; seditious.
rip, n. rent, tear.
ripe, a. mature, ripened; consummate, complete, perfect.
ripen, v. mature, maturate.
ripeness, n. maturity, completeness, consummateness,
development.
rise, v. ascend, mount, arise,
levitate; tower; swell, increase.
rise, n. ascent, spring, source,
origin, beginning.
rising, a. ascending, ascendant.
rising, n. ascent, ascension, rise,
levitation, levee, emergence.
risk, n. unsafety, danger, peril,
jeopardy, hazard, imperilment.
risk, v. hazard, endanger, peril,
imperil, jeopard, jeopardize.
rite, n. ceremony, ordinance.
ritual, n. liturgy, consuetudinary.
rival, n. competitor, emulator,
antagonist. —a. competing,
competitive, emulative.
rival, n. competition, emulation,
contention.
road, n. thoroughfare, avenue,
highroad, highway, street, lane.
roam, v. ramble, stray, rove,
range, wander.
roar, n. bellow, bellowing.
roar, v. bellow; boom, peal,
resound, thunder.
roast, v. bake; torrefy, patch;
banter.
rob, v. plunder, pillage, fleece,
despoil, rifle.
robber, n. bandit, brigand,
buccaneer, burglar.
robbery, n. larceny, burglary,
theft, plundering, piracy.

robe, n. gown.

robust, a. strong, sinewy, muscular, brawny, stalwart, vigorous, sound.

rocking-horse, n. cockhorse.

rogue, n. knave, miscreant, scamp, rascal.

roll, n. scroll; roster, record; convolution.

roll, v. wheel, whirl, revolve, rotate, turn, gyrate, spin.

rolling, a. rotating, circumrotary; undulating.

romantic, a. imaginary, impractical, chimerical, picturesque, fanciful, fantastic.

room, n. space, compass, range, scope, latitude; apartment.

roomer, n. lodger.

roomy, a. spacious, capacious, commodious.

roost, n. perch.

root, n. etymon, stem, radix, radical.

rooting, n. radication; burrowing; implantation.

rope, n. cordage, cable, hawser, lasso, lariat.

rose-colored, a. roseate, rosy; alluring.

rosery, n. rosarium, rosary.

rosy, a. rose-colored, roseate, ruddy, alluring.

rot, n. decomposition, decay, putrescence, corruption, putridity. *Antonyms*: preservation, imputrescence, incorruption, soundness.

rotary, a. turning, rotating.

rotate, v. revolve, turn, gyrate, whirl.

rotation, n. turning, revolution; succession.

rotten, a. decayed, putrid, putrescent, carious, corrupt, decomposed.

rouge, n. ferric oxide, crocus; cosmetic.

rough, a. uneven, jagged, craggy, rugged, cragged, scraggy.

rough, n. bully, ruffian, rowdy.

round, a. circular, spherical, orbicular, orbed, globular.

round, n. revolution, cycle, rotation, series, succession.

roundabout, a. circuitous, indirect, tortuous; encircling, ambient.

roundness, n. circularity, globularity, sphericity, rotundity.

rousing, a. exciting, stirring; astounding, startling.

route, course, way, road, passage.

routine, n. custom, round, course.

rove, v. range, ramble, straggle.

rowdy, n. ruffian, rough, bully, hoodlum.

royal, a. kingly, regal, imperial, monarchical.

royalty, n. kingship, sovereignty, regality, regency; sovereign, majesty.

rub, n. friction; hindrance, impediment, obstruction.

rub, v. abrade, chafe, scrape, grate, fret; embrocate.

rubbing, n. friction, abrasion, attrition, chafing, fraying.

rubbing out. erasure, obliteration, effacement.

rubbish, n. trash, litter, lumber, refuse, debris, garbage.

rude, a. crude, unpolished, raw, rough, indelicate, unrefined, coarse.

rudiment, n. element; embryo; pl. elements, accidence.

rudimentary, n. rudimental, elementary, initial; embryonic, embryo.

rue, v. regret, deplore.

rueful, a. woeful, sad, lugubrious, mournful.

ruffian, n. monster, villain, rowdy, desperado.

ruffle, n. ruff, frill, flounce.

rugged, a. irregular, rough,

P
R

uneven, scraggy.

ruin, n. bane, pest, plague.

ruin, n. wreck, destruction, undoing, dilapidation, disorganization.

ruin, v. overthrow, subvert, destroy, wreck, ruinate, impoverish.

ruination, n. ruin.

rule, n. regulation, prescript, prescription, order, ruling; standard.

rule, v. govern, dominate; restrain, influence, sway, prevail.

ruler, n. governor, sovereign, monarch, president, king.

ruling, n. government, regnancy.

ruminate, v. meditate, muse, ponder, reflect.

rummage, v. ransack.

rumor, n. hearsay, gossip.

rump, n. buttocks.

rumple, v. crumple, wrinkle, pucker, crease.

rumpus, n. disturbance, quarrel, affray, brawl, row, fracas.

run, v. sprint, lope, scamper, scud, speed.

run, n. running, spring, sprinting; course, series.

run after. pursue, follow, tag.

runaway, n. fugitive, absconder, deserter, truant, renegade.

runaway, a. fugitive, absconding, truant.

run away. flee, escape, desert, elope, abscond.

run away with. accompany.

run down. decline, deteriorate; decry, belittle, disparage, derogate.

run into. collide.

runner, n. racer, sprinter, messenger, courier.

running, a. successive, consecutive; flowing, easy, cursive; continuous.

running after. pursuit.

running away. desertion, fleeing, absconding, elopement.

running down. decline, deterioration; decrial, disparagement.

running into. collision.

run out. expire; extend, spread; expatiate, descant; become extinct.

run over. overflow.

runt, n. dwarf, pygmy.

run through. squander, dissipate; transfix, impale, pierce.

ruption, n. breach, rupture.

rural, a. rustic, country, countrified, pastoral.

ruse, n. artifice, wile, trick, stratagem, maneuver.

rush, v. press, hurry.

rush, n. activity, demand.

rust, n. corrosion.

rust, v. corrode; degenerate.

rustic, a. rural, country, agrestic; unpolished, countrified,uncouth, rude.

rusticate, v. ruralize.

rustling, a. whispering, susurrous.

rusty, a. aeruginous; ferruginous; reasty, rancid, musty.

rut, n. groove; roaring [of waves], rote.

ruthful, a. pitiful, tender, compassionate, merciful.

ruthless, a. pitiless, cruel, truculent, relentless, implacable, fell, hard-hearted.

ruthlessness, n. truculence, implacability, cruelty, mercilessness.

ruttish, a. lustful, salacious, lascivious.

S

sack, n. bag, pouch.

sacred, a. consecrated, hallowed; venerable, sainted, religious, inviolable.

sacrifice, n. oblation, immolation; surrender, loss, giving up;

holocaust.

sacrifice, v. offer, immolate; surrender, give up, forego.

sacrilege, n. desecration, profanation, violation.

sacrilegious, a. impious, profane, irreverent.

sad, a. sorrowful, pathetic, plaintive, doleful, piteous.

sadden, v. depress, dishearten; tone down, subdue.

sadness, n. melancholy, pathos, sorrow, gravity, soberness, seriousness.

safe, a. unharmed, intact, unscathed, immune; trustworthy, reliable. *Antonyms*: unsafe, endangered, insecure.

safe-conduct, n. convoy, guard, escort; pass, passport.

safeguard, n. defense, security, palladium, protection.

safeguard, v. guard, defend, protect, shield.

safekeeping, n. guardianship, care, custody, charge, preservation.

safety, n. security, custody; immunity, exemption.

sagacious, a. intelligent, knowing, shrewd, discerning.

sagacity, n. intelligence, shrewdness, cleverness, ingenuity, wisdom.

sail, v. navigate, cruise, embark. —n. sailing, cruise, embarkation.

sailcloth, n. canvas, duck, tarpaulin.

sailor, n. mariner, navigator, seaman, seafarer.

sainted, a. holy, pious, saintly, consecrated; canonized.

salable, a. vendible, marketable. *Antonyms*: unsalable, unmarketable.

sale, n. vendition, market; auction; handsel.

salient, a. prominent, conspicuous, noticeable, striking.

saliva, n. spittle, sputum, spit.

salt, n. chloride of sodium.

salt, n. seasoning, flavor, savor, taste.

salty, a. saline, brackish, saltish, salt, briny, saliferous.

salute, v. address, greet, hail, welcome, accost. —n. salutation.

salvation, n. redemption.

salve, n. ointment, cerate, embrocation, emollient, balm.

same, a. identical, invariable, uniform, analogous, similar.

sameness, n. identity, identicalness, similarity, correspondence, uniformity.

sample, n. specimen, example, illustration, exemplification, instance, pattern.

sanction, n. confirmation, ratification, authorization; penalty, punishment.

sanction, v. confirm, ratify, approve, countenance.

sanctity, n. godliness, saintliness, inviolability, sacredness.

sanctuary, n. shrine, sanctum, adytum; Holy of Holies, church, temple.

sand, n. sandy soil; quicksand.

sandy, a. sabulous, gritty, arenaceous, arenose.

sane, a. underanged, ration, sound, lucid.

sanitarium, n. sanatorium, health retreat.

sanity, n. saneness, rationality.

sappy, a. juicy, lush, succulent.

sarcastic, a. satirical, taunting, ironical, derisive, sneering.

Satan, n. devil, Belial, Apollyon, Abaddon, Prince of Darkness.

satchel, n. handbag, valise.

satire, n. irony, sarcasm, ridicule.

satirical, a. bitter, sarcastic, ironical, caustic, mordacious.

satisfaction, n. gratification; contentment, complacency, content, comfort; reparation.

S
T

satisfactory, a. sufficient, satisfying, conclusive, gratifying, atoning.

satisfy, v. gratify, content, appease, satiate, suffice.

saucy, a. impertinent, insolent, pert, impudent, malapert, flippant.

savage, a. uncivilized, barbarous; ferocious, ravenous, fierce, untamed.

savage, n. barbarian; cannibal.

save, v. rescue, deliver, redeem; preserve, conserve, keep.

save, prep. or conj. except, excepting, reserving.

saving, a. preserving, redemptory, redeeming; preservative, conservative; frugal. *Antonyms*: lavish, extravagant, prodigal, unthrifty, profuse, wasteful.

savory, a. gustable, palatable, toothsome, fragrant. *Antonyms*: unsavory, impalatable.

savvy, v. understand, comprehend. —n. understanding, comprehension.

say, v. utter, express, mention, pronounce, speak, declare, tell, articulate.

saying, n. utterance, declaration, statement, pronunciation, mention.

scaffold, n. staging, scaffolding; gallows.

scramble, v. sprawl, wabble, shamble; scramble, jostle.

scamp, n. rascal, knave, miscreant.

scamper, v. hasten away, scud, hie, run, scuttle, scatter.

scandal, n. reproach, opprobrium, disgrace, odium, shame; slander.

scandalize, v. shock, offend, displease; disgrace; slander, defame, vilify.

scandalous, a. defamatory, libellous, slanderous; infamous, disgraceful.

scant, a. scanty, meager, insufficient, inadequate; sparing.

scantness, n. smallness, narrowness, inadequacy; insufficiency, meagerness, scantiness.

scarce, a. rare, unplentiful, deficient.

scarcity, n. dearth, deficiency, insufficiency, lack, drought, rarity.

scare, v. frighten, intimidate, terrify, daunt, cow, appall. *Antonym*: reassure.

scare, n. fright, alarm, terror, panic.

scarecrow, n. guy, effigy; ragamuffin.

scary, a. timid, apprehensive, alarming, frightful.

scatter, v. dissipate, disperse, dispel, separate.

scatter-brained, a. giddy, thoughtless, flighty, careless.

scattering, a. scattered, sporadic.

scattering, n. dissipation, dispersion; interspersion.

scene, n. spectacle, show, exhibition, display, view, scenery.

scenery, n. view, landscape, prospect.

scent, n. odor, smell, perfume.

scepter, n. royal mace, sovereignty.

schedule, n. list, catalogue, table.

scheme, n. design, plan, project, machination, intrigue.

scheme, v. devise, excogitate, plan, machinate, plot, design.

schismatic, n. nonconformist, dissenter, separatist, heretic, sectary.

scholar, n. pupil, student, learner, disciple.

scholarly, a. scholarlike, erudite, scholastic.

scholarship, n. erudition, learning, knowledge, attainments.

school, n. institute, academy, seminary, college, gymnasium.

school, v. train, educate, drill, teach.

schooling, v. education, training, nurture, discipline; tuition.

scientist, n. savant.

scoff, v. deride, ridicule, mock, sneer, gibe, jeer, contemn.

scold, n. shrew, vixen, virago, termagant, rixatrix.

scolding, n. chiding, censure, rating, reprimand, reprehension, rebuke, berating.

scoop, n. ladle; cavity, hollow.

scope, n. design, purpose; opportunity, space, room, liberty.

scorch, v. singe, char, torrefy, burn, parch.

score, n. tally, account; notch, incision; motive, account.

score, v. notch, scratch, cut; record, enter.

scorn, n. contempt, disdain, derision, contumely, mockery, slight.

scorn, v. despise, reject, contemn, disregard, scout, spurn.

scornful, a. disdainful, contemptuous, contumelious, defiant.

scoundrel, n. villain, knave, rascal, scamp, rogue.

scout, n. spy.

scowl, v. glower, frown, lower. — n. frown.

scraggy, a. scragged, craggy; scrawny, lank, gaunt, skinny.

scramble, v. scrabble, clamber; struggle, contend, strive.

scrap, n. bit, fragment, morsel, crumb; excerpt, extract. pl. cracklings.

scrapbook, n. commonplace book, album.

scrape, n. difficulty, predicament, dilemma.

scrape, v. abrade, rasp, grate, rub; gather, collect; erase, remove.

scrawl, n. scribble.

scrawny, a. angular, lank, meager, scraggy, bony.

scream, n. shriek, screech, yell, outcry.

screech, n. shriek, scream, screak.

screechy, a. discordant, unmelodious, unmusical, strident.

screen, n. shield, protection, guard, defense, traverse, fender.

screw, v. twist, wrench, force, squeeze.

screw, n. extortioner, skinflint.

scribe, n. writer, scrivener, amanuensis, copyist.

scrimmage, n. skirmish, scuffle, scrabble, row, fight.

scrimp, a. scanty.

scrub, n. jungle, thicket, brushwood.

scrubby, a. stunted, dwarfed, undeveloped, scrub, insignificant.

scrumptious, a. fine, elegant, excellent, fastidious, particular.

scrupulous, a. conscientious, exact, strict, punctilious, particular.

scuffle, n. tussle, struggle, encounter, contest, fight, fray.

sculpture, n. statuary.

scurry, v. hurry, scamper, scuddle, scuttle.

scurry, a. despicable, abject, low, mean, contemptible.

scuttle, v. scuddle, hurry, bustle, run.

seacoast, n. seaboard, seashore, seaside, beach.

sea cow. manatee; dugong; walrus.

seal, n. signet; assurance, ratification, attestation, authentication.

S
T

seal, v. ratify, authenticate, confirm, attest.

sealing, n. confirmation, ratification, authentication, attestation, obsignation.

seaman, n. sailor, seafarer, mariner.

sear, v. cauterize, scorch.

search, v. examine, explore, hunt, seek, overhaul; rummage.

search, n. quest, research, pursuit.

searcher, n. seeker.

searchless, a. unsearchable, impenetrable, inscrutable.

seashore, n. seacoast, seaside, seaboard.

seasickness, n. nausea.

season, v. habituate, inure, harden, accustom, acclimatize.

seasonable, a. opportune, timely, suitable, apropos, convenient.

seasoning, n. condiment, spice, relish, sauce, flavor, salt.

seat, n. site, abode, situation, station; fundament, buttocks.

seat, v. usher.

secluded, a. sequestered, isolated, retired, withdrawn, covert, lonely.

seclusion, n. sequestration, isolation, solitude, loneliness, retirement.

second, n. backer, supporter, assistant. —v. back, support, abet.

secondary, a. subordinate, second, inferior, minor, collateral.

secondary, n. subordinate, deputy, delegate, proxy, underling, auxiliary.

second-class, a. inferior, second-rate.

second sight. prophetic vision, deuteroscopy.

second thought. reconsideration.

secrecy, n. seclusion, privacy, retirement, concealment, confidence.

secret, a. hidden, concealed, unrevealed, mysterious. *Antonyms*: overt, revealed, open, exoteric, manifest.

secretary, n. amanuensis, clerk, writer, scribe; writing-desk.

secrete, v. bury, hide, conceal, shroud, disguise, cloak.

secretive, a. uncommunicative, taciturn, reserved, silent, wary.

secrets, n. pl. confidences, mysteries.

sect, n. school, party, denomination.

section, n. portion, part, division, segment, piece; paragraph.

secular, a. temporal, worldly, laic, civil.

secure, a. safe, confident, assured, fast, immovable, stable, indemnified. *Antonyms*: insecure, risky, hazardous.

secure, v. gain, procure, obtain, get, acquire.

security, n. safety, confidence, assurance, certainty, warranty.

sedate, a. staid, demure, imperturbable, composed, calm.

sedative, n. anaesthetic, narcotic, opiate, hypnotic.

sediment, n. precipitate, dregs, lees, settlings, grounds, feculence.

seduce, v. entice, tempt, betray, allure.

seducement, n. seduction, enticement.

seductive, a. alluring, attractive, siren, enticing.

see, v. perceive, descry, view, behold, witness. *Antonyms*: overlook, ignore, miss, skip, connive at.

seed, n. semen, sperm; first principle, origin, source.

seed, n. kernel, grain, pip, ovule.

seedy, a. shabby, tacky, threadbare; spiritless.

seeing, n. perception, viewing, espial, descrying, beholding; discernment. *Antonyms*: imperception, blindness, connivance.

seek, v. search for, hunt; aim at, strive after, attempt.

seeming, n. appearance, show, semblance, speciousness, guise, look.

seemingly, adv. apparently, ostensibly.

seemly, a. becoming, suitable, proper, appropriate, meet, befitting.

seep, v. percolate.

seer, n. prophet, vaticinator, predictor, diviner.

segment, n. section, part, portion, piece.

seize, v. apprehend, snatch, clutch, catch, gripe, grasp.

seizure, n. apprehension, grasping; capture; confiscation, usurpation.

seldom, adv. infrequently, rarely.

select, v. pick out, choose, prefer, cull, single out, elect. — a. choice. *Antonyms*: promiscuous, indiscriminate.

selecting, a. elective, eclectic.

selection, n. choice, election, preference, pick; collection, assortment. *Antonyms*: promiscuity, indiscrimination.

self, n. ego, person, individual.

self-abuse, n. masturbation, onanism, secret vice, self-pollution.

self-conceit, n. egotism, overweening, priggishness, vanity.

self-denial, n. self-abnegation, asceticism, self-sacrifice, abstemiousness. *Antonyms*: self-indulgence, sensuality, voluptuousness.

self-denying, a. self-sacrificing, unselfish, ascetic, abstemious.

self-evident, a. axiomatic, obvious.

self-examination, n. introspection; autoscopy.

self-explanatory, a. obvious.

self-importance, n. pompousness, pomposity, vanity, conceit.

self-righteous, a. pharisaic, sanctimonious.

self-sufficiency, n. self-complacency.

sell, v. vend, barter, exchange, betray; deceive, impose upon, cheat.

sell, n. mposition, cheat, hoax, deception, trick, fraud.

seller, n. vender, vendor.

selling, n. vendition, barter, vending, sale.

semen, n. sperm, seed.

send, v. dispatch, commission, delegate; transmit, forward.

send back. return, remand, recommit.

senile, a. decrepit, feeble, aged, infirm.

senility, n. dotage, decrepitude, old age.

seniority, n. eldership, superiority.

sensation, n. consciousness, feeling, perception; excitement.

sensational, a. melodramatic, emotional, exciting, thrilling.

sense, n. perception, sensation, sensibility, feeling.

sense, v. perceive, recognize.

senseless, a. insensible, unconscious; absurd, silly, nonsensical.

senselessness, a. insensibility, unconsciousness; fatuity, absurdity.

sensible, a. apprehensible, perceptible; susceptible, impressible; conscious. *Antonyms*: insensible, unconscious.

S
T

sensitive, a. susceptible, impressible, sentient, irritable.

sensual, a. unspiritual, carnal, fleshly, sensuous; voluptuous.

sensuality, n. voluptuousness, carnality, sybaritism; wantonness.

sensuous, a. sensual. *Antonym*: insensuous.

sentence, n. opinion, decision, determination, judgment.

sentiment, n. thought, feeling; judgment, notion, opinion.

sentimental, a. romantic, impressible, emotional, lackadaisical. *Antonyms*: unsentimental, matter-of-fact, pragmatical.

sentinel, n. guard, sentry, watchman, picket.

separable, a. divisible, detachable, severable, partible. *Antonym*: inseparable.

separate, v. divide, dissolve, detach, sunder, sever, disconnect.

separate, a. detached, disconnected, disjoined, separated, apart.

separation, n. division, segregation, disunion, disconnection, sequestration.

sequel, n. continuation, conclusion, consequence, result, outcome.

sequence, n. succession, series, following; result, sequel, consequence.

sequestered, a. secluded.

serene, a. calm, placid, composed, tranquil, unruffled, unclouded.

serenity, n. calmness, composure, tranquillity; cloudlessness, clearness.

serious, a. grave, earnest, thoughtful, solemn, staid, sober.

seriousness, n. gravity. *Antonyms*: levity, frivolity, triviality.

sermon, n. homily, exhortation [religious], discourse.

serpent, n. snake, reptile.

servant, n. dependent, subaltern, subordinate, helper.

serve, v. attend, wait upon; promote, advance, contribute.

service, n. labor, employment, office, duty, business, function.

servile, a. slavish, abject, cringing, groveling.

servitude, n. bondage, enslavement.

set, v. place, put, fix, establish, locate, station.

set, a. fixed; immovable, rigid, firm, obstinate, inflexible.

set, n. clique, group, class, party.

set aside. displace, supersede.

setback, n. backset, check, repulse, reverse, relapse.

settle, v. fix, establish; ordain, install; adjust, determine.

settlement, n. establishment; ordination, installation; colonization.

settler, n. pioneer, colonist.

sever, v. part, divide, disunite, separate, disjoint, detach, disconnect.

several, a. various, diverse, manifold, divers, sundry.

severe, a. drastic, harsh, stern, rigorous, exact, cruel.

severity, n. rigor, rigorousness, harshness, exactness, cruelty; seriousness.

sew, v. stitch; baste.

sexual desire. lust, venereal appetite, sexual appetite, carnal appetite, lasciviousness.

sexual intercourse. coition, copulation, venery, sexual conjunction. *Antonyms*: continence, chastity, virginity.

shabby, a. seedy, threadbare, tacky.

shackle, n. handcuff, manacle, fetter.

shade, n. umbrage, shadow; pl.

darkness, obscurity, gloom.

shade, v. screen; obscure, dim, obfuscate, cloud, darken, eclipse.

shadowy, a. unsubstantial, visionary, illusory, chimerical.

shake, v. agitate, jar, jolt, convulse, concuss, jounce.

shake, n. jar, shivering, jolt, shaking, shudder.

shallow, a. shoal; superficial, frivolous, senseless.

sham, n. pretense, feint, delusion, imposition, mockery, fraud.

sham, a. counterfeit, spurious, pretended, dummy, unreal, false, mock, simulated.

shame, n. ignominy, dishonor, reproach, derision, contempt.

shame, v. humiliate, mortify, disconcert; disgrace, degrade.

shameful, a. indecent, immodest, obscene; scandalous, disgraceful.

shameless, a. immodest, unabashed, indelicate, indecent, unblushing, audacious.

shanty, n. hut, hovel, shack.

shape, v. form, mould, fashion, frame; adjust, regulate.

shape, n. form, figure, guise, appearance.

shapeless, a. misshapen, unsymmetrical, unshapely, formless,, amorphous.

shapely, a. symmetrical, well-formed, comely, well-proportioned.

share, v. apportion, divide; partake, participate in.

share, n. portion, allotment, quota, dole, proportion.

shark, v. sharper, trickster, cheat, swindler; fraud, trickery.

sharp, a. pointed, trenchant, incisive, keen; poignant, piercing.

sharpen, v. intensify, aggravate, quicken; hone, grind.

sharpness, n. keenness, poignancy, acuity, acuteness, edge; asperity.

shatter, v. shiver, demolish; disorder, derange.

shave, n. shaving; spokeshave, drawshave.

sheath, n. case, scabbard; covering.

shed, v. diffuse, emit, radiate, spread; cast.

shed, n. outhouse, lean-to, shack, shanty.

sheen, n. shine, luster, gloss, brightness, splendor.

sheep-dog, n. collie, shepherd dog.

sheepish, a. bashful, shy, overmodest.

sheer, a. thin; unadulterated, pure, unmixed; precipitous.

shelf, n. mantel, mantelpiece; bracket, console; ledge.

shell, n. armature, case, exoskeleton, shale.

shell, n. framework; bomb, torpedo, shrapnel, grenade.

shelter, n. protection, screen, cover, shield, defense.

shelter, v. shield, protect, defend, screen, ensconce, cover. *Antonym*: expose.

shield, v. defend, protect, safeguard; ward off, repel.

shift, v. veer, change, turn; quirk, quibble.

shift, n. subterfuge, device, contrivance, evasion, stratagem.

shifting, a. unstable, variable, changeable.

shiftless, a. improvident, unthrifty, thriftless, wasteful. *Antonyms*: thrifty, industrious.

shine, v. beam, radiate, gleam, irradiate, glisten.

shine, n. luster, polish, gloss, sheen, radiance.

shining, a. radiant, beaming, lustrous, luminous, glowing.

S T

ship, n. vessel.

ship, v. transport; deport; dismiss, send away.

shipment, n. shipping, transportation; consignment.

shipping, n. shipment, transportation, navigation.

shipwreck, n. wreckage; disaster, destruction, ruin, subversion, miscarriage.

shirk, v. avoid, evade, neglect.

shiver, n. splinter, sliver; shivering, tremor, horripilation.

shock, v. dismay, horrify, appall, terrify, frighten.

shock, n. impact, blow, collision, concussion, onset.

shocking, a. scandalous, appalling, offensive, outrageous, heinous, dire.

shoddy, a. sham, spurious, mock.

shoestring, n. shoelace.

shoot, v. discharge, fire; eject, hurl, emit, ejaculate.

shooting, a. darting, piercing.

shop, n. workshop, factory; store; warehouse; atelier, studio.

shore, n. beach, coast, strand, marge.

short, a. brief, contracted, terse, concise, condensed. *Antonyms*: diffuse, prolix, long.

shortage, n. deficiency, insufficiency, inadequacy, deficit.

shortcoming, n. defect, imperfection, fault, foible, failure.

shorten, v. abridge, abbreviate, curtail, reduce, epitomize.

shortening, n. abbreviation, abridgement, contraction, curtailment, reduction.

shorthand, n. phonography, stenography.

short-lived, a. ephemeral, mushroom, transitory.

shortness, n. brevity, briefness, conciseness, laconism; inadequacy.

short-sighted, a. myopic, near-sighted; unwise, imprudent, indiscreet.

shot, n. discharge; projectile, bullet, ball; marksman.

shout, n. vociferation, halloo, outcry, call, hoot, clamor, acclamation.

show, n. exposure, exhibition, exposition, demonstration, representation.

show, v. exhibit, present, display, uncover, reveal, disclose.

showing, n. demonstration, exhibition, presentation, revelation, disclosure.

showy, a. spectacular, pageant, ostentatious, pompous, garish, gaudy. *Antonyms*: inconspicuous, modest, unostentatious, quiet, subdued.

shred, n. fragment, tatter, rag, strip, frazzle.

shrewd, a. astute, sharp; cunning, crafty.

shrewdness, n. acumen, astuteness, sharpness, long-headedness.

shriek, n. screech, yell, scream.

shrill, a. piercing, acute, strident.

shrink, v. contract, shrivel, decrease, dwindle; flinch.

shrinkage, n. contraction; depreciation.

shrinking, a. coy, shy, diffident, bashful, modest, retiring.

shroud, n. winding-sheet, grave-clothes, cerements.

shroud, v. mask, screen, cloak, conceal.

shrub, n. bush; pl. shrubbery, thicket, boscage, bosket.

shudder, n. tremor. —v. tremble, shake, shiver, quake.

shuffle, v. jumble, intermix; equivocate, prevaricate.

shuffle, n. artifice, evasion, prevarication, trick.

shun, v. avoid, elude, evade, eschew.

shut, v. close; debar, exclude, preclude.

shy, a. timid, coy, backward, retiring, diffident, wary.

shyness, n. diffidence, coyness, timidity, bashfulness.

shyster, n. knave, impostor, rogue, cheat.

sick, a. ill, unwell, ailing, indisposed, diseased, morbid.

sicken, v. nauseate, disgust, pall, surfeit, decay, languish.

sickening, a. nauseating, disgusting, fulsome, nauseous, revolting.

sickly, a. invalid, unwell, unhealthy, ailing; unwholesome.

sickness, n. illness, malady, ailment, complaint, disorder, distemper.

side, a. lateral, collateral, incidental.

side by side. in apposition.

sidetrack, v. shunt; switch off, divert.

sideways, adv. sidewise, askance, obliquely, laterally.

siege, n. investment, blockage, besiegement.

sieve, n. strainer, sifter.

sift, v. bolt, cribble, riddle; investigate.

sight, n. vision; seeing, view, perception; visibility; spectacle.

sightly, a. comely, attractive, handsome.

sign, n. omen, auspice, portent, prodigy.

sign, v. signify, mark, indicate, betoken; subscribe.

signal, n. sign, ensign, beacon.

signal, a. memorable, remarkable, noticeable, notable.

signature, n. autograph, sign-manual.

signer, n. subscriber, signatory.

significance, n. meaning, import; consequence, importance, force.

significant, a. momentous, important; indicative, significative. *Antonyms*: insignificant, unimportant, meaningless.

signification, n. meaning, import, acceptation, sense.

signify, v. indicate, betoken, denote; mean; matter.

silence, n. stillness, quietness; taciturnity, muteness, reserve, secrecy.

silence, v. still, hush, quiet, suppress, lull.

silent, a. still, quiet, noiseless, inaudible.

sill, n. threshold; window sill.

silliness, n. folly, foolishness, puerility, stupidity.

silly, a. witless, foolish, simple, fatuous, imbecile, half-witted.

similar, a. like, corresponding, resembling, homogeneous, analogous.

similarity, n. analogy, homogeneity, likeness, similitude, correspondence.

simple, a. incomplex, uncompounded, single, elementary, uncombined, mere. *Antonyms*: complex, complicated, intricate, artful, crafty, elaborate.

simpleton, n. dolt, dunce, numskull, lackbrain, oaf.

simulate, v. pretend, feign.

simultaneous, a. contemporaneous, synchronal, synchronous.

sin, n. iniquity, transgression, wickedness, delinquency.

sin, v. do wrong, trespass, transgress.

sincere, a. heartfelt, genuine, unfeigned, undissembling.

sincerity, n. honesty, unaffectedness, frankness. *Antonyms*: insincerity, dissimulation.

sinful, a. iniquitous, wrong, immoral, wicked, depraved.

sinfulness, n. iniquity, immorality, depravity, wickedness.

sing, v. carol, warble, chant,

S
T

hymn, hum.

singe, v. sweal, swale, scorch.

singer, n. vocalist, songster, songstress, minstrel, chanter.

single, a. individual, alone, particular, isolated, sporadic, solitary.

single, v. single out, choose, select, separate, isolate, segregate.

single-hearted, a. sincere, honest, guileless.

single-minded, a. artless, undesigning, guileless.

singular, a. unusual, unconventional, uncommon, strange, peculiar.

singularity, n. peculiarity, idiosyncrasy, individuality; curiosity, freak.

sinister, a. left; unlucky, inauspicious, evil, wrong, forbidding.

sink, v. subside, descend, decline, fall; immerse.

sinking, n. subsidence, fall, decrease, decline.

sinless, a. innocent, guiltless, undefiled, perfect, blameless, faultless.

sinner, n. wrong-doer, delinquent, miscreant, trespasser.

site, n. location.

situation, n. position, place, post, employment, job, location.

size, n. magnitude, volume, dimensions, amplitude, bulk.

skedaddle, v. run away, flee, decamp, scuttle.

skeptic, n. unbeliever, infidel.

skeptical, a. doubtful, disbelieving, incredulous. *Antonym*: credulous.

skepticism, n. doubt, incredulity, infidelity. *Antonym*: credulity.

sketch, n. draught, outline, plan, drawing, design, scenario.

skill, n. adroitness, ingenuity, cleverness, technic, dexterity. *Antonyms*: maladriotness,

empiricism, quackery, inexpertness, clumsiness.

skillful, a. skilled, expert, adroit, dexterous, adept, masterly. *Antonyms*: unskillful, empirical, maladroit.

skimpy, a. scant, skimp.

skin, n. integument, tegument, derm; epidermis. *Antonyms*: pulp, flesh.

skin-deep, a. superficial.

skinflint, n. miser, niggard.

skinny, a. emaciated, gaunt, rawboned, poor.

skip, v. omit, pass, disregard; caper, gambol.

skit, n. reflection, jeer, gibe, satire, squib.

skittish, a. timorous, shy; volatile, restless, wanton.

sky, n. firmament, welkin, empyrean, azure, the heavens.

slack, a. lax, loose, relaxed; remiss, negligent, careless.

slacken, v. moderate, retard, slack, reduce; loosen, relax.

slackness, n. looseness, laxity, negligence, remissness, carelessness.

slander, v. malign, defame, traduce, asperse, vilify.

slanderous, a. defamatory, malicious, vituperative, calumnious, libellous.

slant, n. slope, incline, inclination, obliquity. —v. slope, incline.

slap, adv. suddenly, violently, unceremoniously, instantly.

slash, n. incision, gash, cut, slit.

slaughter, n. butchery.

slave, n. vassal, bond servant, bondslave, bondman.

slave, v. drudge, toil, moil.

slavery, n. bondage, enslavement, servitude, inthrallment, captivity.

sleazy, a. flimsy, thin, gauzy.

sled, n. sleigh, sledge, toboggan.

sleek, a. smooth, glossy.

sleep, v. slumber, repose; doze, drowse; lie dormant; hibernate.

sleep, n. slumber, repose; nap, doze, drowse, snooze, dozing.

sleepiness, n. drowsiness, somnolence.

sleeping, a. asleep, slumbering, dormant.

sleepless, a. wakeful, insomnious, insomnolent.

sleepy, a. drowsy, somnolent, dozy; soporiferous, somniferous.

sleigh, n. cutter, sled, sledge, bobsled, toboggan.

sleight of hand. prestidigitation, jugglery, legerdemain, magic.

slender, a. slim, slight, thin, spare, lank.

slice, n. chop, collop.

slick, a. sleek, sleeky, smooth.

slide, n. slip; flume, shoot, chute.

slide, v. slip, glide, lapse, elapse, skid.

slight, a. inconsiderable, trivial, insignificant, trifling, petty.

slight, n. neglect, inattention, disregard, snub.

slight, v. overlook, neglect, disregard, ignore.

slightly, adv. somewhat; superficially, cursorily, hastily.

slim, a. thin, gaunt, poor, lank, spare, spindling, meager.

slip, n. lapse, error, indiscretion, transgression.

slippery, a. smooth, glib; inconstant, unstable; loose.

slipshod, a. slovenly, careless, negligent.

slit, n. gash, incision.

sliver, n. splinter.

slobber, v. drivel, drool, slabber, slaver; smear.

slogan, n. war cry, rallying cry.

slope, v. slant, incline.

slope, n. inclination, slant, obliquity; acclivity; declivity.

sloping, a. oblique, slanting; acclivous; declivous.

slosh, n. slush, sludge.

sloth, n. sluggishness, indolence, laziness.

slothful, a. dronish, lazy, indolent, supine, sluggish, idle, inactive.

slouchy, a. slouching, ungainly, awkward.

slow, a. deliberate, moderate, gradual; dilatory, languid.

slow, v. slacken, relax, moderate, delay, retard.

sluggish, a. idle, lazy, slothful; inactive, slow, inert.

slump, n. depreciation.

slur, n. stain, mark; innuendo, reproach, brand.

sly, a. cautious, nimble, skillful, arch, wary, knowing, shrewd.

smack, n. taste; kiss, buss; crack, snap.

small, a. little, minute, diminutive, petty, slight, inconsiderable.

smallpox, n. variola.

smart, v. sting, prick, suffer.

smart, a. acute, bright, clever, apt, brilliant, gifted. *Antonyms*: dull, inapt, dowdy, tawdry.

smash, v. shiver, crush. —n. destruction, ruin, wreck; bankruptcy.

smell, n. olfaction; odor, savor, scent. *Antonyms*: inodorousness, scentlessness, anosmia.

smell, v. scent; savor; stink.

smelling, n. olfaction, osmesis.

smile, n. smiling; propitiousness, favor.

smirk, n. simper, sneer.

smite, v. strike, buffet; blast, destroy, afflict, chasten, visit.

smoke, n. fume, reek, effluvium; smudge.

smoke, v. reek; fume; infumate; fumigate; suffumigate; smolder.

smoky, a. fumid, fumy, sooty, reeky, fumacious, fuliginous.

smooth, v. level, plane, sleek, flatten.

S
T

smooth, a. even, plaint, flat,
level, abraded, levigated.

smoothness, n. evenness,
levelness, sleekness; volubility.

smooth-spoken, a.
smooth-tongued, adulatory;
plausible, glib. *Antonyms*:
brusque, abrupt.

smother, v. suffocate, stifle;
extinguish, repress, suppress;
smolder.

smuggler, n. contrabandist.

smut, n. soot, dirt, smutch;
mildew, blight.

smutty, a. obscene, lewd, ribald,
indecent, gross.

snake, n. serpent, reptile.

snaky, a. serpentine, winding;
insinuating, subtle, deceitful.

snap, n. spell, period, season,
interval.

snappish, a. captious, irascible,
testy, petulant.

snare, n. catch, wile, trap, gin,
lure, decoy.

snarl, v. entangle, complicate,
involve, knot; confuse. *Antonyms*: disentangle, unravel,
extricate.

snarl, n. complication, entanglement, intricacy, knot; confusion;
growl.

snarler, n. growler, grumbler,
fault-finder, cynic.

snatch, v. seize, grasp, gripe,
wrest, pluck, grab, twitch.

sneak, v. skulk, slink, lurk,
snoop.

sneaking, a. lurking, skulking,
slavish, underhand, covert,
stealthy.

sneer, v. mock, gibe, scoff, flout,
jeer.

sneezing, n. sternutation.

snicker, n. giggle, titter, snigger.

snide, a. tricky, deceptive,
dishonest, fraudulent.

sniff, v. snuff; scent, smell. —n.
snuff, breath.

snob, n. upstart, pretender,

parvenu; rat, knobstick.

snobbish, a. pretentious,
assuming, overbearing, uppish.

snotty, a. snively, mean, despicable.

snub, v. slight, ignore, disregard.

snub, n. slight, check, rebuke.

snug, a. cozy; concealed, close;
comfortable, compact.

snuggle, v. nestle, cuddle.

soak, v. drench, saturate; absorb,
imbibe.

soaked, a. drenched, saturated,
sodden.

soaking, a. drenching, saturat-
ing.

sob, v. weep.

sober, a. temperate, abstinent,
abstemious; unintoxicated.

sobriety, n. soberness; gravity.

sociable, a. affable, friendly,
companionable, genial, social,
unreserved. *Antonyms*:
unsociable, inaffable.

social, a. civil, civic; sociable;
festive, convivial.

society, n. sodality, association,
fraternity, club, confraternity.

sod, n. sward, turf; peat.

soft, a. mellow; yielding, impressible, impressionable.

soften, v. intenerate, mollify,
palliate, extenuate, qualify.

softness, n. mellowness,
impressibility, plasticity,
flaccidity.

soil, n. ground, earth, dirt,
humus, land.

soil, v. dirty, defile, pollute,
besmear, contaminate, taint.

soldier, n. warrior; private; cadet;
recruit; veteran.

solemn, a. serious, sober, grave;
impressive.

solemness, n. solemnity, gravity,
impressiveness, seriousness.

solicit, v. ask, seek, request.

solicitation, n. request, instance,
entreaty, invitation.

solid, a. dense, compact, hard,

impenetrable, firm.

solidness, n. solidity, firmness, compactness, stability.

solitary, a. unfrequented, secluded, lonely; single, individual.

solitary, n. recluse, anchoret, hermit, eremite.

solitude, n. loneliness, isolation, seclusion, eremitism.

solution, n. dissolution, melting, liquefaction, resolution.

solvent, n. menstruum, dissolvent, resolvent.

somersault, n. somerset.

sometimes, adv. at intervals, now and then, occasionally.

song, n. hymn, chant, lay, ditty, ballad.

soothe, v. compose, tranquilize, pacify, assuage, mollify, calm.

soothing, a. bland, emollient, demulcent, gratifying.

soothsayer, n. seer, prophet, diviner, haruspice, foreteller.

sophistical, a. fallacious, unsound.

soprano, n. descant, treble.

sorcerer, n. conjurer, necromancer, magician, enchanter, juggler, wizard.

sorcery, n. necromancy, magic, enchantment, witchcraft, black art.

sore, a. ulcerated, cankered, ulcerous, raw, inflamed, irritated.

sore, adv. grievously, sorely, severely, greatly.

sorrow, n. grief, regret, remorse, misery, heaviness.

sorrow, v. grieve, mourn, regret, deplore, bewail, lament.

sorry, a. melancholy, mournful, dismal, depressing, sad.

sort, n. kind, species, character, description.

sort, v. assort, classify; conjoin; choose, select.

so-so, a. middling, passable,

tolerable, mediocre, ordinary, average.

soul, n. spirit, psyche.

sound, a. whole, intact, perfect, flawless, unimpaired.

sound, n. strait, narrows, channel.

sound, v. fathom, gauge; examine, try, test, probe.

sounding, n. bathymetry; examination; proclamation; resonance, reverberation.

soundless, a. unfathomable, abysmal; silent, noiseless.

soup, n. broth, bouillon, consomme.

soup dish. tureen.

sour, a. acid, tart, acetose, acerbitous, acrid.

source, n. origin, spring, fountain, rise.

sourness, n. acidity, tartness, acerbity, sharpness.

souvenir, n. keepsake, reminder, memento; trophy.

sovereign, a. supreme, chief, paramount, predominant.

sovereign, n. ruler, monarch.

sovereignty, n. dominion, supremacy, sway, empire.

sow, v. propagate, disseminate, scatter, plant.

space, n. extension, vacancy; vacuum; distance, interval.

spacious, a. capacious, roomy, vast.

spare, v. forbear, refrain, be merciful.

spare, a. thin, lean, poor, gaunt, meager.

sparing, a. economical, frugal, saving, parsimonious, chary.

spark, v. court, woo, philander.

sparkle, v. glitter, coruscate, glisten, scintillate, twinkle.

sparkle, n. scintillation, glitter, gleaming, brilliancy.

sparkling, a. glittering, flashing, brilliant, twinkling.

sparse, a. scattered, thin,

S
T

innumerous, meager.

spasm, n. convulsion, paroxysm, fit, throe.

spasmodic, a. intermittent, fitful, convulsive.

spat, n. tiff, quarrel, dispute, dissension.

speak, v. utter, pronounce, say, articulate, enunciate, express. *Antonyms*: repress, suppress, refrain.

speaker, n. orator, discourser, spokesman, prolocutor.

spear, n. lance, javelin, harpoon.

special, a. particular, especial, specific, exceptional.

specialty, n. particularity; speciality.

species, n. group, class, kind, brood, sort, variety.

specific, a. definite, precise, specified; characteristic, particular, special.

specify, v. designate, particularize, individualize, name.

specimen, n. example, sample, model, copy, pattern.

speck, n. spot, stain; atom, mite, particle.

spectacle, n. scene, sight, show, exhibition, pageant.

spectator, n. beholder, witness, bystander, onlooker, observer.

speculate, v. theorize, meditate, conjecture, guess, think.

speculation, n. theory, supposition, conjecture; contemplation, thought.

speculative, a. contemplative, meditative; theoretical, supposititious.

speech, n. utterance, speaking; language, talk, conversation.

speechless, a. dumb, mute, aphasic, inarticulate.

speechlessness, n. dumbness, muteness, obmutescence, taciturnity.

speed, n. velocity, swiftness, rapidity, celerity, haste.

speed, v. hurry, hasten; accelerate, expedite, quicken.

speedy, a. swift, quick, fast, rapid, fleet, hasty.

spell, n. charm, incantation, exorcism; period, season, interval.

spell, v. orthographize; decipher, read, unravel, unfold.

spellbound, a. fascinated, charmed, enchanted, bewitched.

spelling, n. orthography.

spend, v. expend, disburse.

spender, n. prodigal, spendthrift.

spending, n. expenditure, disbursement.

spendthrift, n. waster, spender, prodigal, squanderer.

spent, a. exhausted, tired, consumed, worn out.

sphere, n. globe, ore, ball; province.

spice, n. condiment; piquancy, pungency.

spicy, a. aromatic, fragrant; piquant, pungent, sharp.

spider, n. araneidan; scorpion, tarantula.

spin, v. whirl, twirl, revolve, gyrate.

spindling, a. tall and slender.

spineless, a. invertebrate.

spinning, n. whirling, twirling.

spiral, a. winding, cochleate, helical, turbinated.

spire, n. steeple; shoot, stalk, blade, spear.

spirit, n. soul; shade, apparition, specter, ghost.

spirit, v. inspirit, animate, encourage; spirit away, carry off, kidnap, abduct.

spirited, a. animated, lively, ardent, mettlesome, fervent, passionate.

spit, n. spittle, sputum, saliva.

spite, n. malignity, malice, rancor, hate, resentment.

spiteful, a. malicious, malign,

malignant, rancorous, hateful.

spleen, n. milt; anger, spite, malice, choler; melancholy, depression.

splendid, a. bright, brilliant; magnificent, grand, superb.

splendor, n. brilliancy, brightness; magnificence, pageantry, pomp.

splice, v. interweave, unite, braid together.

splinter, n. sliver, flinder.

split, v. crack, rent, fissure, rift.

split, a. cleft, riven, divided, sundered.

splitting, n. fission, cleavage, riving, sundering, rupture.

spoil, v. plunder, rob, pillage, ravage, depredate, despoil.

spoil, n. plunder, pillage, booty, prize, gain, loot.

spoke, n. radius, ray; rung, round.

spoken, a. oral, nuncupative, parole.

spokesman, n. speaker, mouthpiece, prolocutor.

sponsor, n. godparent; surety.

spontaneous, a. instinctive, voluntary, impulsive, unforced.

spook, n. ghost, spirit, specter, apparition.

sporadic, a. separate, single, isolated.

sport, n. amusement, game, recreation, fun, play, diversion.

sport, v. frolic, play, caper, disport; exhibit.

sportive, a. frolicsome, merry, boon, frisky, sprightly, prankish, gamesome.

spot, n. speck, speckle, mark, blot, discoloration.

spotless, a. immaculate, unspotted, stainless, unsullied.

spout, n. nozzle; conduit, trough.

spread, v. extend, stretch, expand, dilate; unfurl, unroll.

spreading, n. extension, expansion, dilation; dissemination, propagation.

spree, n. carousal, debauch, revelry, orgies.

sprig, n. shoot, slip, twig, spray.

sprightliness, n. animation, liveliness, vivacity, activity, briskness.

sprightly, a. lively, brisk, animated, debonair, vivacious, sportive, gay.

spring, v. dart, shoot; bound, leap, jump, hop, vault.

springy, a. elastic, resilient, rebounding, recoiling.

sprinkle, v. scatter; strew; besprinkle, bedew, asperse.

sprinter, n. runner.

sprout, v. germinate, pullulate, bourgeon, grow, vegetate.

spry, a. agile, nimble, quick, brisk, sprightly, alert.

spunky, a. mettlesome, plucky, spirited.

spur, v. goad, incite, urge, stimulate, instigate, impel.

spurious, a. counterfeit, sham, false, mock.

spurn, n. rejection, disdain, scorning.

spurt, n. gushing, spouting, jet, ejection. —v. gush, spout, jet.

spy, n. scout; emissary [disguised]. —v. espy, see.

spying, n. espionage, espial.

squabble, n. wrangle, dispute, altercation.

squad, n. band, gang, knot, bevy, company.

square, a. equitable, true, just, honest, impartial.

square, v. adjust, fit, suit; balance, settle; conform.

squat, v. crouch, cower.

squeak, v. creak; betray, tell, confess.

squeal, v. cry, yell; tell, betray, confess.

squeeze, v. compress, gripe, pinch; oppress, extort.

squeeze, n. compression,

S
T

pressure; exaction, extortion.

squelch, v. crush, silence, quell, stifle, abash.

squinting, n. strabismus; cross-eye.

squirm, v. wriggle, writhe, twist.

stab, v. pierce, thrust, gore, transfix; backbite, malign.

stability, n. fixedness, firmness, permanence, constancy, steadiness. *Antonyms*: instability, unsteadiness.

stable, a. steady, firm, immovable, unwavering, constant, permanent.

stable, n. barn; mews.

stack, n. pile, rick.

staff, n. rod, stick, cane.

stage, n. platform, rostrum; scaffold, staging; theater.

stagger, v. reel, totter, sway; shock; astound, dumfound.

stagnant, a. motionless, standing; quiet; inactive, dull, sluggish.

stain, v. soil, sully, defile, taint.

stainless, immaculate, spotless.

stairway, n. stairs, staircase, flight of stairs; escalator.

stake, n. picket, pale, post; pledge, wager.

stake, v. venture, risk, hazard, wager, bet, pledge.

stale, a. vapid, musty, fusty, flat, insipid.

staleness, n. vapidity, mustiness, insipidity; triteness.

stall, n. stable; booth, stand; seat.

stamp, v. impress, imprint; stomp.

stamp, n. impression, imprint, die; hallmark; pestle.

stamp out. extinguish, crush, quell.

stanch, a. loyal, steadfast, constant, true, unwavering, sound.

stand, v. endure, bear, weather, brook, suffer, tolerate.

stand, v. halt, stop, pause; stay.

standard, n. criterion, model, type, pattern, norm.

stand by. befriend, vindicate, advocate, defend, maintain.

standing, a. erect; stagnant; lasting, permanent, persistent.

standing, n. status.

standing out. prominent, projecting, protuberant, jutting out; conspicuous, salient.

standing up for. defense, justification, support, advocacy.

stand it. endure, tolerate, bear, brook.

stand off. keep aloof; refrain; refuse, resist, withstand.

stand out. project, overhang, jut out, bettle; resist, withstand.

standpoint, n. point of view, viewpoint.

stand up for. defend, support, espouse, champion, advocate.

star, n. luminary, planet; asterisk, asterism.

starched, a. stiff, ceremonious, prim, formal.

start, v. set out, go, initiate, launch, institute, embark.

startle, v. scare, surprise, affright.

starvation, n. famishment.

starve, n. famish.

state, n. condition, plight, category, situation, pass, predicament.

state, v. assert, affirm, aver, allege, say, specify, declare.

statehouse, n. capitol.

stately, a. imposing, dignified, august, pompous, majestic, formal.

statement, n. assertion, affirmation, specification, avowal.

station, n. standing, rank, status; depot; situation, place.

statue, n. image; acrolith, caryatid; xoanon.

status, n. standing, rank, station, condition.

statute, n. law.

stay, v. sojourn, tarry, lodge, remain, continue, abide.

stay, n. sojourn, abidance, stop; dependence, support, upholder.

steadfast, a. firm, fixed; constant, unswerving, unwavering.

steady, a. steadfast, constant; stable, firm, fixed, unremitted.

steal, v. pilfer, filch, peculate, purloin, poach, abstract.

stealing, n. theft, larceny, robbery, pilfering, peculation, thievery.

stealthy, a. clandestine, sly, secret, furtive, skulking, underhand.

steam, v. vapor, reek, fume, emanation, effluvium.

steel, v. fortify, brace, nerve.

steep, a. precipitous, abrupt, sheer, perpendicular; excessive, immoderate.

steep, n. precipice, cliff, abrupt declivity; escarpment, scarp.

steep, v. soak, macerate, imbrue, infuse.

steeple, n. spire, tower, turret; minaret.

steer, v. guide, pilot, control, govern.

steering, n. guiding.

steersman, n. helmsman, pilot.

stem, n. trunk, body.

stem, v. oppose, withstand, breast, resist, check.

stench, n. fetor, stink.

stenography, n. phonography, shorthand.

step, n. pace; stair, round; footstep, footprint, footmark.

step, v. pace, stride.

steps, n. pl. stairs; stile; perron.

sterile, a. barren, infecund, unproductive, unfruitful, unprolific.

sterility, v. barrenness, infecundity, unproductiveness.

stern, a. austere, rigorous, exacting, strict, hard-hearted.

sternness, n. austerity, severity, rigor, strictness.

stew, n. confusion, agitation.

stick, n. switch, rod, birch.

stick, v. pierce, stab, penetrate, impale, transfix, gore.

sticker, n. poster; label; adhesive, glue, cement.

stickiness, n. adhesiveness, viscosity, tenacity, cohesiveness, glutinousness.

sticking, n. adhesion, adherence, coherence, cleaving.

sticking out. projecting, protruding, prominent. —n. projection, protrusion, prominence.

stickle, v. contend, altercate, dispute, quibble, scruple, haggle.

stickler, n. haggler, higgler, contender.

stick up for. assert and defend, vindicate.

sticky, a. adhesive, viscous, viscid, mucilaginous, glutinous.

stiff, a. inflexible, rigid, firm, unbending, inelastic, stark. *Antonyms:* limber, flaccid, limp, flexible, lithe.

stiffness, n. inflexibility, rigidity, firmness; prudery, constraint. *Antonyms:* pliability, limpness, flexibility, flaccidity, ease, relaxation, informality.

still, n. motionless, unruffled, stagnant, quiescent, inert, stationary.

still, v. calm, compose, quiet, silence, hush.

stimulant, n. excitant; provocation, stimulus, spur, goad.

stimulate, v. excite, incite, instigate, arouse, provoke, goad, spur.

stimulus, n. incentive; pl. stimuli.

sting, n. aculeus, prick; goad, incitement.

stinginess, n. parsimony, illiberality, penuriousness,

S
T

closeness, avarice. *Antonyms*:
liberality, generosity.

stingy, a. parsimonious, illiberal,
close, penurious, miserly.
Antonyms: liberal, generous.

stink, n. stench, fetor.

stinking, a. fetid, malodorous,
offensive, noisome, ill-smelling.

stint, n. limit, restraint, restriction;
assignment, allotment.

stir, v. move, budge.

stir, a. agitation, tumult, bustle,
commotion, flutter, ado.

stirring, a. animated, lively,
strenuous, active, enterprising.

stock, n. goods, merchandise,
wares, reserve.

stock, v. replenish, supply,
furnish.

stockings, n. pl. hosiery, hose.

stocky, a. stout, plump.

stolen goods. booty, loot, spoil,
plunder, pillage.

stomach, v. resent, dislike; bear,
brook, tolerate, stand, endure.

stomach-ache, n. colic.

stone, n. rock, pebble; calculus,
concretion; flint, granite.

stone, n. gem, jewel, diamond,
brilliant, beryl, emerald.
Antonyms: paste, strass,
gewgaw, gimcrack, tinsel.

stony, a. rocky, flinty, adaman-
tine, petrous; unrelenting,
pitiless.

stool, n. footstool, cricket,
hassock, ottoman.

stoop, v. bend; condescend,
deign, descend.

stoop, n. condescension,
descent; porch, veranda,
piazza.

stop, v. obstruct, close up;
stanch; arrest, hinder, impede.
Antonyms: continue, persist.

stop, n. cessation,
discontinuation, surcease,
pause, suspension, intermission.

store, n. shop; accumulation,

stock, abundance, plenty,
hoard, supply.

storehouse, n. warehouse,
repository, depot, store,
magazine.

storm, n. tempest. *Antonyms*:
calm, subsidence, serenity,
tranquillity.

storm, n. assault, attack,
besiege, expugn; rage, fume,
rant.

storminess, n. inclemency,
tempestuousness, boisterous-
ness, violence.

stormy, a. tempestuous, boisterous, inclement, rugged,
impetuous; violent, furious.
Antonyms: calm, pacific,
serene.

story, n. fiction, tale, anecdote,
romance, novel, fable, legend.

stout, a. strong, powerful,
vigorous, enduring, durable,
tough.

straight, a. perpendicular,
vertical, plumb, erect, upright.
Antonyms: indirect, oblique,
crooked, devious, circuitous.

straightway, n. immediately; at
once, directly, forthwith.

strain, v. stretch, tighten; sprain,
wrench; percolate, filter.

strain, n. pedigree, race, lineage,
extraction; sort, kind.

strained, a. tense, unnatural,
forced, artificial, agonistic,
farfetched.

strait, n. narrows, channel;
dilemma, difficulty,
pinch,exigency, restriction.

strait-laced, a. uncompromising,
rigorous, strict, prudish, prim,
precise.

stranded, a. wrecked, aground,
beached.

strange, a. foreign, unfamiliar,
exotic, outlandish; novel, odd.
Antonyms: familiar, accustomed, wonted, commonplace,
conventional.

strangle, v. choke, throttle, suffocate; stifle, suppress; garrote.

strangling, n. strangulation, choking, suffocation, suppression, constriction.

strap, n. thong, strop, leash.

strapping, a. stalwart, able-bodied, large, muscular, brawny.

stray, v. wander, rove, roam, swerve, deviate; err, sin.

stray, n. estray, waif.

streak, n. stripe, wale, whelk, ridge, vein.

stream, n. current, river, creek, brook.

streamer, n. ensign, pennon, banner, banderole, flag.

street, n. highway, avenue, thoroughfare, boulevard.

strength, n. force, vigor, power, might, hardihood, potency. *Antonyms*: debility, delicacy, fragility, weakness, impotency, frailty, infirmity.

strengthen, v. invigorate, brace, nerve, steel, fortify, harden.

strengthening, a. invigorating, roborant, tonic, fortifying.

strenuous, a. zealous, ardent, valiant, intrepid, vigorous, active, energetic.

stress, n. urgency, pressure; emphasis, accent; severity, inclemency.

stretch, v. extend, elongate, lengthen, spread; overstate, exaggerate.

strict, a. rigorous, stringent, exacting, rigid. *Antonyms*: lax, remiss, indulgent.

strife, n. conflict, struggle, contention, emulation, competition, battle.

strike, v. hit, smite, buffet, knock, beat, thump, whack.

striking, a. impressive, noticeable, astonishing, surprising, forcible.

string, n. cord, line, twine, warp.

stringent, a. binding, restrictive, rigid, severe, rigorous, exact.

strip, v. deprive, divest, dispossess, dismantle; plunder, desolate.

stripping, n. deprivation, divestiture, divestment, dispossession, dismantling.

strive, v. struggle, try, endeavor, contend, vie, cope.

stroll, v. ramble, rove, range, stray, straggle, wander.

strolling, a. wandering, nomadic, itinerant, roving, vagrant.

strong, a. firm, tough, enduring, hale, sound, robust. *Antonyms*: weak, vulnerable, frail, fragile, delicate, faint, mild, frangible.

stronghold, n. fastness, fort, fortress.

struggle, n. conflict, contest, strife.

struggle, v. strive, cope, grapple, labor.

stubborn, a. unyielding, obstinate, obdurate, mulish, refractory.

stuck-up, a. proud, arrogant, haughty, vain, overbearing, cavalier.

study, n. research, excogitation, lucubration, cogitation.

stuff, n. material, fabric, cloth; trash, refuse, rubbish, goods.

stuffing, n. filling, forcemeat, dressing, farce.

stumbling-block, n. difficulty, obstruction, hindrance, barrier, stumbling-stone.

stun, v. overcome, stupefy, dumfound, bewilder.

stunning, a. overpowering, stupefying; astonishing, striking, fine.

stunted, a. dwarfed, atrophied, undeveloped, scrubby, under-sized.

stupefier, n. stupefacient, narcotic, opiate.

S
T

stupefy, v. dull, benumb, hebetate, blunt, besot.

stupid, a. dull, stolid, obtuse, sluggish, inept. *Antonyms:* shrewd, sharp, apt, spirited, lively, exciting, interesting.

stupor, n. lethargy, insensibility, unconsciousness, narcoma.

sturdy, a. obstinate, stubborn, pertinacious; strong, hardy, robust.

style, n. mode, vogue; fashion; manner, way, method.

stylish, a. modish, fashionable, in vogue.

suave, a. urbane, courteous, debonair, bland, affable.

subdue, v. conquer, vanquish, subject, overpower, subjugate.

subdued, a. vanquished, conquered, submissive, tame.

subject, a. exposed, liable, prone; answerable, amenable. *Antonyms:* exempt, immune, independent, free.

subject, v. subordinate, expose.

subject, n. dependant, subordinate; topic, subject, matter, theme.

subjection, n. subjugation, conquest, subordination, subserviency.

sublime, a. exalted, grand, magnificent, glorious, majestic.

submerge, v. plunge, immerse, sink, submerse; overflow, flood.

submerging, n. submergence, submersion, immersion, inundation.

submission, n. compliance, acquiescence, surrender, resignation, obedience.

submissive, a. yielding, obedient, tractable, meek, resigned, passive. *Antonyms:* insubmissive, defiant, intractable, rebellious, refractory.

submit, v. yield, surrender, succumb, acquiesce, comply, tolerate, stand. *Antonyms:* resist, rebel, disobey, revolt.

subservient, a. subordinate, subject, inferior; serviceable, conducive.

subside, v. decrease, sink, abate, fall.

subsidence, n. decrease, abatement.

substantiate, v. verify, corroborate, confirm, prove.

substantiation, n. corroboration, confirmation, verification.

substitute, v. exchange, commute.

substitute, n. deputy, proxy, representative, agent.

subterfuge, n. artifice, evasion, shift, sophistry, excuse.

subtle, a. artful, cunning, sly, designing, crafty, refined, discriminating.

succeeding, a. subsequent, following.

success, n. prosperity, triumph, victory, good fortune.

successful, n. prosperous, victorious, triumphant, fortunate.

succession, n. sequence, consecution; chain, line, series.

successive, a. consecutive.

successor, n. *Antonym:* predecessor.

sudden, a. unexpected, abrupt, unlooked for.

sue, v. prosecute.

suffering, n. distress, agony, misery, pain, discomfort, torture, sufferance.

sufficiency, n. enough, adequacy, competence. *Antonyms:* insufficiency, inadequacy.

sufficient, a. adequate. *Antonyms:* insufficient, inadequate.

suffocate, v. choke, stifle, smother, asphyxiate.

suffocation, n. smothering, asphyxiation.

suggest, v. allude to, hint, intimate, insinuate, propose, recommend.

suggestion, n. intimation, hint, allusion, proposal, instance, insinuation.

suicide, n. self-murder, self-destruction; self-murderer.

suit, n. wooing, courtship, addresses; prosecution, action, lawsuit.

suit, v. fit, adapt, adjust; please, gratify, satisfy.

suitable, a. fitting, accordant, proper, becoming.

sulky, a. sullen, morose, surly, moody.

sullen, a. morose, unamiable, sulky, intractable.

sum, n. amount, total, aggregate, sum total; problem, example.

sum, v. cast up, add, compute; summarize.

summary, n. recapitulation, epitome, resume, synopsis.

summing up. resume, recapitulation, peroration.

sunburnt, a. tanned; blowzy, bronzed.

sunrise, n. daybreak, dawn, aurora.

super, n. supernumerary.

superabundance, n. redundancy, excess, surfeit, superfluity.

superb, n. magnificent, grand, august, elegant.

superintendent, n. overseer, guardian, supervisor, custodian, intendant, manager.

superior, a. more excellent, surpassing, paramount, predominant.

superiority, n. predominancy, preeminence, ascendency, supremacy.

supernatural, a. miraculous, preternatural, hyperphysical.

supersede, v. replace, displace, supplant.

supple, a. flexible, plaint, lithe.

supplement, n. continuation, appendix, postscript, addition, addendum.

supply, v. furnish, afford, yield, replenish, recruit, stock.

support, v. prop, brace, bolster, uphold, sustain. *Antonyms*: desert, undermine, weaken, repudiate, oppose.

supporter, n. advocate, adherent, defender, pillar.

suppose, v. assume, conjecture, presume, imagine, believe, imply, surmise.

supposed, a. assumed, presumed, putative.

supposition, n. hypothesis, conjecture, surmise, assumption.

suppress, v. quell, overpower, put down; check, repress, restrain.

suppression, n. quelling, overthrow; repression, restraint; concealment, secretion.

supreme, a. transcendent, preeminent, superlative, paramount, predominant.

sure, a. certain, inevitable; positive, confident, assured. *Antonyms*: uncertain, doubtful, dubious.

sureness, n. certainty, inevitability, assurance, certitude, safety, positiveness.

surety, n. sureness, certainty; security, pledge, guaranty.

surface, n. exterior, outside, superficies.

surmise, v. suppose, conjecture, suspect, guess, opine.

surmount, v. overtop; conquer, overcome, vanquish.

surmountable, a. superable, conquerable. *Antonyms*: insuperable, unsurmountable.

surpassing, a. exceeding, superior, preeminent, transcendent, supereminent.

S
T

surplus, n. surplusage, excess, overplus, residue, remainder.

surprise, v. amaze, astonish, astound.

surprise, n. amazement, astonishment.

surprising, a. astonishing, amazing, astounding, marvelous.

surrender, v. relinquish, yield, abandon, capitulate, waive, remit.

surrender, n. relinquishment, capitulation, yielding.

surround, v. enclose, encircle, encompass, environ.

surrounding, a. circumambient, encompassing, encircling, ambient, enveloping.

susceptible, a. sensitive, impressionable, impressible, tender.

suspect, v. mistrust, distrust, doubt; conjecture, surmise.

suspense, n. uncertainty, wavering, hesitation, irresolution.

suspension, n. pendency; delay, respite, postponement, abeyance.

suspicion, n. mistrust, misgiving, distrust; surmise, conjecture, supposition.

swallow, v. ingurgitate; gulp, bolt, engorge.

swallowing, n. deglutition, ingurgitation, absorption. *Antonym:* aglutition.

swap, v. exchange, trade.

swarming, a. teeming.

sway, n. dominion, domination, rule.

swear, v. blaspheme, curse, imprecate, use profane language.

swearing, n. profanity, oath, blasphemy.

sweat, v. perspire; exude.

sweet, a. saccharine, honeyed, sugary, nectarean. *Antonyms:*

bitter, acrid, tart, sour.

sweetheart, n. [male] lover, inamorato, beau; [female] ladylove, mistress.

sweets, n. pl. confectionery, sweetmeats.

sweet-smelling, a. fragrant, redolent, balmy, aromatic, savory, sweet-scented.

swell, v. distend, dilate, expand, bloat, puff up.

swell, n. swelling, augmentation, increase; protuberance, bulge.

swell, a. fashionable, elegant, distinguished, exquisite. —n. exquisite, fop, dandy.

swelled, a. swollen, tumid, enlarged, bloated, protuberant.

swelling, n. intumescence, turgescence, prominence, protuberance. *Antonyms:* subsidence, detumescence.

swerve, v. deviate, deflect, diverge, turn aside.

swift, a. fleet, rapid, fast, speedy, quick.

swiftness, n. celerity, velocity, speed, rapidity, fleetness, quickness.

swine, n. pl. hogs.

swing, v. oscillate, vibrate; sway, brandish, flourish, wave.

swipe, v. strike; steal, pluck, snatch.

switch, v. whip, flog; shunt, shift.

swollen, a. tumid, tumefied, bloated, puffed up.

sword, n. rapier, saber.

swordfight, n. fencing, swordplay.

symbolic, a. typical, emblematical.

symmetry, n. proportion, shapeliness. *Antonyms:* asymmetry, disproportion.

sympathetic, a. compassionate, commiserating, pitiful, kind, tender.

sympathize, v. have sympathy, commiserate, condole with;

agree, be in accord.

sympathy, n. fellow-feeling, tenderness; pity, commiseration, compassion. *Antonyms*: antipathy, incompassion, inclemency, disagreement, incompatibility.

symptom, n. indication, mark, sign, evidence, diagnostic.

synopsis, n. syllabus, compendium, abstract, summary, epitome, digest.

system, n. method, order. *Antonyms*: chaos, confusion, disorder.

systematic, a. methodical, orderly. *Antonyms*: unsystematic, chaotic, immethodical.

systematize, v. methodize, classify.

T

tab, n. account, reckoning, check, tally, score.

table, n. tablet; schedule, synopsis, index, list.

taboo, a. prohibited, forbidden, interdicted, proscribed.

tackle, n. gear implements, equipment, rigging, apparatus.

tacky, a. sticky, adhesive; dowdy, shabby, unkempt, seedy.

tadpole, n. polliwog.

taffy, n. toffy, candy.

taint, v. imbue, impregnate, corrupt, infect, vitiate, sully.

taint, n. infection, contamination, vitiation, defilement, pollution.

take, v. seize, grasp, clutch, procure, clasp; catch; confiscate.

take back. recant, retract, recall, revoke, rescind, disavow, resume.

take in. comprise, encompass, comprehend, include, embrace.

take-in, n. imposition, fraud,

deception, swindle, cheat, hoax.

taken, p.p. charmed, captivated, enamored, fascinated.

take the place of. supplant, supersede, displace, substitute.

take upon one's self. assume, undertake; arrogate, usurp.

taking, a. alluring, fascinating, winning, charming, captivating.

taking, n. seizure, apprehension; reprisal; prehension.

taking back. recantation, retraction, resumption, disavowal, revocation.

tale, n. story, romance, parable, apologue, legend, fable.

talent, n. endowment, faculty, gift, forte, knack, genius.

talented, a. gifted, endowed, clever.

talk, v. speak, converse, confer, confabulate, consult; babble.

talk, n. conversation, converse, colloquy, conference, confabulation, chat, parley.

talkative, a. garrulous, loquacious, communicative, voluble, unreserved. *Antonyms*: reserved, reticent, uncommunicative, silent, still.

talkativeness, n. garrulity, loquacity, communicativeness, multiloquence. *Antonyms*: reserve, reticence, taciturnity.

talker, n. conversationalist; interlocutor; chatterer, babbler, magpie, chatterbox.

tall, a. lofty, high, towering.

tally, n. mate, match, counterpart; score, account, record.

tally, v. match, conform, agree, correspond, coincide.

tame, v. domesticate, reclaim, break; discipline, subjugate, conquer, repress.

tame, a. docile, domesticated, gentle; prosy, dull.

tamper, v. meddle, tinker.

S
T

tangible, a. palpable, tactile, material; substantial, evident, perceptible, obvious.

tangle, v. snarl, entangle, interweave. *Antonyms*: disentangle, unravel, extricate.

tangle, n. snarl, complication, intricacy, *Antonyms*: disentanglement, extrication.

tangled, a. entangled, complicated, tangly, snarled, intricate, involved.

tantalize, v. torment, plague, vex, disappoint.

tardy, a. slow, sluggish; dilatory, reluctant, behindhand, late. *Antonyms*: punctual, prompt.

tarnish, v. dim, sully, besmirch, blacken, deface.

task, n. work, labor, assignment, stint; study, lesson, exercise.

taste, n. tasting, gustation, degustation; flavor, savor, tang. *Antonyms*: dowdiness, tawdriness, distaste, vulgarity.

tasteful, a. palatable, savory, relishable, toothsome, gustable, delicious.

tasteless, a. insipid, flat, unpalatable, vapid.

tasty, a. tasteful, neat. *Antonyms*: dowdy, tawdry, meretricious, inartistic.

tattle, v. tell, divulge, blab, peach.

tattler, n. tale-bearer, gossip, quidnunc, news-monger, busybody.

taunt, v. ridicule, deride, mock, reproach, revile, jeer, twit, gibe.

taunting, a. reviling, derisive, jeering, sarcastic.

tax, n. assessment, toll, excise, levy, tribute, custom, duty.

taxable, a. assessable.

teach, v. instruct, inform, educate, discipline, train, indoctrinate, school.

teachable, a. docile, tractable, apt, bright.

teacher, n. instructor, tutor, master, pedagogue, preceptor.

teaching, n. instruction, education, breeding, enlightenment.

tear, n. rent, fissure, rip.

tearful, a. lachrymose, weeping, maudlin.

tearing, n. rending, laceration, lancination, ripping, dismemberment.

tease, v. torment, plague, tantalize, hector, taunt, harass, badger.

tedious, a. tiresome, wearisome, irksome, humdrum, monotonous.

teeth, n. pl. biters, incisors, molars, bicuspids, grinders.

teetotaler, n. nephalist, total abstainer.

tell, n. mention, recount, relate, narrate, enumerate, advise. *Antonyms*: suppress, reserve, withhold, forbear.

telling, n. notification, apprising, communication, relation, narration, recital, divulgement.

telltale, n. tattler.

temper, v. qualify, modify, moderate, appease; anneal.

temper, n. mood, disposition, humor; passion.

temperament, n. constitution, nature, temper, disposition.

temperate, a. moderate; dispassionate, calm; abstemious, sober, self-denying.

temple, n. fane, church, sanctuary, tabernacle.

temporal, a. secular, worldly; temporary; political, civil.

temporary, a. transitory, transient, temporal, impermanent, ephemeral, fleeting.

tempt, v. seduce, entice, decoy, allure, induce; provoke, incite, instigate.

temptation, n. seduction, allurement, enticement, attraction.

tempting, a. enticing, alluring, seductive.

tenacious, a. retentive; cohesive, tough; pertinacious, persistent.

tend, v. conduce, contribute; attend, accompany, guard; incline, lean.

tendency, n. drift, inclination, proclivity, proneness, propensity,, bent, predisposition.

tender, a. delicate, fragile, sensitive, susceptible; pathetic,touching, sympathetic. *Antonyms*: tough, strong.

tender, n. attendant; offer, proposal, overture, proposition.

ten years. decade.

terms, n. pl. stipulations, conditions; terminology, nomenclature.

terrace, n. esplanade, plateau.

terrible, a. dreadful, formidable, shocking, horrible, frightful, dire.

terrify, v. appall, intimidate, daunt, horrify, alarm, shock, frighten.

territory, n. province, region, district.

terror, n. alarm, consternation, dismay, panic, fright, affright.

test, n. trial, ordeal; standard, touchstone, criterion; crucible.

test, v. try, prove, assay.

testicles, n. pl. testes.

testify, v. depose, attest, asseverate, verify.

testimonial, n. credential, certificate, voucher.

testimony, n. attestation, deposition, corroboration; witness, evidence.

testy, a. irritable, choleric, captious.

text, n. passage, pericope; subject, topic, theme.

texture, n. fabric, web; grain, structure, contexture.

thankful, a. grateful.

thankfulness, n. gratitude. *Antonyms*: unthankfulness, ingratitude.

thankless, a. unthankful, ungrateful; unacceptable, unappreciated.

theater, n. playhouse; odeon, lyceum; arena, stage.

theatrical, a. dramatic, histrionic, scenic; stagy, artificial.

theory, n. hypothesis.

thick, a. dense, coagulated, crass, gross, inspissate.

thicken, v. coagulate, condense, inspissate, curdle.

thickness, n. denseness, density, compactness; grossness.

thick-skinned, a. pachydermatous; obtuse, dull, unimpressible.

thief, n. robber, pilferer, filcher, peculator; embezzler, defaulter.

thievery, n. theft, larceny; embezzlement, peculation; shoplifting.

thievish, a. light-fingered, pilfering, predatory; stealthy, sneaking.

thin, a. emaciated, slender, poor, wasted, peaked, gaunt, scrawny.

thing, n. object, article.

things, n. pl. clothes, furniture, appurtenances, belongings, goods, luggage, accessories.

think, v. meditate, cogitate, ponder, contemplate, brood, reflect, muse.

thinkable, a. conceivable, cogitable, imaginable, presumable.

thinking, a. rational, pensive, reflective, contemplative, cogitative, introspective.

thinking, n. cogitation, meditation, contemplation, thought.

thinness, n. emaciation, slenderness, gauntness, spareness, meagerness.

S
T

thirst, n. dryness, aridity, drought. *Antonym*: adipsy.

thorough, a. complete, profound. *Antonyms*: superficial, cursory, partial, sciolistic.

thought, n. reflection, cogitation, revery, musing, meditation, consideration.

thoughtful, a. contemplative, meditative, reflective, cogitative, wistful, pensive.

thoughtless, a. inconsiderate, careless, unmindful, remiss, rash, inadvertent, indiscreet.

threat, n. menace, threatening, commination, fulmination, intimidation.

threaten, v. menace; augur, forbode, portend; impend, be imminent.

three months. trimester.

threshold, n. doorsill.

thrift, n. frugality, economy, thriftiness, providence; prosperity.

thriftless, a. wasteful, improvident, extravagant, prodigal.

thrifty, a. sparing, economical, provident, frugal; thriving, prosperous; luxuriant.

thrilling, a. moving, exciting, sensational.

thrive, v. flourish, prosper.

thriving, a. flourishing, thrifty, prosperous.

throb, n. beating, pulsation, palpitation. —v. palpitate, pulsate, beat.

throne, n. sovereignty.

throw, v. pitch, hurl, fling, cast, toss, sling, heave.

throw away. squander; reject, decline, refuse.

throw out. expel, evict, oust, reject; emit; discharge. *Antonym*: retain.

throw up. resign; vomit, puke.

thrust, v. push, force, impel, shove, stab, pierce, protrude.

thunder, v. detonate, roll, boom.

thundering, n. fulmination. —a. fulminatory.

thunderstruck, n. dumfounded, astounded, amazed.

tickle, v. titillate; please, delight, gladden.

ticklish, a. difficult, critical, delicate.

tidy, a. orderly, neat, trim.

tie, v. secure, fasten, bind, tether, leash.

tie, n. knot, fastening; bond, obligation.

tight, a. taut, tense; snug, close-fitting.

till, v. cultivate.

tilt, v. slant, slope, incline, tip, cant.

time, n. duration; while, spell, season, interval, interim, lapse.

timely, a. seasonable, punctual, opportune. *Antonyms*: untimely, inopportune.

timid, a. timorous, shy, diffident, meticulous, faint-hearted, cowardly.

timidity, n. diffidence, shyness, timorousness, cowardice.

tip, v. incline, lean, cant, tilt; careen, capsize.

tire, v. fatigue, weary, jade, fag, bore, irk, tucker, exhaust.

tiresome, a. irksome, wearisome, fatiguing, tedious, toilsome, arduous.

tissue, n. fabric, stuff, cloth, texture.

together, adv. unitedly, jointly, concertedly, simultaneously.

toil, n. labor, drudgery; toils, snare, trap. —v. labor, moil, drudge.

token, n. sign, symbol, index, indication.

tolerable, a. sufferable, endurable; passable, mediocre, so-so, ordinary.

tolerance, n. endurance, toleration, sufferance. *Antonym*: intolerance.

tolerant, a. indulgent, forbearing, charitable. *Antonym*: intolerant.

tolerate, v. endure, suffer, brook; allow, permit, admit.

toleration, n. tolerance, endurance, sufferance; allowance, permission.

tomb, n. sepulchre, crypt, vault.

tombstone, n. monument; cenotaph.

tone, n. sound, note; cadence, modulation; force, vigor, energy.

tone down. subdue, moderate, soften.

toneless, a. aspirated, surd, atonic, unintonated.

tool, n. implement, utensil, instrument.

top, n. summit, crest, apex, vertex, pinnacle, zenith.

topic, n. subject, theme; division, head, subdivision.

torment, n. pain, anguish, distress, torture; bane, infliction.

torment, v. persecute, hector, tease, tantalize, harry; torture.

torn, a. rent, lacerated, ripped.

tornado, n. hurricane, cyclone, whirlwind.

torpid, n. numb, benumbed, unfeeling; lethargic, dull.

touch, v. meet, impinge; graze.

touch, n. touching, contact, contiguity, juxtaposition, osculation.

touching, a. pathetic, affecting, moving, tender.

touching, prep. respecting, concerning, regarding.

touchy, a. irascible, irritable, petulant, testy, choleric, snappish.

tough, a. tenacious, unyielding; cohesive, adhesive, obdurate, refractory, stubborn.

tour, n. journey, trip, excursion, expedition.

tousled, a. disordered, dishev-

eled.

tower, n. steeple, campanile, minaret, spire, belfry.

tower, v. overtop, rise above.

toy, n. gimcrack, plaything, trinket.

track, n. trace, vestige, footprint, footmark.

trade, n. commerce, barter, traffic, business; handicraft.

trade, v. exchange, barter, traffic, swap.

trader, n. trafficker, dealer, merchant, tradesman, monger.

tradesman, n. trader, merchant; artisan, craftsman, mechanic, journeyman, handicraftsman.

trading, a. commercial, mercantile; venal, corrupt, jobbing.

trail, n. train; track, wake, spoor, footmark, foil, trace.

trailing, a. procumbent, prostrate. *Antonyms*: upright, erect.

train, v. discipline, nurture, drill; accustom, habituate, familiarize.

trained, a. skilled, practiced, disciplined, competent. *Antonym*: untrained.

training, n. discipline, nurture, drilling, exercise.

traitorous, a. perfidious, treasonable, recreant, faithless.

tramp, n. vagrant, vagabond, landloper, walleteer, nomad, hobo, derelict.

trample, v. crush; scorn, spurn, disregard.

transaction, n. procedure, affair, deal, business.

transform, v. transfigure, metamorphose; transmute.

transformation, n. transfiguration, metamorphosis; transmutation.

transgress, v. violate, infringe, disregard.

transgression, n. violation, infringement, infraction.

transient, a. fleeting, transitory,

S
T

temporary, impermanent.

translate, v. construe, render, interpret.

translation, n. rendering, interpretation.

transparency, n. diaphaneity, translucency. *Antonyms*: opacity, intransparency.

transparent, a. diaphanous, translucent, pellucid. *Antonyms*: opaque, intransparent.

trap, n. snare, toil, gin, springe; pitfall; artifice, stratagem.

trap, v. entrap, ensnare, trapan, catch.

trash, n. rubbish, refuse, trumpery.

travel, v. journey, itinerate, peregrinate.

traveler, n. wayfarer, itinerant, voyager, pilgrim, tourist.

traveling, a. wayfaring, itinerant, wandering, peripatetic.

travesty, n. burlesque, parody, caricature, take-off.

tray, n. salver, waiter, plateau, server.

treacherous, a. traitorous, perfidious, faithless.

treachery, n. treason, perfidy, disloyalty.

treat, v. regale, feast; negotiate; behave toward, deal with.

treaty, n. covenant, agreement, compact, concordat, pact, protocol.

tree, n. [young] sapling, seedling.

tremble, v. quake, quiver, shudder, dodder, quaver, totter, vibrate, oscillate.

trembling, n. tremor, quivering, quaver, trepidation, rigor, oscillation.

trend, n. tendency.

trespass, v. encroach upon, infringe, intrude.

trial, n. test, experiment, proof, essay, examination; probation; ordeal.

trick, n. ruse, artifice, stratagem,

sleight, hoax, maneuver.

trick, v. deceive, cheat, defraud, cozen, impose upon.

trickery, n. deception, chicanery, artifice, duplicity.

trickster, n. rogue, cheat, impostor, scoundrel.

tricky, a. trickish, knavish, unprincipled, treacherous.

trifle, n. triviality, bagatelle, doit.

trifling, a. trivial, paltry, piddling, insignificant, piffling, frivolous.

trim, a. spruce, smart; neat, tidy.

trim, v. adjust, arrange; decorate, adorn, garnish, embellish.

trip, n. jaunt; lapse, slip, stumble, misstep.

triumph, n. victory, conquest; exultation, ovation.

triumph, v. overcome, prevail, succeed; exult, rejoice.

triumphant, a. exultant, jubilant; victorious.

trivial, a. trifling, frivolous, insignificant, unimportant.

troop, n. company, battery, squad, band, throng, crowd.

trouble, v. vex, disturb, distress, inconvenience, incommode, pester, worry.

trouble, n. tribulation, adversity, reverses, affliction, calamity, misfortune.

troublesome, a. vexatious, burdensome, afflictive, harassing, galling, wearisome.

trousers, n. pl. pants.

true, a. correct, exact, accurate, veritable, authentic, real, genuine.

trueblue, a. incorruptible, loyal, true.

trump, v. impose, palm off, obtrude, deceive.

trumpet, n. horn.

trust, n. credence, confidence, belief, reliance, affiance, faith; credit. *Antonyms*: distrust, doubt.

trust, v. depend upon, rely upon;

give credit to; tick; intrust, commit.

trustee, n. fiduciary, regent.

trustful, a. unsuspicious, confiding, credulous, confident.

trusty, a. trustworthy, faithful, reliable.

truth, n. veracity, truthfulness; accuracy, precision, exactness, correctness.

truthful, a. veracious, undissembling, ingenuous, veridical.

try, v. test, examine, prove; attempt, essay, endeavor.

try, n. attempt, essay, trial, experiment.

trying, a. severe, distressing, hard, irksome, afflictive, ordeal.

tug, n. trace; pull, effort.

tumble, v. heave, toss, roll, pitch; topple.

tumor, n. sarcoma; myoma; carcinoma; lipoma.

tumult, n. commotion, hurly-burly, turbulence.

tumultuous, a. disorderly, turbulent, noisy, riotous.

tune, n. air, melody; order, harmony, unison, concord, accord.

tune, v. attune, modulate, harmonize.

tuneful, a. melodious, harmonious.

tuneless, a. inharmonious, discordant, dissonant.

turmoil, n. commotion, uproar, tumult, turbulence, agitation.

turn, v. revolve, spin, gyrate, rotate, wheel, veer.

turn, n. bend, winding, meander, curve, detour, deflection.

turned away. averted.

turning, n. rotation, revolution, spinning, gyration; eversion, extroversion.

turning, a. revolving, rotary, rotating, gyratory, winding, circumrotary.

turning back. retroversion, retroflexion.

turning point. crisis; pivot.

turn upside down. invert, reverse.

turtle, n. tortoise; terrapin.

twelve, n. dozen.

twig, n. spray, branch, sprig, switch.

twilight, n. dusk, evening.

twine, v. entwine, encircle, wreathe.

twinkle, v. blink, wink; flash, sparkle, scintillate.

twinkling, n. sparkling, scintillation, flash, twinkle.

twist, v. contort, writhe, squirm, convolve, pervert.

two, n. couple, pair.

twofold, a. double, duplicate.

two-sided, a. double-faced, bilateral.

two weeks. fortnight.

type, n. symbol, token, representation; model, exemplar, prototype, archetype. *Antonyms*: atypical, abnormal, variant, unique.

typesetter, n. compositor; typograph.

typhoid fever. enteric fever.

typical, a. emblematical, prefigurative, representative, indicative. *Antonyms*: atypical, abnormal, variant, unique.

typify, v. represent, prefigure.

typographer, n. printer.

typography, n. printing.

tyrannical, a. despotic, arbitrary, autocratic, imperious, absolute.

tyrannize, v. domineer, persecute, oppress.

tyranny, n. despotism, absolutism, oppression, rigor, severity.

tyrant, n. despot, autocrat; oppressor, persecutor, usurper.

S
T

U

ubiquitous, a. omnipresent.
ugly, a. repulsive, unsightly, loathsome, hideous, grewsome, frightful.
ulcer, n. fester, gathering, imposthume, pustule, ulceration.
ultimate, a. final, farthest, extreme.
ultimately, adv. finally.
ultra, a. extreme.
umpire, n. referee, judge, arbitrator, arbiter.
unabated, a. undiminished, unassuaged.
unable, a. incapable.
unabundant, a. scarce, deficient, rare.
unacceptable, a. objectionable, unwelcome, undesirable.
unaccountable, a. incomprehensible, inexplicable, inscrutable.
unaccustomed, a. unfamiliar, unwonted, unused.
unacquainted, a. unfamiliar, strange.
unadulterated, a. unsophisticated, unalloyed, pure.
unadvised, a. imprudent, unwise, indiscreet, inconsiderate.
unaffected, a. unmoved, untouched, unimpressed; artless, naive, sincere, natural, unfeigned.
unafraid, a. undaunted, unappalled, unabashed, undismayed.
unalterable, a. immutable, unchangeable.
unambitious, a. unenterprising, indifferent.
unamiable, a. cross, ungracious, surly, unfriendly.
unanimity, n. unison, accord, agreement.
unanswerable, a. irrefutable, incontrovertible.
unappeasable, a. insatiate, insatiable, unquenchable, implacable.
unappreciable, a. imperceptible.
unapproachable, a. inaccessible, distant.
unarmed, a. defenseless, unguarded, unprotected.
unasked, a. unsolicited, voluntary, free-will.
unassailable, a. impregnable, invincible, secure, invulnerable.
unassorted, a. mixed, promiscuous, indiscriminate.
unatonable, a. inexpiable, irremissible.
unattainable, a. unachievable, impracticable, impossible.
unauthentic, a. spurious, supposititious, uncanonical, apocryphal, fictitious.
unavailing, a. futile, nugatory, ineffectual, abortive, vain, bootless.
unavoidable, a. inevitable, unpreventable, ineludable.
unaware, a. unconscious, unmindful, insensible.
unbearable, a. intolerable, insufferable, unendurable.
unbecoming, a. inappropriate, unseemly, unsuitable, indecorous.
unbegotten, a. self-existent.
unbelief, n. incredulity, skepticism, doubt, infidelity, distrust, suspicion.
unbelievable, a. incredible, implausible, fabulous.
unbeliever, n. doubter, skeptic, infidel, free-thinker, nullifidian.
unbelieving, a. incredulous, doubtful, skeptical, nullifidian.
unbend, v. relax.
unbending, a. inflexible, unyielding, rigid, unpliant, resolute, incompliant.
unbiased, a. unprejudiced, impartial, unjaundiced, neutral,

disinterested.

unbidden, a. unasked, uninvited; spontaneous, voluntary, volitional.

unblamable, a. blameless, inculpable, irreprehensible, innocent.

unblushing, a. shameless, unabashed, brazen-faced, indecent, immodest.

unbounded, a. illimitable, boundless, unlimited, limitless, immeasurable, vast, infinite, immense.

unbreakable, a. infrangible; inviolable.

unbreathable, a. irrespirable.

unbridled, a. unrestrained, uncurbed, uncontrolled, licentious, immoderate.

unbroken, a. whole, intact; inviolate, inviolated; undisturbed, sound.

unbury, v. exhume, disentomb, disinter.

uncanny, a. weird, eerie.

uncanonical, a. apocryphal, unauthentic.

unceasing, a. incessant, perpetual, perennial, ceaseless.

unceremonious, a. informal, unconstrained; bluff, blunt.

uncertain, a. distrustful, hesitating; dubious, precarious, problematical, insecure.

uncertainty, n. distrust, hesitation, doubt, dubiousness, dubiety, incertitude.

unchangeable, a. immutable, invariable, changeless, stereotyped, unalterable.

unchanging, a. unvarying, permanent.

uncharitable, a. illiberal, intolerant, ungenerous, bigoted, censorious.

unchaste, a. incontinent, impure, lewd, wanton, immoral.

unchastity, n. incontinence,

wantonness, lechery, licentiousness, lewdness, impurity.

unchecked, a. unbridled, unrestrained, unhampered, untrammeled, uncurbed.

uncivil, a. discourteous, rude, churlish, boorish, brusque, impolite.

uncivilized, a. savage, barbarous, unreclaimed, benighted.

unclassifiable, a. nondescript.

unclean, a. soiled, dirty, foul, filthy, nasty, uncleanly.

uncommon, a. unusual, singular, rare, unique, queer, strange, odd.

uncommunicative, a. reserved, taciturn, reticent, secretive.

uncompelled, a. voluntary, spontaneous, gratuitous, unconstrained, volitional.

uncomplaining, a. resigned, patient, forbearing, long-suffering, meek.

uncomplimentary, a. unflattering, frank, derogatory, blunt.

uncompromising, a. inflexible, irreconcilable, intransigent, firm.

unconcern, n. indifference, nonchalance, apathy, disinterestedness.

unconcerned, a. indifferent, nonchalant, cool, apathetic, disinterested.

unconditional, a. absolute, unqualified, unrestricted, *carte blanche*.

uncongenial, a. disagreeable, unpleasant.

unconnected, a. disconnected, separate, isolated, abrupt, incoherent.

unconquerable, a. invincible, insuperable, impregnable, indomitable, inexpugnable.

unconscionable, n. unreasonable, inordinate, exorbitant, excessive.

unconscious, a. unaware,

U
Z

insensible; comatose; ingenuous, artless, naive.

unconsciousness, n. insensibility; coma.

unconstrained, a. spontaneous, uncompelled, voluntary, natural.

uncontradictable, a. incontrovertible, indisputable, incontestable.

uncontrollable, a. ungovernable, irrepressible.

unconvincing, a. inconclusive.

uncouple, v. disconnect, detach, disjoin, loose.

uncourtly, a. rude, gawky, ungraceful, awkward, inelegant.

uncouth, a. awkward, clumsy, rude, ungainly, loutish, gawky, ungraceful.

uncover, v. disclose, reveal, expose, show.

uncultivated, a. untilled, fallow.

uncultered, a. unlettered; ignorant; philistine.

undecaying, a. imperishable, amaranthine, perennial, undying.

undeceive, v. disabuse, disillusionize, disillusion.

undeceiving, n. disillusion, disillusionment.

undecided, a. unsettled, pending; wavering, irresolute, dubious, controvertible.

undecipherable, a. illegible.

undefinable, a. unexplainable, undeterminable.

undefined, a. vague, indefinite, obscure; boundless, limitless.

undemonstrative, a. staid, quiet, demure, phlegmatic, sedate.

undeniable, a. incontestable, indisputable, unquestionable, indubitable, irrefragable.

under, prep. beneath, below, subordinate, inferior, subject to.

underbrush, n. undergrowth, jungle.

underground, a. subterranean, subterraneous, subterrene, subterrestrial.

underhand, a. underhanded, surreptitious, clandestine, covert.

underline, v. underscore.

underling, n. subordinate, inferior, understrapper.

underlying, a. fundamental, basic.

underrate, v. underestimate, undervalue, underprize.

understand, v. comprehend, apprehend, grasp, discern.

understandable, a. comprehensible, intelligible.

understanding, n. comprehension, discernment, apprehension; accord.

undervalue, v. depreciate, vilipend, despise; underrate, underestimate.

under water. submarine, subaquatic, subaqueous, submerged.

underwear, n. underclothing; lingerie.

underwrite, v. insure; subscribe.

undeserved, a. unmerited, unjust.

undeserving, a. unworthy, unmeritorious, indign.

undesigned, a. unpremeditated, unintentional, accidental.

undersigning, a. artless, guileless, sincere.

undesirable, a. inexpedient; objectionable, unacceptable, ineligible.

undetermined, a. unsettled, irresolute, wavering, indeterminate, abeyant.

undeveloped, a. in embryo, embryonic, immature, abeyant.

undevelopment, n. immaturity; atrophy, abortion; embryo.

undignified, a. unseemly, unbecoming, groveling, servile, obsequious.

undiminished, a. unabated, unlessened.

undiscernible, a. imperceptible, indiscernible.

undisputable, a. incontrovertible, incontestable, indisputable, undeniable.

undissolvable, a. insoluble, indissolvable, indissoluble.

undo, v. reverse, annul, nullify, abrogate, neutralize, invalidate.

undoing, n. reversal, annulment, invalidation, abrogation; impoverishment, ruin.

undoubted, a. indubitable, unquestioned, unchallenged, undisputed.

undoubting, a. sure, confident, sanguine, implicit.

undress, v. disrobe, strip, divest.

undressing, n. disrobing, stripping.

undue, v. unreasonable, immoderate, exorbitant, excessive, disproportioned.

undutiful, a. disobedient, unfilial.

undying, a. deathless, immortal.

unearth, v. uncover, disclose, ferret out.

unearthly, a. weird, supernatural, preternatural, eerie.

uneasiness, n. restlessness, inquietude, perturbation, anxiety, agitation, malaise.

uneasy, a. restless, restive, anxious, perturbed, impatient.

uneducated, a. illiterate, benighted.

unemotional, a. phlegmatic.

unendurable, a. intolerable, insufferable.

unequal, a. unmatched, uneven, disparate; ill-balanced, disproportioned.

unerasable, a. indelible, inerasable, permanent.

unescapable, a. inevitable, unavoidable.

unessential, a. nonessential, immaterial, unnecessary.

uneven, a. jagged, rugged, rough.

unexcelled, a. unequaled, unsurpassed, superior, supreme.

unexcitable, a. imperturbable, phlegmatic.

unexhaustible, a. exhaustless, inexhaustible.

unexpected, a. unforeseen, unanticipated, unlooked for.

unexperienced, a. inexperienced, unpracticed.

unexplainable, a. inexplicable, inscrutable, uninterpretable.

unexpressible, a. inexpressible, unutterable, ineffable.

unextinguishable, a. unquenchable, insuppressible.

unfading, a. perennial, amaranthine, permanent, enduring.

unfailing, a. sure, certain, constant, inexhaustible, infallible, inevitable.

unfair, a. unjust, partial, unconscionable, inequitable, disingenuous.

unfairness, n. injustice, inequity, partiality.

unfaithful, a. disloyal, faithless, perfidious, undutiful.

unfaithfulness, n. disloyalty, perfidy, apostasy, recreancy, inconstancy, treachery.

unfaltering, a. steadfast, unwavering, unswerving.

unfamiliar, a. unaccustomed, strange, novel; inconversant, unacquainted.

unfathered, a. fatherless; bastard, illegitimate.

unfavorable, a. adverse, inimical, unpropitious, inauspicious, malign, derogatory, hostile.

unfeeling, a. insensible, insensate, insentient, numb, apathetic, impassible.

unfeigned, a. genuine, sincere, unaffected, unassumed.

U Z

unfinished, a. incomplete.

unfit, a. unsuitable, ineligible, inappropriate, unqualified, incompetent, inapt, inept.

unfit, v. disqualify, incapacitate, disable.

unflattering, a. uncomplimentary, derogatory, frank.

unflinching, a. resolute.

unfold, v. unfurl, expand, evolve, unroll; disentangle, unravel, resolve.

unforced, a. spontaneous, voluntary, optional, unconstrained.

unforgivable, a. unpardonable, irremissible, inexpiable.

unforgiving, a. implacable, irremissive, relentless.

unfortunate, a. unlucky, unsuccessful, disastrous, ill-starred, ill-fated.

unfounded, a. baseless, groundless.

unfriendliness, n. enmity, hostility, disfavor, antipathy.

unfriendly, a. hostile, ill-disposed, inimical, malign, unamicable.

unfruitful, a. unproductive, effete, unprolific, infertile, acarpous.

ungainly, a. awkward, gawky, ungraceful, lumbering, loutish.

ungenerous, a. illiberal, narrow, sordid, uncharitable, stingy.

unglue, v. deglutinate.

ungodly, a. godless, impious, irreverent, profane, unrighteous.

ungovernable, a. unruly, unmanageable, refractory, intractable, mutinous, impotent.

ungraceful, a. awkward, uncourtly, clumsy, uncouth, lumbering, ungainly.

ungrateful, a. ingrateful, unthankful; disagreeable, offensive.

ungratefulness, n. ingratitude.

ungrateful person. ingrate.

unguarded, a. defenseless, unprotected; incautious, unwary.

unhallowed, a. unsanctified, profane.

unhandy, a. inconvenient; clumsy, awkward, maladroit.

unhappiness, n. infelicity, misery, distress, sorrow, woe.

unhappy, a. infelicitous, unfortunate; miserable, wretched, sad, sorrowful.

unharmed, a. unscathed, inviolate, uninjured, unhurt, intact, scatheless.

unhealable, a. insanable, incurable.

unhealthful, a. unwholesome, insalubrious, unsanitary, unhealthy, morbific, pestiferous.

unhealthy, unhealthful, unwholesome, insalubrious, noxious, noisome, pestiferous.

unheard of. unprecedented, exceptional; unknown, obscure.

unheeded, a. disregarded, ignored, unnoticed.

unholy, a. unhallowed, unconsecrated, profane, impious, evil, ungodly.

unhonored, a. inglorious, unsung, unrenowned, obscure.

uniform, unvarying, invariable, constant, undeviating; consonant, consistent. *Antonyms*: diverse, difform, anomalous, variant, heterogeneous, variable.

uniform, n. livery, dress, regimentals.

uniformity, n. sameness, even, tenor; invariability, regularity, equableness. *Antonyms*: diversity, variation, anomaly.

unimaginative, a. matter-of-fact, prosaic, literal, practical, unromantic.

unimportance, n. immateriality, insignificance, triviality, paltriness.

unimportant, a. immaterial, insignificant, trivial, paltry.

unimpressible, a. unimpressionable, impassible, stoical, impassive.

unintentional, a. accidental, unpremeditated, fortuitous, undesigned.

union, n. coalition, combination, merger, fusion, unification, incorporation. *Antonym*: disunion.

unique, a. unmatched, unexampled.

unite, v. join, combine, annex, associate, link, couple, yoke, slice.

united, a. combined, incorporate, federated, confederate, affiliated, unified.

unity, n. oneness, singleness; concord, harmony, agreement, uniformity.

unjust, a. unfair, inequitable, iniquitous, unmerited.

unjustifiable, a. indefensible, inexcusable, unwarrantable.

unkind, a. cruel, harsh, austere, rigorous, incompassionate.

unkindness, n. cruelty, brutality, severity, incompassion, incivility, disfavor.

unknowable, a. incognizable, incognoscible, unascertainable, unintelligible, incomprehensible.

unknown, a. obscure, inglorious, unrenowned, nameless, undistinguished; unascertained.

unknown person. stranger, ignote.

unladylike, a. hoidenish, pert, ill-bred.

unlawful, a. illegal, illicit, contraband, illegitimate, unlicensed.

unlike, a. dissimilar, different, diverse, sundry, variant.

unlikelihood, n. improbability, unlikeliness.

unlikely, a. improbable; unpromising.

unlikeness, n. dissimilarity, dissimilitude, difference, contrast.

unlimited, a. limitless, illimitable, infinite, absolute, unbounded.

unload, v. disburden, unlade, relieve.

unlovely, a. uncomely, homely, plain, unattractive, repulsive.

unlucky, a. unfortunate, luckless, ill-starred, unhappy.

unmaidenly, a. hoidenish, rude, boisterous, pert.

unmanageable, a. ungovernable, intractable, refractory, fractious.

unmannerly, a. impolite, discourteous, boorish, uncivil, rude.

unmarried, a. single, celibate.

unmarried man. bachelor, celibate, agamist.

unmarried woman. spinster.

unmatchable, a. peerless, matchless, incomparable, inimitable, unique.

unmeaning, a. meaningless, senseless; insignificant, inexpressive.

unmeant, a. unintentional.

unmelodious, a. discordant, harsh, dissonant, inharmonious, unmusical.

unmerciful, a. cruel, pitiless, merciless, inclement, unsparing, stern.

unmindful, a. oblivious, inadvertent, inattentive, heedless.

unmistakable, a. manifest, palpable, obvious, patent, evident, distinct, unambiguous.

unmovable, a. fixed, stable, immobile.

unmoved, a. calm, dispassionate, indifferent, unstirred,

U
Z

impassive.

unnatural, a. abnormal, monstrous, anomalous, aberrant, variant.

unnecessary, a. superfluous, useless, needless, uncalled for, expletive, redundant.

unneighborly, a. unsociable, exclusive, distant, unaccommodating.

unnoticed, a. unheeded, unnoted, surreptitious.

unobjectionable, a. unexceptionable.

unobtainable, a. unprocurable, unattainable, inaccessible.

unobtrusive, a. unpretentious, unassuming, modest.

unorthodox, a. heterodox.

unpacifiable, a. implacable, unappeasable, unreconcilable.

unpaid, a. outstanding, payable, due, unliquidated.

unpardonable, a. inexpiable, unatonable, irremissible, unforgivable.

unpassable, a. impassable.

unpenetrable, a. impenetrable, impervious, imperforable.

unpleasant, a. disagreeable, uncongenial.

unpopular, a. disliked, obnoxious, odious, offensive.

unpractical, a. impractical, visionary, Utopian.

unpraiseworthy, a. uncommendable, illaudable, indign.

unprejudiced, a. impartial, unbiased, unjaundiced.

unpretending, a. unobtrusive, modest, unpretentious, unostentatious.

unpretentious, a. unpretending.

unpreventable, a. unavoidable, inevitable.

unprincipled, a. unscrupulous.

unproductive, a. unfruitful, barren.

unprofessional, a. amateur.

unprofitable, a. unremunerative, profitless; futile, fruitless, unavailing.

unpromising, a. unlikely; inauspicious, unpropitious.

unqualified, a. incompetent, ineligible; absolute, unconditional.

unquestionable, a. incontrovertible, irrefutable, incontestable, indubitable, obvious, indisputable.

unquestioned, a. undoubted, implicit.

unravel, v. disentangle, extricate, ravel; decipher, unfold.

unreachable, a. inaccessible.

unreadable, a. illegible.

unreal, a. fanciful, imaginary, visionary, unsubstantial, shadowy.

unreasonable, a. irrational, absurd, unwise, preposterous, senseless; excessive.

unreclaimable, a. irreclaimable, irretrievable, hopeless, incorrigible.

unrecognized, a. ignored, disregarded, unacknowledged.

unreconcilable, a. antagonistic, incompatible, irreconcilable; implacable, unpacifiable.

unrecoverable, a. irrecoverable, irreparable, irretrievable, irrecuperable.

unredeemed, a. forfeited, unransomed, unfulfilled.

unreformable, a. irreformable, incorrigible.

unrelenting, a. relentless, implacable, inexorable, remorseless, pitiless, unmerciful.

unreliable, a. untrustworthy, undependable, uncertain.

unremitting, a. indefatigable, persevering, unceasing, constant.

unrepairable, a. irreparable.

unrepentant, a. impenitent,

incontrite.

unreserve, n. frankness, candor, ingenuousness.

unresistible, a. irresistible.

unresisting, a. passive, submissive, long-suffering.

unrest, n. unquietness, restlessness, uneasiness, disquietude, inquietude.

unrestrained, a. unbridled, ungoverned, uncurbed, riotous, impotent.

unrestraint, n. freedom, liberty, license, abandon.

unrestricted, a. unlimited, unfettered, uncircumscribed.

unrevivable, a. irrevivable, irresuscitable.

unrighteous, a. unholy, evil, iniquitous, wicked, vicious.

unroll, v. unfold, unfurl, evolve.

unromantic, a. prosaic, pragmatical, matter-of-fact, practical, literal.

unruly, a. turbulent, ungovernable, refractory, insubordinate, fractious.

unsafe, a. insecure, risky, perilous, dangerous, hazardous.

unsafety, n. insecurity, danger, risk, peril, hazard, jeopardy.

unsatisfactory, a. disappointing, insufficient.

unsatisfiable, a. insatiable, insatiate.

unsavory, a. offensive, rank, unpleasant; insipid, savorless.

unsay, v. recall, retract, recant.

unscrupulous, a. unprincipled, unconscientious, dishonest, dishonorable, knavish.

unseasonable, a. inopportune, ill-timed, untimely, premature.

unseemly, a. unbecoming, improper, indecorous.

unseen, a. invisible, unperceived, secret, unnoticed, unobserved.

unselfish, a. magnanimous, disinterested, altruistic, charitable.

unsentimental, a. matter-of-fact, prosaic, pragmatical, practical.

unserviceableness, n. inutility.

unsettle, v. disorder, derange, upset, unhinge, disconcert.

unsettled, a. undetermined, dubious, unadjusted, controvertible, disputable.

unshapely, a. misshapen, deformed.

unsheltered, a. exposed, unprotected.

unsightly, a. offensive, repulsive.

unskilled, a. unpracticed, unskillful, empirical.

unsociable, a. morose, uncompanionable, inaffable, ungenial, taciturn.

unsolvable, a. insoluble, inexplicable.

unsophisticated, a. unadulterated; innocent, guileless, gullible, ingenuous.

unsound, a. defective, impaired; sophistical, fallacious, illogical.

unsparing, a. liberal, ungrudging, profuse; severe, unmerciful.

unspeakable, a. ineffable, unutterable, inexpressible.

unspotted, a. spotless, pure.

unstable, a. insecure, unsteady, irresolute, inconstant, erratic.

unsteadfast, a. unstable, inconstant, wavering, irresolute.

unsteady, a. inconstant, precarious, wavering, variable, vacillating.

unstudied, a. extemporaneous, extempore, impromptu, offhand.

unsubmissive, a. insubordinate, refractory.

unsuccessful, a. unfortunate, unlucky, unprosperous; abortive, fruitless.

unsuitable, a. inappropriate,

U
Z

incongruous, incompatible.
unsupplied, a. destitute.
unsurmountable, a. insuperable.
unsurpassed, a. peerless,
transcendent, superior,
unrivaled, matchless.
unsusceptible, a.
unimpressionable, unfeeling.
unsuspecting, a. unsuspicious,
gullible, indubious, unsophisticated.
unsustainable, a. untenable,
controvertible.
untangle, a. unravel, disentangle.
untaxed, a. scot-free, exempt.
unteachable, a. indocile,
intractable.
unthankful, a. ungrateful.
untidy, a. disorderly, slatternly,
littered.
untimely, a. premature, unseasonable, inopportune, ill-timed,
malapropos.
untiring, a. indefatigable,
unceasing, tireless, unremitting, unwearied.
untrue, a. inveracious, mendacious, false, untruthful,
unfaithful.
untruth, n. falsehood, fiction,
fabrication, lie.
untruthful, a. inveracious,
mendacious, lying.
untwist, v. unravel, disentangle,
feaze.
unused, a. unaccustomed,
unfamiliar.
unusual, a. uncommon, curious,
rare, odd, unique, extraordinary.
unvarying, a. invariable, monotonous, uniform.
unveil, v. expose, uncover,
reveal, disclose.
unviolated, a. inviolate,
inviolated, inviolable.
unwarrantable, a. unjustifiable,
indefensible.
unwavering, a. steadfast,

resolute.
unwholesome, a. baneful,
insalubrious.
unwieldy, a. ponderous, cumbersome, clumsy.
unwilling, a. reluctant, indisposed, loath, disinclined,
averse.
unwind, v. disentangle, unravel.
unwise, a. imprudent, injudicious, inexpedient, indiscreet.
unwittingly, adv. unknowingly,
undesignedly, inadvertently.
unworthy, a. unmeritorious,
undeserving, despicable,
contemptible.
unyielding, a. inflexible, stiff,
unbending, incompliant,
indomitable.
up grade. ascent, acclivity.
uphill, a. ascending, acclivitous,
rising.
uphold, v. support, sustain,
vindicate, defend.
upkeep, n. maintenance.
upper-hand, n. advantage,
mastery, dominion, control.
upright, a. erect, perpendicular,
vertical; honorable, honest.
uproar, n. turmoil, *fracas*, clamor,
tumult, commotion.
uproot, v. eradicate, extirpate.
upset, v. overturn, overset,
capsize, invert, overthrow;
disconcert.
upside down. inverted; disordered, topsy-turvy.
upward, a. ascending, acclivous.
urge, v. egg, importune, exhort;
impel, force; incite, instigate.
urgency, n. insistence, pressure;
importunity; exigency, stress.
urgent, a. pressing, imperative,
insistent, exigent.
usage, n. treatment; custom,
practice, use.
use, n. employment, application,
service, utilization, exploitation;
necessity. *Antonyms*: disuse,
obsolescence, desuetude,

inutility.

use, v. employ, apply, utilize, exploit; treat, behave toward.

useful, a. serviceable, advantageous, available.

usefulness, n. utility, advantage.

useless, a.unserviceable, futile, worthless, unavailing.

usher, v. show to a seat; introduce, forerun, precede.

usual, a. ordinary, general, accustomed, conventional, prevailing, everyday.

usually, adv. ordinarily, generally, customarily, commonly.

usurp, v. arrogate, seize, appropriate, accroach.

utility, n. usefulness. *Antonym*: inutility.

utilize, v. use, employ, exploit.

utmost, a. farthest out, extreme, last; greatest, maximum, uttermost.

utter, v. speak, pronounce, express.

utter, a. complete, absolute, perfect; unconditional, unqualified, peremptory.

utterance, n. speech, articulation.

utterly, adv. entirety, completely, wholly, unconditional, altogether.

uttermost, a. extreme, utmost, farthest.

V

vacancy, n. emptiness; space, vacuum, chasm, gap.

vacant, a. empty, unfilled, void, uninhabited, untenanted. *Antonyms*: full, filled, occupied.

vacate, v. empty, evacuate, resign, abdicate, annul.

vacation, n. evacuation, resignation, abdication; invalidation.

vaccinate, v. inoculate.

vacillate, v. fluctuate, waver,

veer, oscillate.

vacillating, a. irresolute, changeable, wavering, undecided, inconstant.

vagabond, n. vagrant, tramp, mendicant, beggar; rascal, rogue.

vagrant, n. tramp; beggar, vagabond, rascal. —a. wandering, nomadic, vagabond.

vague, a. indefinite, ambiguous, obscure, uncertain, groundless, hazy, indistinct.

vagueness, n. indefiniteness, ambiguity, obscurity, uncertainty.

vain, a. conceited, arrogant, egotistical, overweening.

valid, a. cogent, logical, justifiable, efficacious, well-grounded.

validity, n. strength, cogency, soundness, force. *Antonym*: invalidity.

valley, n. vale, hollow, bottom, dale, ravine.

valuable, a. costly, precious, rare, expensive; esteemed, worthy.

valuable, n. treasure.

valuation, n. appraisement, appraisal.

value, n. worth, excellence.

value, v. appraise; prize, esteem, appreciate.

vandal, n. destroyer.

vanishing, a. evanescent, disappearing, transient. —n. disappearance, evanescence.

vanity, n. unsubstantialness, unreality, inanity, delusiveness, emptiness.

vanquish, v. overcome, defeat, subjugate, subdue, rout, overpower.

vapor, n. gas, haze, fog, fume.

vaporize, v. evaporate.

variability, n. variableness, mutability, inconstancy, unsteadfastness.

U
Z

variable, a. mutable, change-able. *Antonyms*: invariable, unchangeable.

variance, n. change, alteration; dissension, disagreement, difference, nonconformity.

variation, n. mutation, change; deviation, diversity, discrepancy, diversification.

varied, a. various, diversified, different.

variety, n. diversity, diversification, multiplicity, variousness; assortment.

various, a. manifold, diverse, sundry, numerous, multifarious.

varnish, v. lacquer, japan, enamel, glaze; gloss over.

vary, v. diversify, variegate, modify; deviate, depart.

vast, a. spacious, immense, monstrous, huge, extensive, immeasurable.

vault, n. crypt, tomb, catacomb.

vault, v. leap over, spring, bound, jump; tumble.

vegetate, v. sprout, grow, germinate, pullulate; rusticate, hibernate.

vehicle, n. conveyance, carriage; medium, instrument.

veil, n. disguise, pretense, cloak, mask.

venerate, v. reverence, revere, honor, esteem.

veneration, n. reverence, honor.

venereal disease. gonorrhea, clap; syphilis.

vengeance, n. retribution, avengement, revenge.

venial, a. pardonable.

vent, v. emit, utter, say, discharge.

venture, n. chance, risk, hazard, contingency.

venture, v. dare, hazard, risk.

venturesome, a. daring, bold, intrepid, undaunted, temerarious.

veracious, a. truthful.

veranda, n. porch, piazza.

verbal, a. oral.

verdict, n. finding, decision.

verification, n. confirmation, corroboration, authentication, attestation, proof.

verify, v. corroborate, confirm, attest, authenticate, prove.

verse, n. stitch; poetry, versification; stanza.

versed, a. acquainted, skilled, proficient, conversant.

version, n. rendition, translation.

vertical, a. upright, perpendicular, plumb. *Antonyms*: horizontal, flat, level.

very, a. veritable, true, real, actual, unquestionable, identical, same.

very, adv. exceedingly, highly, greatly, extremely, excessively, surpassingly.

vest, n. invest.

vestibule, n. hall, lobby.

vex, v. tease, plague, harass, torment, tantalize.

vexatious, a. annoying, troublesome, carking, irritating, provoking, aggravating.

vibrate, v. brandish, flourish, swing; oscillate, librate.

vibration, n. oscillation, swinging, vacillation, libration.

vice, n. sin, iniquity, licentiousness, immorality; defect, fault.

vicinity, n. neighborhood, vicinage; nearness, propinquity, proximity.

vicious, a. immoral, evil; defective, faulty, imperfect.

victorious, a. triumphant, conquering, successful, exultant.

victory, n. triumph, conquest, mastery.

vie, n. contend, compete, emulate.

view, n. scene, landscape, vista, perspective, panorama.

viewy, a. visionary, fanciful,

quixotic; spectacular, panoramic, picturesque.

vigilance, n. watchfulness, circumspection, attention, caution.

vigilant, a. watchful, attentive, circumspect, wakeful.

vigor, n. strength, force, lustiness, energy, endurance, virility.

vigorous, a. strong, lusty, robust; energetic, cogent, forcible, luxuriant.

vile, a. base, depraved, vicious, iniquitous, felonious, atrocious.

villainous, a. unprincipled, knavish, arrant, depraved, atrocious.

vim, n. activity, energy, spirit, life. *Antonyms*: lifelessness, languor.

vindicate, v. justify.

vindication, n. justification, defense.

vindicator, n. justifier, champion, advocate.

vindictive, a. revengeful, implacable, malevolent, rancorous.

violate, v. break, disobey, transgress, contravene, profane, desecrate.

violation, n. transgression, infringement, breach, infraction, contravention. *Antonyms*: inviolability, keeping, obedience.

violence, n. force, impetuosity, vehemence, intensity, severity.

violent, a. passionate, vehement, impetuous, fierce, impotent.

virgin, a. vestal, virgin; chaste, pure, stainless; impregnant.

virginity, n. maidenhood, chastity.

virile, a. masculine, vigorous, strong; potent. *Antonyms*: invirile, emasculated, impotent.

virility, n. manhood, manly vigor.

Antonyms: invirility, impotency, emasculation.

virtual, a. potential, energizing; practical, essential.

virtually, adv. practically, really, substantially, potentially.

virtue, n. excellence, worth, goodness, purity, morality, integrity.

virtuous, a. good, exemplary, moral, pure, continent, upright.

visible, a. perceivable, perceptible, discernible, apparent, evident, manifest. *Antonyms*: invisible, imperceptible.

vision, n. sight; apparition, dream, phantasm, specter.

visionary, a. dreamy, imaginative, romantic, fanciful.

visitor, n. guest. *Antonym*: host.

vitiate, v. debase, corrupt, demoralize, contaminate, deprave, spoil.

voice, n. utterance, speech; vote, choice, election, suffrage.

void, a. vacant, empty, vacuous; destitute, devoid, lacking.

void, v. evacuate, eject, discharge, egest, pass; nullify.

volume, n. book, tome; dimensions, compass, size, bulk, mass.

voluntary, a. free, volitional, unforced, spontaneous.

volunteer, n. *Antonym*: conscript.

voluptuous, a. sensual, epicurean, sybaritic. *Antonyms*: ascetic, abstemious, austere.

vomit, v. puke; spew, emit, belch.

voracious, a. rapacious, ravenous, insatiable, fierce, gluttonous, cormorant.

voracity, n. rapacity, voraciousness, greediness.

vote, n. suffrage; ballot, ticket; referendum.

vote, v. declare.

voter, n. elector, suffragist.

voting place. poll.

vouch, v. attest, corroborate,

U
Z

warrant.

voucher, n. attestator.

vow, n. pledge.

vulgar, a. unrefined, plebeian, ignoble, low-born, coarse, inelegant. *Antonyms*: refined, dainty, pure, chaste.

vulgarity, n. unrefinement, dowdiness.

W

wabble, v. stagger, vacillate, reel.

waddle, v. toddle, totter.

wage, v. stake, bet, wager.

wager, v. bet, stake, pledge, hazard, speculate.

wages, n. compensation, pay, earnings, hire, salary.

waggery, n. humor, facetiousness, pleasantry, drollery, jesting, jocularity.

waggish, a. frolicsome, facetious, roguish, arch, sportive, prankish.

wagon, n. vehicle, wain; caravan, van.

waif, n. estray, stray.

wait, v. tarry, stay, linger, await, abide; delay, postpone.

wait, n. waiting, delay, halt, stop; ambush.

waiter, n. attendant, servitor.

waiting, n. tarrying, lingering, delay; abeyance, suspension, quiescence.

waiting-room, n. station, depot.

waive, v. relinquish, forego, surrender.

wake, v. awake, waken; arouse, rouse, revive.

wakeful, a. sleepless, insomnolent; vigilant, watchful.

wakefulness, n. sleeplessness, insomnia, insomnolence, vigilance, watchfulness.

walk, n. stroll, promenade, constitutional; gait, step, carriage.

walk, v. stroll, tramp, stride, plod, trudge, tread.

walker, n. pedestrian, ambulator, perambulator.

walking papers. dismissal.

wall, n. foundation; partition; defense.

wallet, n. pocket-book, purse.

wallow, v. welter, flounder; grovel.

walrus, n. morse, sea-cow.

wander, v. ramble, range, rove, stroll, roam, stray.

wanderer, n. nomad, vagrant, rover, rambler, stroller.

wandering, n. rambling, ranging, roving, strolling.

wandering, a. nomadic, migratory, itinerant, vagrant, vagabond.

wane, v. decrease, diminish, fade. —n. decrease, diminution, decrescence.

want, n. deficiency, lack, dearth, scarcity, need, default, absence.

want, v. need, require; desire, wish, crave.

wanting, a. absent, lacking, missing, deficient, defective, needy, destitute.

wanton, a. unrestrained, uncontrolled, unchecked, unbridled, undisciplined; luxuriant.

war, n. hostilities, warfare, strife, battle.

war, v. contend, fight, combat, militate, wage war.

ward, n. guardianship, guard.

ward, v. ward off, fend off, avert, parry, repel, forefend.

warden, n. church warden; keeper, custodian, curator, warder.

warding off. parry, evasion, averting.

warehouse, n. storehouse, depot, magazine, repository, depository.

wares, n. pl. merchandise, commodities.

warfare, n. war, hostilities; crusade, struggle, strife, militancy.

warlike, a. military, martial, belligerent.

warm, a. lukewarm, tepid, thermal; zealous, ardent, fervent.

warm v. heat.

warmth, n. heat; ardor, fervor, passion, earnestness, fervency.

warn, v. admonish, caution, notify, premonish, apprise, advise, forewarn, signal.

warning, a. cautioning, monitory, mentorial, monitorial, ominous.

warped, a. twisted, bent, bulging, protuberant, distorted.

warrant, v. guarantee, assure, insure; justify, defend, affirm, attest, vouch.

warrant, n. commission, authority; guaranty, surety; voucher, attestation.

warranty, n. guaranty, guarantee, security, warrant.

wary, a. guarded, cautious, circumspect, careful, vigilant.

wash, v. lave, bathe, absterge, foment, rinse; launder.

waste, v. squander, misspend, fritter away, dissipate, dawdle.

waste, a. refuse, rejected, unused, unproductive, untilled.

waste, n. wasting, squandering, dissipation, decrement, prodigality; wilderness.

wasteful, a. extravagant, prodigal, unthrifty, improvident, infrugal, lavish, thriftless.

waster, n. spendthrift, prodigal, squanderer.

watch, n. vigil, outlook, attention; watcher, patrol, watchman.

watch, v. keep vigil, be on the lookout, keep guard.

watchful, a. vigilant, heedful, attentive, alert, circumspect, wary.

watching, n. vigil, vigilance; espionage, surveillance.

watch-tower, n. observatory.

waterfall, n. cascade, cataract.

wave, n. undulation, surge, eagre, bore, swell, billow, breaker.

wave, v. undulate, float, flutter; flourish, brandish, beckon, signal.

waver, v. vacillate, fluctuate, veer, oscillate, hesitate.

wavering, a. vacillating, fluctuating, oscillating, unstable, irresolute, uncertain.

way, n. manner, method, mode, fashion, style, guise, custom.

way in. entrance.

way out. exit, egress.

wayward, a. disobedient, perverse, froward, willful, intractable, headstrong.

weak, a. feeble, infirm, debilitated, weakly, fragile, delicate, invalid.

weaken, v. debilitate, enfeeble, enervate, unnerve, emasculate, incapacitate.

weakening, a. debilitant; diluent, attenuant.

weak-minded, a. fee__minded, foolish, shallow, witless.

weakness, n. debility, feebleness, infirmity, enervation, debilitation, frailness, fragility.

wealth, n. opulence, affluence, riches, fortune, competence.

wealthy, a. opulent, affluent, rich, capitalistic, independent.

wearied, a. tired, fatigued, exhausted, weary.

weary, a. tired, fatigued, worn, exhausted, wearied, spent.

weave, v. entwine, interlace, mat, plait, braid.

wedding, n. nuptials, marriage, espousals.

weep, v. sob, cry.

weighable, a. ponderable.

weight, n. heaviness, ponderousness, gravity, ponderosity, poise.

weighty, a. heavy, ponderous, massive, onerous; momentous, important.

welcome, n. greeting, salutation.

welfare, n. prosperity, happiness, weal, success, well-being.

well, a. good, desirable, fortunate, expedient, favorable, beneficial, advantageous.

wet, a. damp, moist, humid, soaked.

wet, v. moisten, dampen, soak, imbrue, saturate.

whimsey, n. whim.

whimsical, a. capricious, vagarious, notional, crotchety, fantastic.

whine, n. whimper, puling, complaint, —v. whimper, pule, complain.

whip, v. lash, beat, thrash, flog, drub, punish, chastise.

whipping, n. chastisement, castigation, punishment, scourging.

whirl, v. spin, revolve, twirl, rotate, gyrate, wheel, pirouette.

whirling, n. spinning, rotation, gyration, turbination, pirouette.

whirlwind, n. cyclone, typhoon.

whiskers, n. pl. beard.

whiskey, n. *spiritus frumenti*.

whisper, n. susurrus, susurration, whispering, sibilation; innuendo, suggestion, intimation.

white, a. blanched, bleached, etiolate, pale.

whole, a. all, total, entire; intact, complete, inviolate.

whole, n. sum, total, totality, all, aggregate, gross. *Antonyms*: part, portion, fraction, disintegration.

wholeness, n. entirety, completeness, integrity.

wholesome, a. healthy, salubrious, salutary, nutritious, beneficial.

whore, n. harlot, prostitute.

wicked, a. sinful, iniquitous, evil, immoral, depraved, vicious.

wickedness, n. iniquity, depravity, immorality, sinfulness, vice.

wide, a. broad; extensive, vast; comprehensive.

wide-awake, a. alert, keen, vigilant, watchful, wary, attentive.

widespread, a. prevalent, extended, extensive.

widow, n. relict.

wife, n. spouse, consort, helpmate, partner.

wiggle, v. squirm, wriggle.

wild, a. untamed, undomesticated, feral, ferine; desert, waste.

will, n. volition, preference, choice; command, wish, behest, order.

will, n. testament, devise.

will, v. bequeath, devise, leave; decree, ordain, direct.

willful, a. refractory, headstrong, perverse, disobedient, inflexible.

willing, a. disposed, voluntary, desirous.

willingness, n. readiness, disposition, alacrity.

wily, a. crafty, artful, intriguing, designing, tricky, insidious, politic.

win, v. achieve, attain.

wince, v. shrink, flinch, recoil.

wind, n. breeze, zephyr; draught; gale, squall; hurricane.

wind, v. coil, twine, twist, wreathe; crook, meander.

windfall, n. godsend, boon.

winding, n. convolution, labyrinth, detour, meander.

winding-up, n. conclusion, settlement.

windy, a. squally, gusty, tempestuous; flatulent.

winning, n. achievement, gaining.

winning, a. charming, captivating, winsome, engaging.

winter, v. hibernate.

wipe, v. swab; expunge, efface, obliterate, erase.

wisdom, n. lore, learning, sapience, erudition, knowledge, enlightenment.

wise, a. erudite, sapient, learned, philosophical, enlightened.

wisely, adv. prudently, judiciously, sapiently, sagaciously.

wish, v. desire, aspire; invoke, imprecate; congratulate.

wish, n. desire, longing, aspiration, hankering.

wit, n. sense, understanding; repartee, drollery, facetiousness.

witch, n. sorceress, enchantress; hag; siren.

witchcraft, n. sorcery, enchantments, necromancy, black art, conjuration.

witchery, n. witchcraft, sorcery; fascination, spell, charm, entrancement.

withdraw, v. retire, retreat, quit; recall, retract, recant, disavow.

withhold, v. refrain, abstain; refuse, deny.

witness, v. testify, bear witness, confirm, corroborate, attest.

witness, n. attestation, testimony, evidence; eye-witness, deponent, attestor.

witty, a. facetious, droll, sharp.

wizard, n. wonder-worker, magician, conjurer, sorcerer, enchanter.

wolf, n. coyote; werewolf, lycanthrope.

woman, n. dame, matron; mulier; adult.

womanhood, n. womanliness, femininity, feminality.

womanish, a. effeminate,

feminine.

wonder, n. surprise, astonishment, amazement, awe.

wonder, v. marvel.

wonderful, a. marvelous, wondrous, phenomenal, miraculous, portentous.

wood, n. forest, wold, grove, woodland, timberland.

woods, n. pl. forest.

wooing, n. courtship.

word, n. term, vocable; etymon, root; derivative; signal.

wordbook, n. dictionary, lexicon, thesaurus, glossary.

word for word. *verbatim*, literally.

wording, n. phrasing.

words, n. pl. phraseology; vocabulary.

work, v. toil, labor, strive; drudge, slave; operate, manipulate. *Antonyms*: shirk, idle, dabble, loaf.

work, n. industry, toil, labor, employment, occupation; effort. *Antonyms*: idleness, dalliance, trifling, sloth, sluggardy, truancy.

worker, n. artisan, artificer, craftsman, handicraftsman, journeyman, mechanic. *Antonyms*: idler, drone, dabbler, sluggard, truant.

working, a. industrious.

working man. worker, laborer.

working together. cooperation; collusion; concurrence; collaboration.

workman, n. artisan, artificer, craftsman, journeyman.

world, n. earth, creation, universe, cosmos; globe, planet.

worldly, a. terrestrial, earthly, mundane, terrene; secular, temporal.

worn away. eroded, abraded, attrite.

worry, v. harass, vex, annoy,

U Z

torment, tease, fret.

worry, n. anxiety, fretting, apprehension, concern, solicitude. *Antonym*: unconcern.

worrying, a. anxious, distressing, carking.

worship, v. adore, revere; idolize, deify, apotheosize, glorify.

worst, v. defeat, vanquish, conquer, overcome, overthrow, discomfit.

worth, n. worthiness, excellence, virtue, merit, integrity, honor, value.

worthless, a. valueless, good-for-nothing, futile, trashy, unworthy.

worthy, a. meritorious, excellent, estimable, deserving, reputable, exemplary, upright.

wound, n. hurt, injury, scath, lesion, trauma.

wound, v. injure, scath, hurt, maim, disable.

wrangle, n. altercation, dispute, squabble, brawl, bickering, quarrel.

wrap, n. infold, swathe, bemuffle, envelop.

wreck, v. demolish, destroy, ruin, shatter.

wretch, n. outcast, pariah, pilgarlic, vagabond, knave, rogue.

wretched, a. miserable, unhappy; contemptible, abject, despicable, paltry.

wrinkle, n. corrugation, pucker, crease, furrow.

write, v. inscribe, indite; superscribe.

writer, n. scribe, scrivener, penman, secretary, correspondent, essayist.

writing, n. handwriting, chirography, penmanship, calligraphy.

written above. superscript, suprascript.

written under. subscript, subscribed.

wrong, a. immoral, bad, wicked, sinful, evil, improper, criminal.

wrong, n. injustice, inequity, oppression, disservice, trespass, transgression, injury. —adv. amiss, erroneously.

wrong, v. cheat, damnify, defraud, maltreat, abuse.

wrong-doer, n. sinner, criminal, culprit, delinquent, offender.

wrong-doing, n. misdemeanor, malfeasance, malpractice, malversation, dereliction, iniquity, sin.

wrought, a. worked, elaborated, finished.

wry, a. twisted, distorted, awry; wrested, perverted.

X

X-ray, n. the Rontgen ray.

Xerox, v. copy, make a copy or facsimile, reproduce. (Trademark)

Xmas, n. Christmas; also holiday season, yuletide.

xylophone, n. marimba, celeste; carillion.

Y

yank, n. pull, jerk, twitch. —v. pull, jerk, twitch, snatch.

yap, n. bark, yelp.

yard, n. three feet; enclosure, court, area, garth, courtyard.

yarn, n. worsted, warp, abb, spinel.

yawn, v. gape; oscitate.

yawn, n. gape, gaping, yawning, oscitation, oscitancy.

yawning, a. gaping, oscitant.

yearbook, n. annual.

yearly, a. annual, anniversary. —

adv. annually.

yearn, v. long, desire, hanker after, pine.

yearning, n. longing, hankering, pining.

yeast, n. barm, leaven, ferment.

yeasty, a. barmy.

yell, n. outcry, scream, shriek, howl, yowl, vociferation.

yell, v. scream, shriek, screech, bawl, howl, yowl.

yellow, a. golden, sallow, tawny, ecru, amber.

yellowbird, n. goldfinch.

yellow race. Mongols, Mongolians.

yellows, n. jaundice; jeterus.

yelp, n. bark, yap, yaup.

yes, adv. yea, aye, ay. —n. affirmative, consent.

yield, v. produce, pay, return; submit, surrender, succumb, give up. *Antonyms*: resist, retain, withhold, refuse, withstand.

yield, n. product, crop, harvest.

yielding, n. production, bearing; surrender, relinquishment, submission, compliance.

yielding, a. compliant, tractable, submissive, amenable, unresisting.

yoke, n. oxbow and bar, crosspiece; team, span, pair, couple.

yoke, v. couple, join, unite, link, hitch together; subject, enslave.

yokel, n. bumpkin, boor, rustic.

yolk, n. yelk, vitellus, oviplasma.

young, a. juvenile, youthful, immature, adolescent.

young, n. offspring.

younger, a. junior.

youth, n. juvenility, youthfulness; adolescence, teens, minority.

youthful, a. immature, juvenile, adolescent, boyish. *Antonyms*: adult, manly, mature.

Z

zany, n. jester, buffoon, clown, harlequin, merry-andrew.

zanyism, n. harlequinism, buffoonery, clownishness.

zeal, n. fervor, ardor, zealotry, intensity, passion, devotion, devotedness.

zealot, n. enthusiast, partisan, devotee, fanatic.

zealous, a. ardent, eager, strenuous, fervent, passionate, intense, devoted, impassioned.

zenith, n. culmination, pinnacle, acme, summit, apex. *Antonym*: nadir.

zero, n. cipher, nothing, naught.

zest, n. relish, flavor, taste; enjoyment, relish, gusto.

zinc, n. spelter.

zip, n. hissing, sibilance, sibilation. —v. hiss, sibilate.

zone, n. clime, region; girdle, belt, band, girth.

NOTES:

U
Z